· · · · · The Mother Side of Midnight

■ ■ ■ ■ ■ Also by Teryl Zarnow

*Husband Is the Past Tense of Daddy
and Other Dispatches from the Front
Lines of Motherhood*

The Mother Side of Midnight

Nocturnal Confessions of a Lunchbox Queen

Teryl Zarnow

Addison-Wesley Publishing Company, Inc.
Reading, Massachusetts   Menlo Park, California
New York   Don Mills, Ontario
Wokingham, England   Amsterdam   Bonn
Sydney   Singapore   Tokyo   Madrid   San Juan
Paris   Seoul   Milan   Mexico City   Taipei

Library of Congress Cataloging-in-Publication Data

Zarnow, Teryl.
    The mother side of midnight : nocturnal
confessions of a lunchbox queen / Teryl Zarnow.
       p.   cm.
    ISBN 0-201-57053-X
    1. Motherhood. 2. Child rearing. I. Title.
HQ759.Z375 1992
649'.1—dc20   91-30729
                                      CIP

Portions of this book have appeared previously in a different form in *The Orange County Register* and *Redbook*.

Jacket design by Diana Coe
Jacket illustration by Bonnie Timmons
Text design by Janis Owens
Set in 10-point Sabon by Shepard Poorman
    Communications Corporation, Indianapolis, IN

1 2 3 4 5 6 7 8 9-MW-95949392
First printing, February 1992

For my mother,
for everything.

Contents

■ ■ ■ Preface

Sometimes—when I am struggling with my children in such classy places as the shopping mall rest room, the grocery store, or the pediatrician's waiting room—other mothers will stare at me with a glimmer of recognition. Usually when this occurs my jeans are dirty, at least one child is screaming, and I do not look like a woman who has life under control.

Other mothers get that glimmer of recognition not because I resemble somebody they know, but because I resemble them. You probably see mothers like me everywhere. My family is ordinary, my children are generic, and out of 31 possible flavors my life is vanilla. As individuals, yes, we are special. But with three kids, two pets, and a garage full of bicycles, we turned out to be just like everyone else.

My son Zachary, seven, is the last one in line with his first-grade classmates as they walk to the library. He is the one flapping his arms like a chicken at a rate exceeded only by his mouth. At preschool, my daughter Rachel, five, is the one coloring rainbows and giggling with her friend. When she comes home she will tell me they were trying to decide whom they will marry. On the playground, my youngest, Noah, three, is the child playing with every truck but the one we brought. He hangs from the highest monkey bar and then screams in panic for me to rescue him. After I take him down, he climbs up again. You've seen my children everywhere.

Likewise, even though you haven't met my husband, David, you probably know him. My husband is the one who comes home from work late and falls asleep early. He lets the children eat corn chips for breakfast after they catch him with the opened bag. And on the days he takes over with the kids, he never remembers to change a wet diaper. As a father he is more hands-on than his own, but he still falls short of my ideal, which I have lifted from the pages of *Kramer vs. Kramer*. He has not yet learned how to do everything my way.

On a typical day, after school, you might have driven past us while we were getting some fresh air. My daughter insists on riding her bicycle with training wheels, which gets stuck every time she tries to lift it over a curb. She brings her tape recorder so she can sing along with the soundtrack to *The Little Mermaid*. My sons are the ones riding in a red wagon and kicking each other while they fight over leg room. My oldest is collecting pine cones that my youngest is trying to throw away. I am the one pulling.

At home, the kids capture ants to feed the Venus flytrap. We are joined by three boys from the neighborhood (who begin to chase one another with baseball bats) and the two-year-old across the street (who tries to find at least one toy my three-year-old will permit him to touch). Once, on such an afternoon, a woman driving by slowed down to inquire whether I offer day care. Inside the house, my daughter refuses to allow her brother to inspect the toy she just received for her birthday. While she gets in the bathtub my son retaliates by throwing its pieces all over the closet. When confronted by the damage, he denies all culpability. In the bathtub, the three-year-old and five-year-old get into a fight over the plastic cups. During the resulting mayhem, I am the one who gets doused with water. I also am the one who pulls the plug.

Even if you've never specifically seen my family, in other words, you would recognize us anywhere—in any front yard, any playground, or any bathtub. My kids and my family, in fact, are a lot like yours. When I write about them, only the names have been changed to protect the innocent.

That is precisely why I write about my family: because we are like everyone else. I take some comfort in being common, and I aspire only to elevate the mundane to the ordinary. My children are special to me because they are mine, but all children are special when they belong to someone who loves them.

In writing about my children, I am attempting to chronicle these years of joy and tribulation. If I am laughing at anyone, it is mostly myself. If I am complaining about everyone, I include myself. In my writing I try to see the humor in everything. In real life, sometimes, I do not.

I do not offer advice. I am feeling my way and cannot claim to always know what I am doing. Since any wisdom I possess is born of hindsight, I can only try to explain how I am learning to manage.

There are not, I have discovered, many books for parents like me who recently have outgrown the baby years. Lots of books told me about my babies; there are plenty to tell me about my future teens. But not so many seem to relate to this stage after layettes but before skateboards. I am in between. I am just wiping my hands of diapers and just getting my feet wet with elementary school. In other words, I used to breast-feed; now I pack lunchboxes. As they grow my children are posing more sophisticated challenges than they did as toddlers. The issues are not so clear-cut as teaching them to use their words. I am feeling my way through these years when my children still will listen, but I do not always know what to say.

My lifestyle has changed. Before we had our babies, my husband and I thought nothing of staying awake past midnight. We stayed up late because we slept late. If we were not out somewhere, then we were home reading, relaxing, or listening to music. Evenings were a private time we saved for ourselves. But after we became parents, the realities of our lives changed. Now we have little time for ourselves. Now we want to be asleep at an early hour. But instead of sleep, as a parent I've discovered a time of day that I have come to call (with apologies to author Sidney Sheldon) the mother side of midnight. At first this was the early morning hours when I was awake nursing my babies in an otherwise sleeping world. Sometimes this is still the time when children seeking comfort come to my bed. But now, most often, these are the hours when my children come to my mind. As my children get older, the mother side of midnight is the time when I review the day and think about them.

I want my writing to be therapeutic for other parents by helping them to discover that they are not alone in the night with the conflict of their feelings. I also want to know I am not alone with mine. Once I spoke to a group of mothers about the cumulative effect of daily aggravations. I described a series of minor occurrences that collected until they had a major effect upon my temper. At the end of the day, when my son refused his carrots, I dumped them on his head. I described this, not with pride, but with rueful recognition that children bring out the brat in all of us. After my talk, another mother came up to me.

"I'm so relieved to hear you tell that story," she said. "Sometimes my two-year-old just drives me crazy. The other day I was watering the garden and she just wouldn't be quiet, not even for an instant. I don't know what came over me, but I turned the hose on her."

As I said, I do not offer advice, but I do offer companionship to mothers who want to know that many of their feelings are common. How can the children we love so much drive us so crazy? I take those feelings and try to put them into perspective. So when I write about my children, I do not eulogize. I know they are wonderful. I accept it as a given that families share a great deal of joy. But during the precious moments it is easiest to cope. My writing is partly for the other times.

I hope this book provides comfort and understanding. I intend to give copies to my children when they themselves are parents so they will understand that life is a circle. I hope these words will bring back their own dimly recalled memories, as well as a new understanding of the way we were. I hope they will recognize that I have tried to paint a true picture as I saw it, and I hope they will feel the love that punctuates each sentence.

▪ ▪ ▪ Acknowledgments

First and foremost, I wish to thank my mother, Ronna, who started it all. I dedicate this book to her.

I also wish to thank the members of my family, all of whom have given me tremendous support. My sister Denna has been behind me every step of the way. Knowing what I do about sibling rivalry, she is terrific.

My father, Melvin, has done an outstanding job taking charge of sales and publicity.

I especially appreciate the enthusiastic encouragement of my Uncle Irving, who is almost more excited about this book than I am.

This book would never have been written without the love and understanding of my husband, David. He is my first critic, my first editor, my biggest supporter, and the best computer jockey I know. I am lucky he has encouraged me every step of the way, and I am grateful for his superb sense of humor.

Likewise my children, Zachary, Rachel, and Noah, have been patient with a Mommy who works when they want to play and who becomes a tad testy when deadlines loom. They are an endless source of material and of joy.

I also wish to thank my editor, Nancy Miller, who wanted me to write this book so that she could read it; and my agent, Carla Glasser, who takes the time to call and talk. Thank you to Michael Nicoletti, who has a way with words.

And special thanks to the many mothers who have let me know when I am on the right track.

■ ■ ■

1

Redecorating the Nursery

▚▚▚▚▚▚

Saying bye-bye to the Baby Years

is head fits neatly into the palm of my hand and his toothless mouth smiles sweetly at a world that has always smiled back. Instinctively, as I cuddle his head in the hollow under my neck, I begin to sway sideways in the rhythmic rocking practiced by mothers through the ages. Holding him feels natural and right.

So does handing him back to his mother.

Among my friends, babies have been busting out all over. For their showers I have painted T-shirts the size of handkerchiefs and marveled at the new generation of baby strollers that dates mine back to the Dark Ages. At their homecomings I have murmured softly over bassinets and waited for my turn to gently hold the new occupants. I have warbled and cooed in an effort to coax smiles from drowsy faces, and I have marveled anew that something so tiny can feel so complete. I love to hold those babies.

But no longer do I long to take them home.

I suspect we mothers never truly get over babies, but the day must come when we stop having them. Sometimes the alarm rings on our biological clocks; sometimes we are simply alarmed at the prospect of having any more. Sometimes we are simply ready to move on. In my case it was all three. This book is about taking those first tentative steps past the baby years. It is a time filled with equal measures of relief and regret.

"You'll know when you're ready to stop," my mother told me, and she was right. I remember when my youngest turned two. Of my three children, his was the first two-year-old party I did not celebrate in conjunction with my third trimester. I felt relief and exhilaration. I knew my time had come.

In some ways I compare my childbearing years to climbing in mud. Each time I have clawed my way to the summit—and enjoyed such amenities as eight hours of sleep and a house free of playpens and toddler gates—I have had another baby and slid back down to the bottom. Each child, I believe, sets you back about two years in terms of progress toward rational family life. Finally, I honestly can say: I am tired of getting dirty.

Parenting, I have come to realize, is seasonal work. It is only a stage of your entire life, but during those years it is totally and absolutely all consuming. I compare it to my plum tree. When the fruit is ripe, it cascades to earth in abundance. I know that I should gorge myself and enjoy the fruit as much as I can because plums have only a short season. But, sometimes, I get sick of plums. Sometimes, in the few short weeks when overripe fruit bombards us, it is impossible to remember when there weren't squishy plums all over the yard. And sometimes it is impossible to remember when there weren't noisy kids rampaging through my house.

I thought about this recently when—without a thought for the consequences—I took two of my children down the street to welcome the new neighbors. I knew very little about them except that they are a young, energetic couple. But I would have known they have no children by how quickly they invited us all to come inside. The parents I know prefer as a defense mechanism to keep visiting children outside whenever possible.

My three-year-old and five-year-old recognize an opportunity when it is handed to them. They ran through the inside of our neighbor's house faster than the birthday boy unwraps his presents. They ran relays on a course through the kitchen, down the hallway, and into the living room. They opened doors and touched everything.

The behavior of my children was not surprising; that is why usually they are kept outside. The behavior of the neighbors was. They did not have the Parent Protective Reflex. By this I mean they did not disengage my three-year-old from the crystal bowl on the coffee table; they did not stoop to rescue the coasters that nearly doubled as Frisbees. They did not even seem to notice. I was mortified by my children's behavior and spent a good deal of our visit trying to calm them down and keep them in line. I tried to tightrope walk between carrying on a conversation and maintaining order. Wherever my children went I tracked them with my eyes. The neighbors did not. They are at a different stage of life.

After a few minutes, I took my children and myself out of there. I figured it was better to leave before the neighbors also began to look nervous. By then it would have been too late to prevent actual damage. When we got outside, I laughed to another mother as I described our visit. I told her I couldn't remember a time when my parental reflexes weren't operating on full-scale alert. She said that she could.

"When I met you," she recalled, "you had no children. I was stuck home covered with baby drool and you were always going off somewhere looking nice."

I glanced down at my jeans and smiled. I recognized what she was saying. Recently I saw a woman I previously had known as childless. Now she has two kids, and she barely looked familiar beneath her diaper bag and portable playpen. She spent most of her time hovering over her crawling baby, her parental reflexes in high gear. I had some difficulty recognizing her as the same woman who used to wear makeup when she was gardening.

Another old acquaintance had that same problem with me. A friend who knew me before I moved away and had children recently tried to convince me to fly across the country for the weekend.

"I can't," I told her as I enumerated my schedule and the ways I am trapped in place by the spider web of my responsibilities.

"I don't understand," she answered. "You used to be able to get away."

I used to do a lot of things that I have put on hold these past few years. But now that my youngest child has made it to three, I look forward to being able to do some of them soon again.

Oh, I know that I will miss these years when I have been the best playmate my children could have. I will miss these years when my daughter begs me to play Barbie with her and my son wants to pitch me a Frisbee. Already now, when I read library books, my youngest is my only child who wants to sit in my lap. And I'm trying to pawn off the job. My seven-year-old is learning to read and I tell him to practice on his brother. When a child of mine scrapes his knee, only my youngest still believes my kisses hold healing power. The others still want hugs, but they know when they also need medical, not emotional, attention.

My daughter says she wishes we had a real baby in the house. Someday, with nostalgia, I know that I will look back and agree with her. I know mothers who experienced an undeniable ache when their youngest turned five. They had another baby. But right now, I do not miss the playpen no longer in my living room; it blocked the doorway. I do not mourn the toddler gate recently removed from the stairway; at the end it was more of a hazard than a help. I do not miss the car seat my five-year-old formerly occupied; now we no longer have to crawl over her seat. Someday my entire family may even be able to go out all afternoon without paying the price for skipping my three-year-old's nap. Some afternoon in my house we will not have to whisper.

I want to look ahead. I fantasize about the day when all my children will be able to sit through a concert or play. I want to take my oldest to museums where the youngest is finally old enough to behave himself. I would like to take a car trip of more than thirty minutes duration that is not planned around nap time. And when I get there I would like to manage without a stroller. I long for a time when jigsaw puzzles can be left safely uncompleted atop a table, or when Lego creations are admired by all, not demolished by some.

Now, I am not looking so far into the future that I no longer need baby-sitters. I'm just gazing a little down the road to the first time in over seven years when maybe I won't have to walk my children across the street. I can't imagine going to bed without reminding someone to potty. Older children may bring their own aggravation, but they also bring liberation. There is something to be said for children who can eat and dress and reach the faucet by themselves. I wouldn't mind being able to send all three children outside to play and not have to stand on patrol and watch them.

I am beginning to enjoy a slight breathing space from constant vigilance. It seems like only yesterday my husband and I would gasp in horror upon discovering one of the children alone in a room. Only recently I believed a baby-sitter capable of coping with my brood had to be at least in college. No longer. I accept anyone as old as the ages of my kids combined. Likewise, when my husband and I have plans now, the children are as delighted to see us go as we are to leave.

And who among us feels regret when the youngest child completes potty training? I felt some nostalgia when my last baby outgrew the smallest size of diapers, but I felt none when my three-year-old filled out his first pair of underpants. By a conservative estimate, I am now saving at least ten dollars per week at the grocery store. Saved up for a year, that's enough for a good-sized celebration—although the point is not so much the money that I save, but the freedom that it represents. No longer must the carpet in the children's bedroom be crushed beneath the weight of the diaper pail. Perhaps the divot won't be permanent. No longer must the window be left permanently cracked open. Perhaps the odor will disperse. I see cause for celebration. For over seven years I have diapered at least one child regularly; for overlapping periods I have even diapered two. Until I am a grandmother, I intend to diaper no more.

I am long past squeamish, so it's not so much the diapers themselves that drove me crazy. I delivered some of my best monologues to children lying flat on their backs. But diapers represent a time in parenting that has been very physically labor-intensive. I am tired of lifting, carrying, and hauling children. I'm ready for kids who can walk by themselves, talk by themselves, and (soon, I hope) shower by themselves. I could do without kneeling every night paying homage to the bathtub.

I know that after diapers will come serious challenges. My children will want to ride their bikes home alone from their friends' houses. They will start to use deodorant and learn to tell convincing lies. Eventually they will become adolescents. I did not say it will be better, but in terms of sheer physical endurance it will be easier. I'm at the age when my back starts to hurt easily. I really shouldn't do so much lifting.

■ ■ ■

Despite my brave words, as you might have guessed, I am not thoroughly comfortable with the notion of my kids growing older. Having expressed my delight at how my children are no longer small, let me also admit to my misgivings that they are growing big. I like my children smaller than I am. Size provides an obvious clue as to who is supposed to be in charge. But I am much shorter than my husband. This means my authority will be the first to go.

As the children grow it means we are leaving familiarity behind. My three-year-old, difficult at times though he may be, holds no surprises. I essentially know what to expect from the early years of life. But anything my oldest does is new to me; I do not know what to expect of him. Soon, each of my children will be heading off to school, choosing friends I haven't met and learning things I didn't teach them. Their problems will become more serious, the repercussions will be felt long after bedtime. Certainly, the day will come when junior high feels comfortable to me, when my children will baby-sit for others. But for now adolescence is a faraway, frightening prospect.

That prospect was brought home to me one day at the park. The park was cooking exactly the way I like it. The sand was not so hot we couldn't go barefoot; the air was not so cool we needed jackets. The crowd was seasoned just right. Not so many babies that the infant swings were monopolized; not so many big kids that the traffic was hazardous to a toddler. The children with sand toys were willing to share and the sole dog tied to a bench was friendly.

I was enjoying the modest euphoria that comes after the lunches are packed, the car is unpacked, and it is too soon to worry about cleaning the sand off everyone to go home. I was feeling particularly good because the incredibly youthful and fit woman by the slide with three children in tow turned out to be only their baby-sitter.

Suddenly, without warning, a summer recreation program dumped its cargo of charges into the park. Like a toxic spill, they polluted the day. Now, I would rather wave the flag than burn it. I believe in democracy. I believe public parks belong to everyone. Yet as I watched those kids swarm across the sand, my emotional reaction was undeniable: I wanted the big kids out. They were, first of all, grotesque and threatening compared to the preschoolers. Tall and ungainly in the early throes of adolescence, these kids were old enough, I imagined, to have police records.

"I shot you," crowed one boy, holding his fingers like a gun and wearing a T-shirt for a product of which I have never heard.

My oldest watched, fascinated, as they proceeded to give chase in the sort of tackle game I have never encouraged him to play.

"You can't catch me, pig!" shouted another boy as he bounded across the swaying wooden bridge to which my toddler clung for dear life.

"Let's see you bomb off the swing," one of the girls challenged a friend, using her feet to kick sand near my daughter's head.

My children, usually fearless, cowed together subdued. Intent on watching my own children, I did not notice another mother protecting hers.

"Who brought those kids to the park? I'm ready to tell them where to go," she muttered, plopping down next to me on the bench. "I'm ready to smack 'em."

"I know what you mean," I replied. "Did they do something to you?"

"They were making fun of Robbie," she answered with a gesture toward her son. "He's four, and he can hold his own against five- and six-year-olds. But these kids are just too big."

I thought about that while I hovered over my children and argued with myself. Part of me pointed out that big kids have every right to come to the park; the rest of me said there comes a time to realize they have outgrown it. It was their size, I decided, that threw me off balance. Although my oldest is gaining on me, I have not yet had to discipline a child whose shoe size is bigger than mine. These kids were too big. A terrorist at age two is redeemed by his cuteness and excused by his youth. Nothing redeems an obnoxious adolescent. He is a testament to his hormones and somebody's failure.

Then, as quickly as they descended, the pack of youngsters left. The mood at the park lightened perceptibly, and we mothers relaxed at our posts. I enjoyed that all's-right-with-the-world sense of well-being I usually feel each week when the garbage goes out.

Later, as I wiped sand off tiny toes and adjusted seat belts and car seats, I relished the smallness of my children. At this age they represent a promise. It's no more possible to take a peek at their final characters than to discern the ultimate shapes of their noses. Both will flesh out in time.

I was glad, in short, that my children bore no relationship to the adolescents at the playground. It didn't occur to me until later that when my children grow bigger, of course, adolescent is exactly what they will become.

In the same way, I have no desire to plunge into the male-female relationships of grade-school children. Dating seems beyond my comprehension. I once saw a nine-year-old boy gesture at a girl standing nearby who apparently had gotten a new haircut.

"What happened to your hair?" he asked insolently.

The girl shrugged mutely in answer and the boy turned away.

The girl's friend nudged her excitedly. "See?" she said. "I told you that he likes you."

Do not ask me to explain the courtship rituals of children. I count myself lucky to have had no experience with them and do not relish the eventual prospect. The closest my children have come to the subject is a discussion about why Bambi got "twitterpated" in the spring. The children I know are mercifully too young for torrid passion. The oldest girls are just starting to "like" the boys. They are at the stage of discovering that boys are different from girls—but they can't stop giggling long enough to do anything productive about it.

My three-year-old son has nothing against girls. Except for his sister, he doesn't know a thing about them. He simply ignores all girls while he concentrates on the boys. (Because my son is adorable, I suspect his strategy is correct. Someday, without any effort on his part, the girls will come after him.)

My five-year-old daughter uses her sexuality as a powerful weapon.

"Ben was coming to get us," she tells me, "so I chased him instead and told him I was going to give him a kiss. He ran away." (She will, I suspect, employ this strategy even as she gets older.)

But my seven-year-old son is already giving me second thoughts about my ability to handle what lies ahead. He knows that there is something about girls, but just like his father he cannot quite put his finger on what it means to him. He was nonplussed when a girl picked him to be her computer partner. He was stoic when one of the girls in his class began calling him at home nightly and asking him to play. But he never wavered as he repeatedly turned her down.

At recess he has been gainfully employed as a bodyguard.

"James pays me a quarter to be his bodyguard," he explained. "Jessica wants to kiss him."

Valentine's Day was a bit traumatic for him in first grade. His class has two Julies. One Julie dared the other to write him a love note. She did and left it on his desk. He didn't know which one sent the valentine. In an act of extreme innocence, he showed the note to the substitute teacher, who should have known better.

"*Ooohh,*" she said, quite audibly. "Somebody has a crush on you!"

"*Oooh,*" imitated every child in the classroom.

"They were laughing at me," my son told me later, his eyes brimming with tears of humiliation. "So I got even. I chased Julie all across the playground. She won't write me any notes again!"

We talked.

"The kids were just joking around. They weren't laughing at you," I said. "The point is that Julie wanted to send you a valentine because she thinks you're cute."

He glared at me suspiciously.

"It's really a compliment when somebody likes you," I told him. "I think you're pretty cute myself. Just like Daddy when I first saw him."

My son stared at me.

"When somebody thinks you're cute, do you have to let them kiss you?" he asked.

"Sometimes. It depends," I replied, thinking of a grandma.

"Depends on what?" he asked, thinking of a Julie.

That, I told him, was another story. When he's nine maybe, maybe, I'll be ready to tell it.

■　■　■

As my children grow, I feel not only unease about where life is taking me, but some regret as well. Each passing day takes me farther away from the baby years. Although I have been anxious to leave them behind, that does not mean I am glad they are over. I will miss them even though I no longer want them.

When my daughter turned four, we gave her a pink bicycle with training wheels. As she wobbled by, swaying from training wheel to training wheel high above the ground, she seemed vulnerable and old at the same time. I suddenly missed the sight of her chubby legs pumping furiously on the red tricycle. A year later, she confidently rides her bicycle without hesitation and it doesn't seem too big for her at all. The training wheels will come off soon.

The other day my seven-year-old wanted to tape a poster of some singers onto his bedroom wallpaper.

"Don't tape it there. You'll hurt the wallpaper," I said.

"I don't see anything special about the wallpaper," he answered.

I do. I remember agonizing over its selection as my husband and I created a nursery for a baby we hadn't met. His future seemed to be riding upon our choice between pastel and primary colors. We invested our hopes and dreams in that room. Any day now, my children will ask me to take out the rocking chair because it takes up too much space. They won't miss it, but I will. I'm the only one who will remember how cozily I rocked them as babies, companionably together, in the hush of the night.

I remember once when my oldest was six and he was playing tag at the playground with an older boy he had just met. The bigger boy was old enough to think while he ran; my son was not. He could barely change direction without tripping. The bigger boy kept tagging my son with ease.

"Swing across on the rings," he told my son in an effort to be helpful and to perhaps even the odds.

"I can't," my son ruefully admitted.

Disdain chased disbelief across the boy's face as he contemplated my son, whom he evidently had thought was much older.

"Hey," I started to interject—and then I stopped. "My son is only six," I was going to say. But then I realized that by the time you turn six, age is no longer an automatic excuse. When my youngest would shove another child, I used to make excuses. "He's only two," I would explain apologetically to the other mother. But I suddenly realized I could no longer say that about my oldest. Excuses for him were starting to wear thin.

He was not "only" six any more than he still wears size seven. When I had to march across the aisle and buy his clothes in the youth department—where decor tends toward surfboards rather than stuffed animals—I knew my son was growing up. He also knows it. I was once his favorite playmate; now he has his own circle of friends. Now he can open the new applesauce jar when I cannot budge it. We once took baths together; now he showers alone.

Just as his body is his own, so is his mind. The issues become more challenging once your child outgrows size seven. Whereas before I imposed discipline largely from an authoritarian standpoint, now I also strive for understanding. I want my son to understand why I do the things I do. I want him to know the reasons for the rules.

Sometimes now I can discern glimmers of adult response. But even when he understands, my son still flaunts the rules to the best of his ability. One morning my son dug through the box of Cheerios in order to get the sample roll of Life Savers inside. I took the candy away and put it on the kitchen counter. Not so long ago my son would have left it there. But as we were leaving the house, I noticed the candy was gone. As we pulled up at school, my son was fussing with his lunchbox. He couldn't get it closed and asked me to help. The lunchbox was too full because he had crammed the roll of Life Savers inside it. I took them away again and forgot about it. A week later I discovered the empty wrapper under his bed. This happened when my son was six. Now that he is seven, I suspect he would be smart enough to throw the wrapper in the garbage. I will miss the days when he was so easy to catch.

Once your child outgrows size seven, it becomes easier to visualize the adult he is going to become. Sometimes I feel nostalgic because I miss the child he used to be. I miss shopping on the stuffed animal side of the aisle. I like little boys with clean hands who wear shirts with collars and coveralls with snaps.

When he was in kindergarten, however, my son showed me that while he may have outgrown size seven, he still hadn't outgrown his mother. At the school I met his class walking back from the library and fell into step alongside my son. Almost reflexively, it seemed, he reached out to hold my hand—and he held it as we walked all the way back to his classroom. I can't tell you how happy I felt.

If my oldest is the first to show the signs of growing up, then my youngest is the last to show the signs of babyhood. By definition, he is the last to sit in the high chair, the last to wear diapers, and the last to occupy a crib. I rushed my two oldest children through these stages. For each of them, a new baby was nipping at their heels. So at age two, they went up, over, and out of whatever equipment it was I needed for the next child.

My youngest, of course, has no successor. His was a lingering toddlerhood. Because he was the last, he nursed longer, wore diapers longer, and generally took longer to leave the trappings of infancy behind. His brother and sister awaken and run to the television set. He still runs to be cuddled.

But now that he is three, the last vestiges of his baby years are tumbling like blocks. Recently I found a teething ring behind moldy cheese in the back of my refrigerator. Time was when my oldest son wouldn't let it out of his sight. He used to cry for a "ting" after every "owie," as though a teething ring possessed curative powers. It took me years to ignore the printed warnings and go ahead and freeze those things. Along with pacifiers I used to buy them in quantity. Now in my household neither serve any purpose.

Already I have pushed the stroller to the back of the closet and packed up the bibs because my youngest refuses to wear them. I have begun weeding out toys labeled suitable for "up to 36 months" because my three-year-old plays only with the toys his seven-year-old brother also likes. I am packing away a few, select favorites for (dare I say it?) my grandchildren. My husband has seriously mentioned removing the few remaining, functioning, safety latches from the cabinets. Our three-year-old is by far the most adept at using them. I do not remember what it is like to open a drawer without pressing down on a safety latch first. Soon I suspect the sipper cups and high chair will be next to go. My youngest has begun agitating for his own seat at the table.

I have discovered something, however, about those families in which only the first-grader is teething. Traces of the early years still remain. Look closely and you will see the five-year-old sucking his thumb while he watches television. Peek under the pillow of a ten-year-old, other mothers have told me, and you will find folded there treasured remnants of his baby blanket. I used to think I would find such behavior immature. Now I'm not so sure.

My youngest, the Linus of southern California, still sucks his thumb while dragging his bedraggled baby blanket. I have had mixed feelings about this so let me tell you about his blanket.

In the beginning, it was an ordinary baby blanket. I purchased it more than seven years ago during my first pregnancy because the layette lists seemed to place great emphasis upon blankets, and I lived in fear of being unprepared. An ordinary blanket, it has satin edging and a loose weave. It is, of necessity, yellow. Its virtues were its softness and the fact that it is machine washable.

I thought its appeal as a blanket was strictly utilitarian, and my first two children agreed. Unless they were cold, they didn't care about it one way or another. For my third-born, however, the whole of that blanket is greater than the sum of its parts. He loves it.

To my youngest that blanket sounds comforting like a lullaby, smells of security like his nursery, and wraps him in a hug like a mother. He needs his blanket when he is tired, hungry, or upset. It is his private tranquilizer, his glass of wine, his cup of tea, or his cigarette. He will have to get rid of it someday, or he's going to want it after he has sex. But for now, when the thumb of his right hand is in his mouth, the fingers of his left hand need to clutch it. He lulls himself to sleep stroking the satin edging of that blanket.

I suspect the edging is his favorite part because when his blanket is unavailable, he goes to my bed and tugs at the edging on mine. I am guessing, of course. Little hard evidence exists about precisely what attracts which child to a particular blanket. I heard about a mother who despaired over her son's blanket. Four years of constant use had left it a bit scraggly. In an effort to tidy it up, she cut off a dangling yarn. Her son threw a royal fit. Turns out that yarn was the part he most loved. The satin edging has mostly come off my son's blanket; it dangles dangerously like a noose. I do not know whether to cut it off, stitch it on, or secretly buy a replacement blanket.

All I know is that my son loves his blankie even more than the raisins he picks out of his toast. He does not want to suck his thumb without it. Ordinarily his clumsy hands blunder their way into places they have no business being, wreaking destruction everywhere. But delicately they stroke his blanket with a feather-light touch. Other times he fingers it like worry beads. His beads, my worry. I worry about whether he loves it too much.

This is my first experience with a security blanket. My other children, who have no such attachments to inanimate objects, think their brother is amusing.

"He's just like Linus," chortles my eldest.

I'm not sure it's funny. Linus, a perpetual toddler, has clutched his thermal life preserver for years. My son is just three, but sometimes a wispy cloud of worry crosses my mind. I wonder how old he will be before he gives up his blanket. Once I watched a friend try to convince her four-year-old to leave the house without her blanket because it was still on the rinse cycle. No way. In desperation, she negotiated a substitute. Now her daughter clings to two blankets.

I personally had not given the matter much thought until I decided to wash my son's blanket. Deciding was easy; finding the opportunity was not. Unthinkable to wash it during nap time or at bedtime. Not so easy to sneak it away at any other time. Some mornings when I dress my son, I have found myself threading the blanket through the sleeve along with his arm. One time when he was sick I faced a real dilemma. He threw up all over his blanket. He needed his blanket for comfort; I needed it for the laundry.

In theory, my son's blanket is supposed to be more an occasional dessert then a steady diet. I do not allow it outside, and it is supposed to be stored inside the crib until times of acute need. But far away I can discern storm clouds of battle. Some mornings my son drags it downstairs. He has become expert at sticking his hand through the slats of his crib to fish for his blanket inside. In his sleep he turns over to find it.

Of course I know the experts would say: Don't worry, be happy. Along with thumb sucking and tantrums, this too shall pass. But I have set a goal for the day my son marches off to kindergarten. When one of the other parents asks me which child is mine, I want to be able to answer nonchalantly: "My son? Oh, he's the one without a blanket."

In the end, whatever happens, I know this blanket will never be ordinary again. My husband says the blanket smells. And it does have a unique odor all its own. But on this one I have to side with my son. The blanket does not stink. It smells of my baby boy. And if my son does not want to keep it forever, I know that I will.

■　■　■

While I may want to save my son's baby blanket forever, please understand that I also am perfectly willing to pack it away. Remember that we are talking about an emotion that is equal parts regret and relief. I have no wish to hustle away my children's childhoods, but I cheer the moments of emancipation that come my way. I remember my exhilaration the first time all three children were gone and I was alone in the house. I marveled that the house was empty. No, that was not literally true. I was there, but my husband and three children were not. Two kids were at school and, for the first time in his memory, I had taken my youngest to a baby-sitter.

I had left my children before, but always before I had left them at home. This was the first day I was home and they were not. They were not throwing pillows on the floor in the family room; they were not in the kitchen asking what else they could eat; and they were not outside chasing a ball into the street. Blessedly, they were not there.

I felt intoxicated by freedom and possibility. My wildest dreams could come true.

"You need to gain weight," the doctor was saying to me. "Eat as many cinnamon rolls as you want."

"Your books strike me as the basis for a screenplay," the director was saying to me. "How much would you like for the rights?"

"I've arranged for a vacation," my husband was saying to me. "How would you like to spend two weeks in Hawaii?"

I also felt paralyzed by freedom and possibility. Like a crazed chicken I darted from room to room, straightening, picking up, organizing—indulging myself in ways previously possible only during my children's naps, behind bathroom doors, or in my dreams. I filled the minutes faster than I can fill a grocery cart—thinking of new closets to clean, new letters to write, and new errands to run. Unencumbered, I dashed to the store and explained myself to no one.

That first day I saved for myself. I reveled in the silence, the calm, and the feeling of being in control. For once, the day would not be a bucking bronco. I would stay in the saddle and get everything done. I would not be thrown by a child.

I know, of course, some parents can take this sensation for granted. To parents whose children have all finished kindergarten, liberation almost comes automatically. They can glory in the knowledge that until 2:30 or 3:00 on school days their houses can be "empty." I know I am waiting in line for my turn at this—but I could not hold on for another three years without relief.

That first day I was alone I wanted to shout with joy that I had some time to myself, for myself. Always before when I had left my children, it had been for a reason. Either they were busy or I had someplace to go. Finally, I came to realize that giving myself a break is also a reason. My friend got to choose between a cleaning lady or a baby-sitter. Her house could use cleaning, but she said it was no contest. She chose freedom. I did not feel guilty for making myself a present of time for myself. I believed even my youngest was old enough to understand that when Mommy leaves, she always comes back. We have a lifetime contract.

So I grasped at my Mom's Day Out, my sanity saver. I had been waiting for that day. It was a small thing, I realize—a personal milestone recorded only on my private emotional growth chart. No, I had not been held captive behind a Berlin Wall, but on my first day alone I understood liberation.

So when my daughter asks me if I've run out of love for any more babies I tell her that just isn't true. But I think I have run out of energy and resources. I don't have what it takes to answer one more voice shouting "Mom!" the second I sit down. I can't remember the shoe size to one more pair of feet or the eating preferences of one more picky person. I know that at certain times I will miss the talcum sweetness of a baby after his bath and the cuddling that nurtures an infant just as much as his milk. But the years have weaned me away from needing them the way I once did.

There comes a time after you pack up the baby clothes and sell that playpen to a neighbor when you take stock of where you stand. Instead of looking back to the childbearing experiences I've already had, I am looking forward to events entirely new. I am putting the baby years behind me. Having reached my decision, I suppose the only thing left to do is give away the baby clothes. I hesitate to do that, however. From what I hear, that's the surest way to get pregnant.

2

Smile, You're on Candid Camera

Family portraits

We are gathered under a tree and we are all supposed to be smiling for the camera. I cannot imagine any of us smiling, however, because we are not having fun yet. Approximately twenty minutes ago I lost all sensation to my lower legs. This is not surprising since I have contorted my legs to become a chair for my forty-pound daughter—and she sits there angrily kicking the furniture.

Storm-warning flags began to fly even before the photographer arrived. First, I had to schedule this family picture-taking session for a day when I could assemble the entire family. That meant playing dodge ball around work, nap, and sports schedules. That was hard. Then, I had to convince the family to do it. That turned out to be harder.

"We are going to take our first picture of this family all together, all in one place at one time," I informed my children. "I expect full cooperation."

I was, as they say, whistling in the wind. I ran into the first squall over what clothes the kids would wear and a full-fledged storm when we tackled the combing of hair. We had moved on to the matter of posing when my daughter announced she didn't want to be in the picture at all. Thus, my legs have become her chair as I attempt to coax her (stunningly crowned by the hair she would not let me braid) into some semblance of a smile.

We cluster around my youngest, perched in his swing, and try to look comfortable beneath the ole backyard tree. Already I fear that the odds of getting a good picture are about as high as the odds that we all will have our eyes open at once. My daughter puts a leaf on her head just as the shutter clicks. In another picture she is beautifully photographed struggling to get off my lap. My instinct is to throttle her. But because there are witnesses, I humor her.

"Stickers if you behave," I promise. She pulls her skirt over her head.

"I'll let you eat dinner on your special china plate," I coax. She stares at the ground. Finally, the photographer lets her take a picture using his camera. She decides to cooperate.

Two frames later, green gooey stuff begins to bubble out of my youngest's nose. Then, a full hour before his earliest conceivable nap time, he begins to get fussy. He does this by alternately crying, rubbing his eyes, and trying to climb out of the swing. I run to get him a raisin box. The photographer shoots the next roll of film between his chews. About the time my son regains his good humor, my daughter starts to lose hers again. Determinedly, I keep my smile plastered in place. My husband, whose legs have cramped from holding our noncomplaining oldest, lobbies for a change of pose.

"How about you take a turn in the swing?" I brightly suggest to my daughter. She thinks that idea is swell. My youngest, who believes property rights is the main issue confronting his generation, does not. Seizing the chance to stand up, I hold him aloft so he can push the swing. But in this position he also can pull his sister's hair. Finally, smiling all the while, I immobilize him in a hammerlock. Eventually the photographer—insisting he has run out of neither film nor patience— says he has had enough. I do not ask of what, preferring to believe that he means enough adequate photo opportunities. To my mind, he is a good photographer. I have not seen his pictures, but I like his style.

My children, set free, are instantly transformed back into adorable, charming creatures as they run off to play. My daughter beams, my toddler is no longer fussy. They probably will photograph far better than I. As I thank the photographer, it occurs to me that the man truly earned his salary. I can think of only a few less stressful lines of work than photographing children—divorce mediation, for one.

In conversation a few days later, I ask another mother how often she has full family portraits taken.

"The children grow up so quickly," she answers. "So I like to do it once a year."

I don't. But while I may not have a series of family photos, I do shoot pages of film with my words. As I write about my children, I try to capture the stages of their lives. I try to describe the way they were—the poses that feel so ordinary when they occur, but which will seem so extraordinary to remember later. When my three-year-old is thirteen, he will not remember how cute he was as a toddler. I write about him so that at least I will. The photo album of my mind is packed with portraits of my children, and I want to share a few.

I have devoted pages to my youngest and his toddler years. This has been a time when I wonder how anyone who looks so cute can act so awful. Here is how he looked at twenty months:

An eager contestant in life, my youngest started each morning convinced he would be a winner. First, I would hear the thunder of his little feet as he barreled down the hallway. His blond curls would bounce as he ran. Then would follow the shout of alarm, the scuffle and screams of protest, followed by the slamming of the door. Even from upstairs, I knew what had happened. My toddler, eager to be with his siblings, once again had been summarily ejected. He saw it as rejected.

"Why can't you let him play with you?" I would chirp with indomitable optimism.

My older children had a million reasons, all of them true. He messes up our fort, they would answer. He changes the channel. He pulls hair. No matter how much I would coax, no matter how many reprieves he received, eventually my youngest ended up out on his ear. For a while they would lock him out with the baby gate originally intended to lock him in. He had the plague; they put him in quarantine.

Ya gotta feel sorry for a fellow like that. My youngest is an intriguing combination of devil and angel. He's a sweet guy even if his favorite toy happens to be the garage door opener. He's a good kid, even if he leaves footprints on the refrigerator shelves as he climbs to reach his cup. Before he would throw his food on the floor, he used to always give a two-second warning. He is the last child in my family to recognize me by my knees.

As far as children go, I try to tell myself he is no worse than any other. Once I took him with me for coffee at a friend's house. The place was crawling with kids. We mothers took turns rescuing precariously placed china cups. Only my child successfully managed to smash one.

"Don't feel bad," another mother said. "Now we all feel good because our own kid wasn't the one to do it."

Periodically I decide to do better than my two other children, who slam the door on my son. Here's another mental picture of my son, twenty-four months old, at his first Mommy & Me class. I thought I could open a few doors by giving my son some special attention. Enough Mommy & Us. So off we went, just the two of us, to a mommy's class. It was a morning of unstructured fun—with just a few problems. At rug time, while the other children sat singing in a circle, mine ran around in one. While the other children stayed behind the gate and off the playground slide, mine viewed climbing over as a new challenge. For entertainment he practiced pushing over the kids he could not reach to bite.

As I drove home, exhausted, I realized that my attitude had altered. I began to think that perhaps there were good reasons why my youngest child was suited to be my third. It required more than one sibling to handle him: One had to push him out the door while the other one slammed it.

These feelings were confirmed when he officially turned two. For a long time I thought my youngest's two-year-old stage was a personal punishment visited upon me for having the audacity to bear three children when deep inside I knew I only had the patience for handling two.

Mentally, I flip the page and conjure a clear image of my son: His body tensing, his eyes sizing up the competition, he would run as fast as he could to claim possession of the red tricycle. His purpose was not to ride it, but to make sure that nobody else did. Six months earlier, of course, he would have let another child help himself to his trike without a murmur of complaint. But six months ago my child was not yet two.

From the child's standpoint, of course, two is not a terrible age. It simply represents a time when a child who never previously had an opinion in his life suddenly expresses one on everything. It is his turn to assert independence. This poses a problem to a mother in the habit of asserting control. It slows you down when your child refuses to be dressed in any clothing that has to be pulled over his head. It tries your patience when your child throws a screaming fit because you looked at him. And it embarrasses you when your child uses the baby next door for target practice.

My husband had a new joke. What's the difference, he would ask, between a terrorist and a two-year-old?

Answer: You can negotiate with a terrorist.

My son had learned a lot in his two years. In two years he had learned, for example, that if he shoved a smaller kid in the chest, the kid would fall over. He had learned that if he wanted something somebody else had, by pulling hard enough he sometimes could take it. So when my son was on the prowl, I was on patrol. He was not my first child to rappel down the bookshelves . . . although he was the first I have found sitting in my bathroom sink. His favorite trick was throwing his clothes in the bath water and peeing on the carpet. He would scream until I let him have the crayons, and then he would proceed to break them.

Since he refused to talk, my son could not really "use his words" to express his desires. When he turned two, however, he perfected one syllable perfectly. A furious scowl darkened his face, his rigid body became an exclamation mark punctuated by two furious fists, and he shouted, "Na, Na, Na!" I believe he meant "No."

Just before he officially turned three, and before I was ready for it, my youngest learned to climb out of his crib. I took it as a sign of another way in which my son's love has been a blessing but his behavior sometimes feels like a curse. Some days my youngest is so cute I just cannot stand it—and some days I just cannot stand it.

I see him that way now. Only the smudged outline of babyhood remains evident in his pudgy feet and the extended curve of his belly. It will be gone entirely in another six months. He looks a lot like his big brother but does not yet act like him. Right now, at least, his nails grow until I cut them. The hair that I comb after bath remains neat an hour later. And although he sticks his fingers in his ears, I have never seen him use them to excavate his nose.

He no longer pushes food out of his mouth with his tongue. He doesn't have to. Now he clamps his mouth shut and pushes himself away from the table. He no longer curls his toes when I try to put on his shoes. He puts his shoes on himself and then uses them to pedal his tricycle around the block. He loves things that go: airplanes and ambulances. The noisier they are, the better. His current ambition, could it be determined, probably would be to drive a garbage truck.

My youngest is a bulldog who cannot take a hint. He interjects himself into every game his siblings try to play without him. He has no fear of punishment and expresses his displeasure by indiscriminately screaming at anyone who gets in his way. His favorite toy is a plastic guitar with missing strings that he plays as he dances and sings. Sometimes, when he isn't playing the guitar, it doubles as a powerful weapon. He has moderated since his terrible twos, but I would not yet go so far as to call him fully civilized.

Oh, but when he is good, he is very, very good.

A thirsty sponge with infinite capacity to absorb, he drinks up affection. Leave-taking at the baby-sitter's is an exquisite extravaganza of kisses, matched only by the smile on his face when I come to take him home. He is not yet too old or too big for me to carry or to hug. After a fire engine, I am his favorite mode of transportation. Unlike his siblings, he still believes his parents are omnipotent. Whatever the calamity—a hole in the roof to a leak in his cup—he believes Daddy can make it all better. And if I pretend to cry after he has hurt me, he tries with his kisses to make it all better.

It confounds me, this beguiling combination of sweet and sour. But only recently did I realize that his brother and sister also can fall under his spell. My husband and I came in one evening just after the sitter had put the children to bed. Our youngest, she said, had been crying for a few minutes but she ignored it and he finally stopped. She assumed he had fallen asleep. I knew otherwise. I could not hear crying upstairs, but I could hear footsteps. I tiptoed up to find the crib was empty. I located my youngest in bed with his brother.

"What's going on?" I asked.

"Mommy, he was in his bed crying for you. Then he was crying for Daddy," explained my seven-year-old, who had spent the better portion of the afternoon slamming doors in his brother's face.

"So how did he get into bed with you?" I asked.

"Well, he stopped crying for you," my son replied with a sheepish grin, "and then he started crying for me."

■ ■ ■

There are several classic ways in which I picture my daughter. She is an animated one: brown eyes flashing, chestnut curls bouncing as she laughs, talks, and issues orders. She is the most mercurial of my children. She alternates between confectionery sweetness and sulking anger. "I never go first!" "I'm running away!" she huffs at a moment's provocation. Yet her smile is the sun and her morning hugs start my day. She works hard at her accomplishments: whistling, snapping her fingers, tying her shoes.

"I'm almost ready for kindergarten," she informs me as she prints her name. She is, I suspect, trying to get the jump on her older brother.

I picture my daughter when she is drawing, hand poised over her markers, carefully selecting the proper color. Most mornings by 7 A.M. she has already logged nearly an hour of sketching. To my five-year-old, drawing isn't a job—it's a passion. At preschool and at home, she colors and she creates relentlessly. My daughter not only draws a picture, but she also decorates the envelope into which it goes. She is productive. We have her work stacked up to the ceiling, decorating every wall, and even more to give away as door prizes to visitors.

My daughter takes it seriously and she is good at it. She worked hard to learn how to draw a tulip. She was proud the day she mastered drawing stars. And she spent weeks perfecting a kitty cat to her satisfaction.

"I'm no good at pumpkins, Momma," she mourns. And she is not much comforted by my reply that this is seasonal work for which there is only spotty demand.

I once heard a psychiatrist explain that you can tell a great deal about a child from his drawings. Look at the distances between people, see if any figures are isolated, and notice their relative sizes, he said. You can tell if a child is happy or if he feels small and powerless. I mentally filed the information away, and now it reassures me. My daughter specializes in family portraits. There are the boys of the family, with big ears, brown pants, and grins from ear to ear. There are we girls of the family, in matching triangle skirts, two eyelashes apiece, and no ears. We all stand, always, side by side with our arms stretched out wide as if we are dancing.

It is a happy world my daughter draws. It is a world full of bunny rabbits, rainbows, flowers, and an occasional butterfly. It is a well-ordered world, with everything in its place. The sun is always shining bright yellow at the top of the page and the grass is always bright green across the bottom. Her colors are vivid and strong. She mixes crayon with marker to striking advantage. I gave her a set of thirty-six markers, and she ponders carefully her choice before setting pen to paper. She is quick to crumple a mistake.

"I messed up," she says.

She not only draws her pictures, but she tells me about them. Each comes with an entire story.

"This is a dog and a cat," she explains. "The dog is eating her bone and the cat is eating her cat food. After they are done eating, they are going to play together on the grass."

Hers is not a world full of coloring books. Those, I am happy to see, stay in the cupboard waiting for the day when coloring inside the lines will be the most important lesson she can learn. I am in no hurry to see that time.

There is an innocence to a child's creativity, but it does not last for long. The children who dress like dragons for the Halloween parade one year, announce they are too old to wear costumes the next. The child who once watched a puppet show with rapt attention, next year is explaining that it's really only people behind the stage. My three-year-old makes uninhibited engine noises as he races cars across the floor. My five-year-old creates stories with her stuffed animals, but she subsides into silence if I walk into the room. And my seven-year-old, who cared little for fantasy, is more concerned now with how things actually work. He discovers with his hands; he imagines less with his mind.

So I treasure my daughter's ability to see things as she wants them to be. All too soon she will see things only as they are supposed to be. I cringe when my seven-year-old accurately but tactlessly points to his sister's self-portrait and informs her that she has forgotten to draw her neck. It does not take a child long to learn the lessons of conformity. I like the way she sees the world. She is far too young to be told that butterflies do not smile.

When I think of my daughter, I also picture her dressed for ballet. She wears a pink leotard with a net tutu and a self-satisfied smile. She thinks she looks beautiful.

It is a scientific fact that a girl's fascination with ballet begins with the costume. Before bedtime come stories, before walking comes crawling, and before ballet lessons come tutus. I have never met a girl over the age of two who does not have her own. Several have entire wardrobes of tutus, complete with fairy wands and crowns. One mother told me that her daughter, who has never had a lesson, walks everywhere on her toes. For my daughter's fifth birthday party all the guests came dressed as ballerinas. They were all beautiful.

When my daughter was four (and able to make a serious commitment to lessons and not just to the idea of them), she began dance class. For many girls, I suspect lessons are a rite of passage. I remember also taking lessons as a child. Today I can carry a child and a bag of groceries while I unlock the door, but I have never been able to carry a beat. Yet I, too, wanted a legitimate excuse to wear the costume.

Now it is my daughter's turn. Each Friday she dons her requisite pink tights and leotard, carries her de rigueur ballet bag, and scampers off to class. I cannot assess her prima potential, but she is entitled to dream. At first she was disappointed. Ballet and tap did not consist mostly of twirls. They are work. But inspired by Angelina Ballerina, she has stuck it out. She earned her reward when her class gave its first performance.

"Rehearsal is over. We're going on the stage!" she greets me, shouting gaily, as I arrive a little early. She wears white feathers in her hair, red velvet ribbons with bells on her wrists, tap shoes, and a megawatt smile.

The six three- and four-year-olds line up on stage. In the center is a petite, porcelain blonde, with pink ribbons in her straight, long hair and her feathers perfectly centered. Standing next to her, towering taller, is my daughter. Her chestnut hair is mussed, her feathers are askew, and I notice that her tights are on backward because I see the bumps for her heels on top of her ankles.

Her excitement increases as the floodlights come on while she practices to the tune of "Walking in a Winter Wonderland."

"Stop!" shouts the teacher. The girls pile up like railroad cars.

"Now, when we dance, what are we going to do?" asks the teacher.

"Don't walk off the stage," my daughter shouts.

"Well, yes," responds the teacher, who clearly had never previously considered the obvious. "But don't forget to smile."

The girls shuffle through their routine. On the chorus, everyone stands with their hands on their knees—expect for my daughter, who is waving happily. As their teacher pantomimes the steps offstage, the chorus line continues. Two girls, carrying on a conversation, walk the wrong way and crash into each other. During the second verse they all turn in circles, each child apparently selecting a different direction. An admiring audience of parents, we applaud mightily. My daughter is the only one who stands there in grand finale, arms flung upward, embracing the world. ("We were all supposed to do that, Mommy," she explains afterward.)

As the other daughters rush offstage toward their mothers, mine stands there enraptured for an extra moment. She has discovered show business.

■　■　■

My oldest son, the trailblazer for his siblings, is sweet, sensitive, hot tempered, and well aware of his responsibilities as firstborn. He is definitely all boy. When I picture my oldest, I think of endless skinny legs, dirty hands, and bulging pockets.

His pockets bulge because my son is a collector. In my mental pictures of my son, I must include the shoebox in which he hides his collections. When I bought my son his Teenage Mutant Ninja Turtles shoes, I did not realize that the real prize was going to be the box in which they came. The shoes long ago were pulverized on the playground, but the brightly illustrated box endures. I know my son values it highly, not only because he stashes it under his bed, but because inside of it he hides his treasures.

They say one man's junk is another man's treasure, and I have only to look inside his shoebox to know that this is true. Like many children, my son has a genetic compulsion to collect. He began young. As a toddler his pockets would bulge after every walk with "treasures" such as shiny rocks, pointed sticks, and unusual leaves. As a youth, he has not changed. He totes home shells from the beach and pine cones from the park. He wants to keep everything that catches his eye and still cannot understand why the tree limb on the grass at the house around the corner does not belong inside our garage.

My seven-year-old is most proud of his collection of colored plastic caps from squeeze juice drinks—junk to those who carelessly drop them on the ground, treasure to my son, who brings them home to his box. Someday, when he has tired of it, I hope my son's juice-cap collection will fade into his past. I am not hostile to his collections; it's just that we see the market differently. I am trying to divest while he is into merger and acquisition. Right now the only things I want to collect are my thoughts. The rest of the time I try to weed out the old clothes, newspapers, and junk mail that threaten to drown the house in a morass of stuff. My son wants to bring home their equivalent.

But I hold my tongue as he indulges his passion. I suspect collections are important to kids who are just encountering the pleasures of acquiring for themselves what they want. Before they have had to content themselves with what others have given them. One day, as I overheard my son and his buddy boast about their collections of collections, I realized that even as grown-ups perhaps we never entirely outgrow the urge.

"Well, I collect juice caps and baseball cards and shells," said my son.

"Well, I collect baseball cards and rocks and cars and butterflies," his friend responded. "Oh, yeah. I also collect money."

I smiled to myself. We're not so different. When it comes to money, I try to do the same thing.

My son collects money as well, but he does not save it. My mental photo album contains a picture of my son clutching his blue Velcro wallet, begging to buy something. This has made an impression on me because up until he was six, money hardly mattered to him. For years, whenever my children would receive checks as gifts for their birthdays, they would turn tortured eyes to me and silently beseech: "Why didn't we get anything?" They never understood that pieces of paper can have value—perhaps because I would always snatch them away to deposit in the bank.

But now all that is changing. I first noticed when my son received a wallet for his sixth birthday. I did not expect him to be thrilled by something into which you put those pieces of paper. To my amazement, he loved it. To my even greater amazement, he began to fill it. Some days he has more cash than I do. His fortune is like the lint in the dryer. I cannot figure out its source.

After he learned the virtue of acquisition, my son began to appreciate the joys of spending. Wherever we go he wants to buy something. He is particularly vulnerable to the lure of vending machines. He will buy sodas, gum balls, or trinkets without discrimination. To him, they are like slot machines; he derives joy just from pulling the levers. His sister is the opposite; she is a born saver. She appreciates money for the mere possession of it. One time she parted with a dollar to buy gum. For days afterward she regretted her action.

"It wasn't worth it," she complained. "I don't like to spend money because then you have less."

Once my son discovered money, he became intensely interested in knowing what everything costs. For obvious reasons, I have been reluctant to disclose the balance on the mortgage or my yearly income. I would prefer that he tell the neighborhood our grocery bill. Conversely my son, who likes to spend so freely, for a long time had no conception of market values. If he saw a numeral 5 on a price tag, he had no idea whether it should be $5, $50, or $500.

Lately, however, I sense he has begun to appreciate the value of a dollar. I know this, first of all, because he now tries to get me to spend my money before he volunteers to spend his own. But also he suddenly has become fascinated with the possibilities for earning income. The other day I told him I had a paying job for him in the garden. I had his complete attention. I told him I wanted some dead plants dug out, deposited in the garbage, and the tomato cages stacked in the garage.

"How much will you pay me?" he asked.

"How much do you want?" I countered.

"Let's see," he said, assuming a bargaining stance. "I need to use the shovel, I'll probably get dirty, and I have to carry everything pretty far, and it's hot outside . . . two dollars."

"A dollar," I countered.

"OK," he said, " . . . for each plant?"

"Total," I snorted.

He agreed—and that's when I realized he has mastered the art of the deal. I had been going to offer fifty cents.

My son is definitely into income. The next day he asked if I had any more jobs. I told the kids they could pick plums from our tree, fill the wagon and deliver them for tips to our neighbors. Then I would take them to a store to spend their money. My son showed an industriousness I wish he would apply to his homework. He and his sister picked, washed, packed, and hawked those plums up and down the street. When we counted their loot, they had each earned $2.50. Ever since then my son, who immediately wanted to pick more fruit, has a new appreciation for nature. As far as he's concerned, money grows on trees.

I have another image of my son. He is smiling into the camera, his front teeth missing. No photo album would be complete without its shots of gap-toothed children grinning proudly during the second time in their lives when they must gum an apple.

"Don't forget to brush your smile," I have admonished my son, only to realize that he has nothing in front to brush and very little more with which to chew. I am always grateful that toothless children, like bald babies, do not realize exactly how silly they look. Fortunately, seven-year-olds consider losing teeth a status symbol.

In my home we had a lot of excitement over the Tooth Fairy. Teeth had never been such a hot topic of conversation before. We hadn't had that much excitement, in fact, since my toddler hid the TV control box. When my son's first tooth began to wobble, our house became bicuspid rumor central.

"Will the Tooth Fairy wake me up?" my son wanted to know. Then he turned mercenary. "How much will I get?"

My kids had other questions.

"How do you chew with your teeth out?" my daughter worried. "Maybe you just don't eat."

My son saw it differently. "Maybe," he offered hopefully, "maybe, if you lost all your teeth at once, you wouldn't have to brush at all." Later he had the nerve to suggest that he get paid more if he brushed a tooth after it fell out. The idea, I corrected him gently, was to brush the tooth before it fell out.

To my son, of course, none of this was theoretical. He saw it as a very personal matter of agony and ecstasy. The ecstasy was knowing he soon would wear the kindergartner's badge of honor every time he flashed his gaping grin. The agony was contemplating how in the heck to remove the loose tooth. My son vacillated, torn between wanting to get it over with dispatch and wanting to get it over without pain.

"I'll just use my hacksaw," my husband offered sadistically.

"We used to tie a string to the tooth and tie it to the doorknob," I offered. "Then we slammed the door."

Our son declined radical measures. He tried chomping on carrots and apples to no avail. Finally, he resorted to that age-old practice of wiggling his tooth with his fingers while he was supposed to be paying attention to his teacher. One morning he wiggled the tooth right off.

With great ceremony that night my son placed his tooth beneath his pillow as bait. Then he lay in wait, hoping to trap a Tooth Fairy. First I poked my head into his bedroom, but even in the darkness I could see my son's eyes fly open. Later, fighting off sleep, my husband tried. He crept in and emerged chastised a second later. Our son heard him, he reported, and sat up faster than a two-year-old can knock over his juice. Finally, early in the morning, my husband sneaked in and slipped two quarters under our son's pillow.

Regardless of its market value, however, my son's first tooth is worth more than fifty cents to me. When it first broke ground in his baby mouth, I greeted that tooth with a lot of excitement. Now I plan to keep it. Finally holding it in my hand, I marveled at the size of the actual tooth. You can't tell it from the photographs, but it's really very little for such a big deal.

■ ■ ■

3
If This Is Tuesday, Then You Need a Bath

The same old thing is getting old

Mothers, perhaps the ultimate beasts of burden, are yoked into place. If you subtract the repetitious from the routine chores of the day, we have very little left that is new or exciting. When it comes to cooking or cleaning, there is very little I do one day that I didn't do the day before. There are always meals to cook, rabbit cages to be cleaned, and bedtimes to enforce. A mother is never at a loss about what to do next.

"Why should I make my bed?" I remember asking my mother as a child. "It will only get messed up again."

My mother made me do it anyway, and now I understand. Like my mother before me, I won't allow any chores to be skipped. Why wash the floor if it's only going to get dirty again? Because standards must be maintained. As a mother now, each morning I wake up, before I put on my makeup, I try to figure out what's going to be for dinner that night. Each night, after dinner, I stand in the kitchen and try to figure out what's going to be for lunches the next day. In between I try to accomplish a few other chores, most notably laundry and grocery shopping.

So let's start with food. Its purchase and preparation gobble up time. Sometimes, deciding what to cook is the biggest part of the battle. When my neighbor went away for the weekend, I envied her not because she was going, but because for two nights she wouldn't have to decide what to cook for dinner. In a poll totally unworthy of Gallup, we mothers frequently cluster outside each evening asking each other what we have resigned ourselves to serving. We give the same tired old answers.

"Tacos," says my neighbor to the right.

"French toast," says my neighbor to the left.

"Pizza," answers a third.

"Chicken," I admit, hastening to add that this reflects not so much my dedication to full-course cooking as my desire to throw out the bones along with the garbage in the morning. (The only reason we no longer have chicken every Monday, in fact, is because my husband began coming home and saying, "This is Monday. Garbage, I mean, chicken again?") I used to make all sorts of interesting dishes, foods that, when my three-year-old sees them now, he refuses to get into his high chair. And, anyway, cooking such dishes requires careful preparation. As it is in my house, some nights I feel my choice is either to let the children rot their minds by watching TV while I cook, or skip cooking and serve Ding Dongs.

My favorite chore, I suppose, is packing three lunches every night. I try to do a good job and I hope my children recognize the care I take with it. If I stuck them with leftover roast one day, I try to reward them with peanut butter the next. Bananas one day means apples another. I try to give each child a treat, some reward for eating (I hope) all the other stuff. I try to tell myself that a lunch packed with care is an expression of love. This makes it hard not to take it personally when the sandwich returns home half-eaten. I dare not wonder what it means that my oldest son brings back his lunchbox full of grass and my daughter never finishes her juice.

I try to tell myself that taking care of my family is a noble calling. But sometimes their responses are daunting. I ask my husband what he wants for dinner.

"It doesn't matter," he answers. "Let's just eat soon."

I ask my son what he wants for lunch.

"Please, Mom," he answers, "can't I just buy a corn dog in the cafeteria?"

I know that food is important to my children, however, far beyond its nutritional value. Likewise, I know that the dinner hour is important to me.

The children stampede screaming into the kitchen, embroiled in a fight staged partly for the benefit of an audience.

"He hit me!" blubbers my daughter. She subscribes to the theory that only the righteous can cry.

"She messed up my cars," snarls my son. He believes that he who wronged first wronged most.

Panting with anger, awaiting my response, it is obvious that two of the three people in the room believe I should settle the matter. But I have no intention of dipping my hand into dirty water.

"Want some cheese?" I respond. They want. And by the time they have consumed, nobody even remembers the fight. Even in primitive cultures, breaking bread together is a sign of friendship.

Eating, I conclude, has done it again. Now I am not saying food is emotional aspirin, something to pop in a feel-good society. It does not relieve every headache; sometimes a nap is in order. But I am saying that 90 percent of the time something to eat can make it all better. A crabby child is a hungry child. When my youngest whines and begins to lose his marbles for no apparent reason, often the trouble is not in his head but in his empty stomach. When a child wakes up grumpy, I no longer try to talk him out of it. I feed him out of it. When my daughter and her friend spend more time squabbling over who gets which Barbie than they spend playing with them, then it's time to serve snacks. Children whose mouths are full find it difficult to argue.

Food is important to children. Youngsters who cannot remember to close the door never forget to ask what you cooked for dinner. It is difficult to say too many good things about food. I should know; I've been eating all my life. Now it seems I spend nearly all my life serving meals and dispensing snacks to children who apparently require nourishment at ninety-minute intervals.

But that is not all. Food, originally intended to fill stomachs, also functions as entertainment. How many mothers honestly can say they have never baked cookies to fill the hours of a rainy afternoon? Grown-ups who dine out recognize that eating can be an event.

Food is also the best bribery. To convince my youngest to sit in the grocery cart, for example, I bribe him with crackers. By the time we reach the checkout counter, I must pay for more empty boxes than I care to admit. But when crackers no longer work, I am fully prepared to graduate to cookies. (Yes, that word was "bribe." Any time you employ food in a capacity beyond purely nutritional value, it enters the realm of bribery. How do I feel about bribery? About the same way I do about spraying bugs. In the abstract I believe ultimately it is a short-sighted response to a problem. In reality, when caterpillars begin devouring my vegetable garden, well, that is a different story.) I read an article once that suggested it is unwise to regularly associate a particular reward with a particular event. I do not care. Crackers get me through the grocery shopping.

And, finally, food is the original source of comfort. It is, after all, the first thing mothers give their babies. Food works, and I understand why. It pleases the palate, fills the tummy, and imparts a sense of well-being. I know that when I am upset no problem is so serious that a pint of Rocky Road won't make it feel better.

Because I attach so much importance to food, it is no wonder I attach a great deal of importance to dinner. I see the dinner hour as a time to pass the peas along with the news of the day. We recount the day's accomplishments; we interact as a family. Since the days when they were babies nursing, my children have had all too much of feeding on demand. We eat breakfast as we straggle downstairs; we eat lunch at countless off-site locations. We have only dinner left at which to gather together.

The evening routine is pretty much standard. One by one, beginning at 5 P.M., my neighbors disappear inside—only to summon their off-spring shortly thereafter. An hour later, mine are the only children left playing. It is not that I like to eat late. Rather, my husband arrives then. Monday is the only night he is punctual, and then he is rushing to see football as much as his family.

Many of the other mothers, whose cooking also reflects their children's culinary tastes, do not wait for their husbands to come home. They eat without them. In some cases this means the husband's microwave meal awaits him in solitary splendor. In other cases this means his wife does. But in many cases, according to another inexact poll, the father does not dine with his children.

For years now I stubbornly have resisted eating in split shifts, viewing it as the sort of trial separation that could lead to divorce. I don't think alternate custody of the meal is good for the family. Well, the theory is great, but in practice the hour grows late. We nearly starve waiting to eat. Long after other mothers are denying their children snacks, mine continue trekking to the kitchen for another quick fix. It is tricky to dole out enough food to diminish their stomach pains but not to dull their appetites. I pass out vitamins before dinner, as though the fruit-flavored chewables are hors d'oeuvres. Hence, when their father appears, our children greet him with true excitement. I have never been quite sure whether this response indicates love or a reflex linked to salivation. They know that when he comes home they get to eat.

Lateness is not the only reason I have begun to waffle in my support for the mandatory dinner hour. Rather, I have come to realize that by delaying dinner everyone gets to eat together but me. No matter how quickly I serve, someone is always ready for seconds before I sit down for firsts. Invariably I am cutting food for my youngest before I have eaten mine—and some nights mine is what he eats. Since I am still standing, usually I answer the telephone that is wired to ring the moment we eat. And, at most meals, at least one child spends part of dinner closeted in the bathroom or begging to be excused to watch television.

So my fantasy of a close family dinner is partly just that. Fantasy. We may all be in the same place at the same time, but we are not necessarily together. Nonetheless, I cling to the dinner hour on the theory that something is better than nothing. I require that my children spend at least ten minutes sitting at the table eating what it took me over an hour to prepare. I cannot see letting children eat without their father.

But I admit that sometimes, when I long for a break, I think a viable alternative would be letting everyone eat without me.

■   ■   ■

If Monday nights used to mean chicken in my household, Fridays meant fish and Saturdays meant rabbit. No, those are not items on the menu. That is the schedule for cleaning up after the family pets. They are, of course, not my particular pets. The fish belongs to my daughter and the rabbit to my son. But when it comes to routine maintenance, they are my pets. They are another of the chores that I take the time to do once, only to have to do again.

My children have always wanted pets, but I have not. I have not wanted the responsibility. I knew before we acquired them that the animals would become my burden, which is one of the reasons why for years I never wanted any living creatures in my house except for my family. How we got the animals in spite of my better instincts makes a story in itself.

I tend to view pets the way many grandparents view children: They are great fun to visit and play with, but when they create a fuss or become a burden, it's wonderful to hand them back to their rightful owners. And I was correct. My feelings were verified two years ago when we pet-sat for our neighbor's two finches, one cat, three turtles, and a goose. I came downstairs one morning to find my daughter sitting there, by dawn's early light, engrossed in earnest conversation with the parakeet. I have no idea what time parakeets prefer to arise in the morning, but I'm willing to bet that in her excitement my daughter woke up this one. For my children, the excitement was overwhelming. This was the closest they had come to owning a pet. For me, it was too close.

"There's so much to do," I had groused to my husband the night before. "In addition to assuming responsibility for the care and feeding of three children, plus fertilizing the flowers, I now have animals depending on me."

"Turtles just eat lettuce," he said in an attempt to defuse my anxiety.

"A lot you know," I responded. "Our refrigerator is full of iceberg and they eat romaine."

Responsibility is, of course, the nub of it. One day I fully intended to own a pet. But I had hoped to avoid taking on any other living creatures until my children were old enough to take on the responsibility for themselves. I had enough on my plate without asking for extra helpings.

My husband almost cracked me once. A beautiful stray collie showed up at our house, eager for affection and food. My husband and son gave him both.

"He's a great dog, isn't he?" my husband asked my son rhetorically as they raided my refrigerator to scrounge a meal.

"Maybe Mommy will decide we can keep him," he continued in a despicable attempt to shuffle the burden of decision over to me.

The dog, fortunately, was addicted to wanderlust. He left us before we could decide whether to keep him. I can't tell you how sorry I was.

Since that time, except for my neighbor's pets, I had held firm. We were going to remain borrowers, not owners, until my children's sense of responsibility caught up to their desires. An incident weeks later confirmed that it hadn't.

I found a caterpillar munching down my petunia and deposited him in my son's bug keeper. (Bugs and crawly things are always good for a day's entertainment to a boy.) My son, who was five at the time, insisted on taking him to school for show-and-tell, so I agreed we could keep him for the night. To tide him over, I served the critter another one of my blossoms. When I picked up my son that evening, proudly he was allowing his classmates to touch his caterpillar.

"Do you want to let him go?" I asked hopefully.

"No way," he replied. "I've always wanted a pet."

"Where is the food I put in there?" I asked.

"I threw it away," he replied. "It looked yucky."

As we climbed into the car, my son dropped his bug keeper and the caterpillar fell out. I can't tell you how sorry I was; we found him. At home, despite my discourse about how all living things require food and water, my son handed me the caterpillar and ran off to play.

Resignedly, I fed the guy another one of my flowers. Later we looked up caterpillars in the encyclopedia together, talking again about the importance of food and water. My son appeared to understand, but then he got distracted without doing anything about it. This continued for two days. By then I had had enough. I informed my son that taking care of the caterpillar was his responsibility. I closed down my catering business for bugs and stopped feeding the guy. Two days later, when my son noticed, the caterpillar was dead. I can't tell you how sorry I was.

My euphoria lasted several months, during which time we had no pets. I had staked out my position, I had dug in, and I was firm. In retrospect I wonder, how did I ever expect to defend such a Maginot Line?

My son breached it first. When he was six, he admired the Venus flytraps at the nursery, and for some reason the man behind the cash register gave him one. I think he did it because they are too much trouble to feed. For a few weeks my son sort of took care of the plant himself. At my suggestion he would place the plant in the sun, water it, and hunt up flies and ants for the trap to eat. But it is not all that easy to serve protein to a carnivore. You must either slaughter insects and place them inside the trap or direct a flow of live traffic in its direction. Suffice it to say my son's interest waned. In a few weeks some of the trap's leaves blackened and died, confirming my worst fears—a slow death by starvation, the cruelty of which now rests upon my conscience.

Not too long after the death of the trap, my daughter, at age four, waged her own successful assault against my no-pets policy. Our experience merely confirmed my worst fears that this pet business was way more than we could handle.

So let me tell you my fish story. My daughter won a twenty-five-cent goldfish at a carnival. I couldn't abide the thought of any more cruelty, so we had to invest twenty times that much to set the fellow up in a comfortable condominium. I even purchased a companion so the fish wouldn't feel lonely. I must admit, my daughter loved her "fishies." She named them Jeff and Jennifer. She watched them with limpid eyes. She could feed them, but, speaking of responsibility, she couldn't clean their bowl.

"The fish water is dirty," she would tell me.

"Tell Daddy," I would tell her.

"Tell Mommy," he would tell her.

And as I cleaned the goldfish bowl, along with the kitchen, my daughter would beg me once again to let her feed the fish. All of which brings us to the issue of funerals—something else with which I had hoped not to deal until the children are older. Without a doubt, the trap died of starvation, but as for the fish, well, I'm afraid their problem was the opposite. No matter how careful we were about food, first the big fish went belly up, then the little guy. After the first fish croaked, I prepared my daughter ahead of time.

"I think the other fish is dying," I told her. "I think we will find him dead in the morning." That way, when we did find him dead in the morning, she did not go to pieces. (I was upset, however, and both times had to prevail upon my husband to bury the creatures at sea down the toilet.) Then, operating under the replacement theory for coping with grief, I quickly bought a black molly and moved her into the condo.

When I had explained my problem to the fish store man—"No more corpses," I told him—he suggested the molly as a hardier fish. He neglected to tell me she was a pregnant fish. We came home one day to discover the bowl full of tiny baby fish, some of whom were just starting to swim. We were excited. I decided maybe I had been wrong about this pet business; it had its compensations. We went outside to tell everyone in the neighborhood we were parents. We came back inside only to discover that what we thought of as babies the mother had perceived as hors d'oeuvres. The babies were gone. And the momma fish, which had been kind of dragging her tail the day before, never looked more chipper.

Nobody told me that mollies eat their babies, but I had to tell my daughter, who was tearfully horrified. (My son, by contrast, was fascinated and planned to tell his entire class the next day.) We looked up mollies up in the encyclopedia together.

"Why did the mommy eat her babies?" my daughter asked.

"She didn't know they were her babies," I answered. "Lots of bigger fish eat little fish, and that is what she did."

We talked some more. It helped, I discovered, to say "young," instead of "babies." By the time my husband came home to the scene of the slaughter, my daughter rather calmly informed him: "Lots of fish eat their young." She was stoic, perhaps because a child's feelings are less intense about an animal she cannot hug. Anyway, we still have the molly. My daughter still feeds her when she remembers, and I still clean out her bowl whenever the stench is unbearable.

Having said all this, I am embarrassed to admit that the rabbit was entirely my fault. I regretted it almost instantly, but by then it was too late.

I cannot explain why, but suddenly I decided the time was right to give my son a pet for his birthday. A feeling came over me, much the same way on some nights I will decide it is absolutely out of the question for me to cook dinner. The certitude was almost palpable and not to be denied. Ironically my husband, that great lover of dogs, did not share it.

"He's seven years old. He really wants a pet of his own, and I think he's old enough to take care of one," I argued.

"I don't agree. We'd end up feeding the animal," my husband said.

"Just some turtles or something easy," I answered.

"No turtles, rats, hamsters, snakes, or gerbils," my husband said stonily. "But maybe a nice bird that could learn to talk and then teach our two-year-old," he added, softening a little.

Our son, of course, loved the idea. He wanted a dog—big, furry, and lovable that he could take for walks. No dog, we answered. A dog would be a pet later for the entire family.

"We want something just for you, like a bird," I chirped.

"I don't want a bird, but maybe a rabbit," he answered immediately.

"No rabbit," my husband answered immediately.

"Bunnies are so cute," I said, disagreeing with my husband. A rabbit, after all, would be the quietest and cleanest member of the household.

I appreciate any creature that can't talk and gives himself a bath. My husband gazed at me frostily.

"Let's go to the pet store and see what they have," I backpedaled, doing my best Donna Reed imitation. And so we did. When we walked into the pet store my husband crossed immediately to the bird section. Our son never made it past the bunnies.

I know it was a rabbit, but I can only describe it as puppy love. Our son stood there, stroking that quivering back, cooing softly, and I knew that he was lost. My husband knew it, too. Nobody else even wanted to look at the birds. The salesman tried to tell us a rat would make a better pet, but nobody listened to him, either. The rabbit would have to stay inside our warm house all winter, he said, but nobody listened. Boy met bunny and the rest, as they say, was history.

"Buy it," my husband sighed, accepting his fate the same way the coyote submits to the roadrunner.

An hour later, we came home with one bunny and more equipment than new parents need to set up a nursery. We named him Bugs (as in Bunny). When Bugs was safely set up in his cage, I left to go shopping. When I came home, Bugs was trying to dig a hole in the family room carpet.

"Who said you could let him out?" I demanded of my son.

"Daddy did," he answered.

"He's pooping on the carpet. Maybe this is not a good idea," I said, mildly I thought.

"But the kids wanted to play with him. He's so cute," my husband answered as he fiddled with the food and water containers. I responded like any mother. I vacuumed and wiped. I am, you must understand, the sort of mother who will buy my child a sandbox and then curse myself daily as I sweep up sand. I began to wonder what had come over me. I began to remember all my previous objections to having a pet. I began to realize that when it came to second thoughts, it was too late. I went upstairs. I came back later. My daughter was entertaining Bugs with her bunny puppet while my son read him "Pat the Bunny." They also had shot an entire roll of Polaroid film of the bunny.

"Who let them do that?" I asked rhetorically.

"I did," my husband answered. "We needed pictures. He's so cute."

That night at bedtime I had to pry the children away from the cage.

"It's hard to say goodnight," my husband explained, as the bunny nuzzled his hand. "He's so cute." Sounds like something I might have said. Once.

Too late now. Bugs is a bona fide member of our family. A few nights ago when my husband came home, I heard him talking downstairs. We were all upstairs, so I went down to check.

"Daddy's home," he was telling the rabbit. "Did you miss me today?"

■ ■ ■

When I don't have another mouth (human or otherwise) to feed, then I'm sure to have another bed to make. Every time I turn around I seem either to be coaxing my children into bed or tugging them out of it. Sleep is another major preoccupation of a mother's life. No sooner do I get my kids to sleep than it's time to get them up. No sooner do I get them to sleep in their own beds than they are worming their ways into mine.

Before I had children, I used to fantasize about how they might bring me pleasure. I thought about sweet smiles, gifts of genius, or research they might undertake to benefit mankind. A cure for cancer wouldn't be bad. In my ignorance, I was filling out college applications for an infant. I never considered something as basic as sleep. I cannot say enough good things about any child who naps or who sleeps through the night and late into the morning. Portions of this book, in fact, were made possible courtesy of my youngest son and the days he had the decency to take a nap long enough for me to write them.

In my house, although several children might benefit, only one of my children still will deign to nap. In my house, although all of us would benefit, only on rare nights do all of us sleep soundly in our own beds. First, I would like to sing the praises of children who nap. Then I would like to sing the blues about the nighttime traffic through my bedroom.

Throughout my life as a mother, I have heard from other mothers about their children who are good sleepers.

"I had to wake him up at four this afternoon," the mother simpers, "but he still was sound asleep again by eight that night."

"I couldn't believe it," gushes another. "We brought her home from the hospital and she started sleeping through the night. I had to check to make sure she was still breathing. And I thought a baby would tire me out!"

"I'm so lucky," sighs a woman I formerly considered my friend. "Most of his friends have outgrown their naps, but he still loves his."

Personally, I believe gloating in public is rude. So I thoughtfully hid my glee from a friend who complained that while her three-year-old took four-hour naps, her second baby barely took one at all. It's not that my children have never slept. Of course they have: in my arms or while the car is moving. It's just that concerning my two oldest, prime time for their afternoon naps was but a brief period of months that was reduced to a memory by the time they hit three. "Quiet time" was invented by a desperate mother whose child refused to nap.

My daughter began going through nap withdrawal at age three and has just now conquered it. She is young enough to still need her nap, but old enough to successfully fight taking it. Many are the times I have "napped" with her, only to have her wake me by announcing that she just cannot fall asleep. So she stays up. This makes late afternoons my personal purgatory. Sometime around 4 P.M. she begins to cry—about the things I said, about the things I didn't say, about her birthday party last year. One look is enough to set her off. Her friends should consider themselves lucky when she orders them to go away and leave her alone.

But my youngest, he is a miracle to behold. Herewith my ode to the afternoon nap—that oasis of time bringing pleasure sublime. (Pardon the poetry.) During my son's Golden Age of Naps, I merged his two short and unproductive naps into one. Some afternoons he would snooze away for three solid hours. As politico Everett Dirksen might have said, a few minutes here, a few minutes there, and pretty soon you're talking real time. I can get something accomplished. But his glories do not stop there. Not only does he go to sleep without argument, but he awakens the same way. He does not scream to announce that he is awake and ready to go. He will lounge cozily with his thumb and his blanket and wait for somebody to notice him. He will cuddle briefly, flash a smile, and then he is ready to resume his exploration of the world.

My eldest, who at age two discarded afternoon naps faster than an empty candy bar wrapper, was the opposite. The slightest sound would disturb his sleep. And when he awakened, he was an angry god I tried to appease. The only way I found to make him stop screaming was to stuff his mouth. I would leave juice and a bowl of Cheerios like a sacrificial offering in front of a TV already tuned to "Dumbo's Circus."

My youngest, by contrast, can sleep serenely through the vacuuming. Doorbells, telephones, and shouting siblings fail to disturb his sleep. I cannot exaggerate the pleasure I derive from his tremendous talent for napping. Unlike his siblings, he appreciates the luscious languor of snoozing in the afternoon. Best of all, sometimes when he has been sacked out taking his nap, I used to get the chance to take mine.

But now, unfortunately, we have begun running into a different kind of a problem. Nap time has begun colliding with soccer, basketball, or ballet. And frequently I am in the unhappy position of having to awaken my youngest because my oldest has to leave. I no longer have a peaceful afternoon to spend at home. We have places to go and, as the third child, he must go with us. My last child has been my best napper. He is also my first child who will have to stop napping because I made him.

I wish there were some way I could continue to take my nap, however, because so often nighttimes in my household have been anything but restful. I do not sleep soundly in the midst of a storm. For a while my youngest, the prince of afternoon naps, was a pauper of the night. Until he was well over two years old he would awaken nightly at 3:30 A.M. and stand erect, screaming in his crib. He did not yet know how to talk but he made clear exactly what he was saying. He was telling me to take him into my bed, a place he has no business being. To press his case, with his relentless cries he would take a jackhammer to my sleep. He was more than old enough to sleep through the night and old enough to understand that he sleeps in his bed and I sleep in mine. I would explain all this to him again each night, as I carried him from his crib and deposited him into my bed. He wouldn't listen to a word as he would snuggle into my pillow on the sheets my body had warmed and instantly fall asleep.

Before I got married, I used to sleep alone. Before I had children, I used to sleep with my husband. Now I am never sure whose body I will find sprawled out beside me when I awaken each morning. I do not sleep around, but my family does. Our house contains six beds, one crib, two couches plus assorted floors upon which a person conceivably could sack out. On any one night it seems most of them are in use, at least briefly.

I realize this is an intimate subject, but I suspect my husband and I are not alone—in not being alone. Our bedroom, I joke to my husband, is like a train station. It bustles with unscheduled arrivals and departures at all hours of the night. Show me a husband who sleeps alone with his wife and I will show you a father whose children have finished teething. In my house many a child creeps in for a short visit and stays the night. They are inspired by insomnia, bad dreams, darkness, wet beds, and asthma attacks. My definition of a bad morning is when I have to change not only the sheets on their beds, but on mine as well.

Sometimes my bedroom is more like a major airport. Lots of people pass through, but it is not their final destination. I am just a connecting hub. Sometimes my children are searching for their father, who believes bed is not where you start the night, but where you finish in the morning. He gets his best night's sleep in front of the television. The only thing that wakes him is when I turn off the set. I can tell where he fell asleep each night by where his shoes are in the morning. Some nights a wandering child will bring him back to bed; some nights he stops where he drops.

I do not sleep soundly amidst all this nocturnal activity. Sharing a bed with children is not comfortable. They sleep soundly, but I do not. We battle ferociously over covers and pillow space. When a child joins me in bed he becomes a human compass pointing perpendicular; that way his feet can use my stomach as a springboard to shift position. Children steal the covers you have just assembled to your satisfaction. Their feet are heat-seeking missiles they warm on the inside of your thighs. They will fight to the death to capture your pillow. When a child sleeps with me it takes forever for us both to get comfortable. Just about that time I realize I have to go to the bathroom.

Trying to sleep in my house is, in short, exhausting. I haven't slept soundly since I brought my first-born home from the hospital. It's hard work, monitoring everyone's whereabouts. Even in my sleep I can tell which bedroom door is being opened or which floorboard is creaking.

Wide awake, evidently, my hearing is not so acute. One night, when my husband worked late, I heaved a sigh of relief after getting two kids to bed. As I rocked my youngest, I heard animated chatter through the bedroom wall. I heaved a second sigh when the talking subsided. A while later, ready for bed, I popped into the children's room for my last-glance check. It took a minute to register that both beds were empty. Stalking downstairs to the family room, I found my children behind closed doors watching television.

"Upstairs!" I barked. "Don't ever try that again."

As I lumbered up the stairs behind them, my son asked me why it took me so long to discover the two of them. He didn't understand my answer. I told him that if I had been asleep, I would have noticed sooner.

4

If This Is Wednesday, What Happened to Tuesday?

Momma said there'd be days like this

Some people worry that their credit cards will be stolen. I worry someone will take my datebook. I dare not make a move without it. In it I have written every practice, game, lesson, paper drive, book sale, jog-a-thon, school holiday, doctor's appointment, and party looming in the immediate three months of my life and four others'. Sometimes I have to play bumper car in order to enter anything new. Sometimes I feel as though my days are full and I cannot enter anything new.

Now that my children are easing out of the preschool years and into the elementary school years, I am beginning to recognize how life has a way of careening out of control and aging parents rapidly. I suspect it gets worse.

The more complicated my days become, the more I am prone to anxieties. It is a chronic condition that comes from being a mother. My husband takes care of "important" things; I feel as if I take care of everything else. My days are crammed with a million small details that, taken one at a time, don't amount to much. But together they add up to busy days. Taking care of details is the way I try to stay on top of things.

This is not easy. Some days I feel as if a schematic of my brain would reveal the circuits are operating on stress overload. They would look like the freeway at rush hour. They would smell something like my old toaster before it finally blew. Part of me is wondering where to try next for the tap shoes my daughter needs before her first lesson; another part clamors for attention because I forgot to check whether my son's soccer shoes are suitable for baseball. I am wondering what to make for dinner, where my son left his homework, how I'm going to return the library books, what to get for a birthday present, and who else I can call to try for a baby-sitter.

I used to think the hard part about three children was taking financial care of them. Now I suspect it's also keeping track of them. You see, I know it is going to get worse. So far my youngest is not entitled to his own social calendar. But soon all my children will have important obligations. I can see my car pool days coming on strong. One of the baby-sitters who recently turned me down couldn't work because she had interpretational roller skating an hour's drive away. I hung up the telephone in total awe. Somewhere there is a mother driving her an hour each way to those lessons.

My husband does not entirely understand my stress. After all, I "get" to stay home instead of working full-time.

"Women have choices, men have responsibilities," the aggrieved husband tells his wife in the film *Parenthood*. "My whole life is have to."

I know what he's talking about. Important things like earning money to keep a roof over his family. But we both earn money. And I know what I'm talking about: the additional responsibility for the daily life that goes on under it. ("What camp are they going to this year?" my husband asks in July.) Mostly I take care of the daily details, and the responsibility weighs upon me. I am worried that I will mess up something important. If life is a dance recital, I am worried that I will trip. Before I bore responsibility solely for myself; now daily I bear responsibility for a family.

My husband, of course, thinks he does. As the major breadwinner, he works hard setting his five-year goals at business. I too work hard setting my morning goals after breakfast. I meet deadlines for my editors and deadlines for my car pools. My husband's objectives may be more global than mine, but trying to meet our separate goals can leave us equally stressed.

I read somewhere that at-home mothering is a hard job because it leaves women so little control over how they spend their time. I thought about this as I waited for my three-year-old to hop like a frog down the driveway on a morning when I was running late.

"You're in control," disagrees my husband, who usually comes home each night after baths. "You're in control of the kids."

I think that is a little bit like saying you won't get burned by a fire so long as you use pot holders. I know that the older the children get, the more serious the complications become. Yes, I am expecting it to get worse. I have only to look back to the beginning to see how my earlier feelings of control have begun to erode:

"Well, sweetie pie," the new mother coos. "What shall we eat today? How about trying some sweet potatoes?"

She fusses with the baby carrier, moving her son out of the sun, into the shade, upstairs and down. She changes his clothes and turns him over. She carries on as though her baby were a doll. That is, of course, a good description of new babies. Except for the mess and the noise they can make, they are a lot like living dolls. You can put them down and pick them up knowing that very little has changed in their lives since you left them.

It is easy for a new mother to feel smug because at first it is easy to feel as if you have this parenthood business under control. After all, you determine just about everything that your child does. (A new mother, in fact, is most likely to look at a three-year-old and wonder why his mother let him get so filthy. My approach tends to be the opposite: How did she keep him so clean?) This delusion of being in control lasts about as long as you can pick out your child's food, pick out his clothes, and pick him up.

Older children are not like that. The amount of control they gain over their lives increases in direct proportion to the amount of control parents lose. The first time you shout at your child is the first time you realize that it's also possible for you to lose control of yourself. You haven't gotten your feet wet until you tell your child to get dressed and he replies, "No way! It's my body!"

Then it's time to get real. When my children were babies, the biggest things I worried about were when I finally was going to get a good night's sleep and what would happen if they never ate green vegetables. At the time, I thought I had it rough. Could it be that I just don't know when I've got it good?

The point is that no longer can I tell my children what to do all the time. They do not believe every word I say. I cannot pick their friends any more than I can keep them out of the refrigerator. I can cover my seven-year-old with the blanket at night, but I can't stop him from kicking it off. As my husband puts it, we're at the stage now where it really doesn't matter how loudly we yell.

This is a rude awakening. I know what has been happening, but it is just starting to sink in how bad it is going to get. It's like the first time I realized my youngest knew when we turned down the street where his baby-sitter lives. It's like the first time I realized my daughter was stacking the deck to cheat at Candy Land. It's like the first time I heard my seven-year-old swear and it wasn't a word he had learned from me.

It's not only losing control over my children's bodies, but also over their minds. They have learned to switch mental channels without my permission. They hear things from teachers and friends that I know nothing about. They have problems I cannot kiss and make all better. They worry about things I never realized they knew. The other night I hid in the closet listening to a fascinating conversation about how my two oldest manage to get ready for bed without letting the baby-sitter see them undress. I hadn't realized they were even modest.

Although I try to manage every detail of our daily lives, the task is, of course, impossible. As my children get older, I find I have real problems to worry about. I feel like the string attached to the end of the kite: I'm just along for the ride. But some days I sure wish I knew where we were going.

Look, I knew this would happen; I just never expected it.

■ ■ ■

At the beginning, for example, I did not anticipate that clothing ever would become the source of so much angst. I did not, after all, consult the baby before purchasing the layette. Sure, as a parent I expected to have to buy clothes, dress my children, and wash the laundry. But I did not realize that finding the right clothes or keeping sufficient quantities of them clean would be so difficult. Now I know otherwise. Major wars have been fought over a dress. Good taste to a seven-year-old can be difficult for a mother to swallow.

With young children, of course, the issue is physically dressing their bodies. My daughter once had an outfit that looked adorable: a cute little sunsuit with a matching dress to wear over it. Together, however, they contained fifteen buttons and not a snap in sight. No problem, if you didn't mind completely undressing your child from two layers every time you changed her diaper.

Dressing a toddler is like clothing slippery spaghetti. Would you try to put tights on a noodle? Would you put buttons down the back? We are not discussing consenting adults. We are talking about children who one day may decide they don't want to get dressed or one night may decide they don't want to get undressed. They balk at anything that goes on over their heads, anything that itches, and anything that doesn't look "right."

As kids get older, it is not easy to find fashions that kids will consent to and moms can stomach. Mom is looking for durability and reasonable prices. She is outfitting a boy who destroys his shoes before he outgrows them. She also wants clothing that a child baffled by buttons can remove easily when he heads for the potty twenty seconds ahead of the puddle. She believes Velcro is the best invention since Scotch tape. And as she unfurls the dirty clothes for nightly deposit in the laundry, she has two concerns: Will the stains come out and has she gotten all the sand?

Kids, who evaluate lunch on the basis of dessert, have different criteria. Every preschooler worth his Legos knows pants are no good without pockets. Children like loud colors and big pictures. The picture on the shirt is more important than how it fits. Girls like frilly dresses they can twirl in—before they proceed to get covered in dirt. Given the choice, your daughter would dress for a tea party and your son for jungle warfare.

When I picked out all the clothes for my children, if I do say so myself, they looked rather cute. If they didn't, at least they looked color coordinated. As time went by, however, my children wanted to choose for themselves. No problem. I would hold up two acceptable shirts and ask which one. Then my children wanted to pick the shirts out of the drawer themselves. No problem. I would stack the shirts in order so that the ones on top were the ones I wanted them to wear. But now they rummage around to the bottom. Some days, depending on what they pick, I consider that a problem. Let's just say that sometimes I don't want to walk next to them in public.

Once a child gets an attitude about clothing fixed in his mind, there is no stopping him. Getting a child to wear something he hates is nearly as impossible as buying pants long enough to last two seasons. It goes without saying that whatever clean clothes remain in the drawer are guaranteed to be the ones your child doesn't want to wear. I'm still depressed by how many cute sweaters my son has refused to wear because they are "fuzzy." Currently he scorns any shirt with a collar. Some of my most infuriating fights have been over misguided and un-successful attempts to get a child to wear something that has fallen from favor. My neighbor's daughter once admired a dress my daughter was wearing.

"That was your dress," her mother exclaimed. "And I never could get you to wear it!"

My daughter has an adorable dress she has refused for over a year to wear. She, too, will change her mind when it no longer fits.

The issue becomes crucial when your supply of clothing fails to keep up with demand for it. Shopping to clothe three growing children can be a full-time job. As newborns, showered with attention and gifts, they boasted wardrobes more extensive than mine. I can remember being tempted to change their outfits several times a day, just to work in equal time for all their clothes. But then they grew, and the remaining number of gifts shrank. By the third child, clothes are hardly ever a gift item. I can recognize my youngest son's clothes, in fact, because they have my oldest son's name on the label.

Some days my children get dressed out of the dryer because demand leaves supply behind like an unwanted little brother. There are two reasons for this. First, children are life's kudzu. They grow so quickly it's impossible to keep up. The pants cuffed in the winter are flapping above the ankles by spring. And, second, children consider changing clothes an athletic event. They try to do it as quickly and as often as possible. My daughter will pull off her pants at record speed if her friend shows up wearing a dress. Any item that has touched their bodies once, no matter how briefly, gets pitched into the laundry basket. Children believe it to be the only container in the house to be emptied by magic.

Likewise, although I believe I am fighting a losing battle in my daily efforts to get and keep them acceptably dressed, my children believe the opposition employs magical powers to win. I recall this conversation as I was stuffing a plastic bag full of emergency clothes for school:

"I don't like that sweater," protested my daughter.

"I don't like that shirt. It's fuzzy," protested my son.

"I know you don't like them," I replied. "Because you don't like them I thought they would be good clothes to pack. You won't have to wear them."

"Well, then," my son asked, "what are they for? Why are you packing them if we don't have to wear them?"

"They are your emergency clothes to keep at school in case there's an earthquake."

"Is there going to be an earthquake?" my daughter wanted to know.

"No, I don't think so."

"Then why are you packing them?"

"Just in case there is an earthquake," I said, "and you have to wear them."

"See!" My son howled triumphantly. "I knew we were gonna have to wear them."

■ ■ ■

As a parent, I expected to buy a lot of clothes for my children—but I never expected to buy so much medicine. Talk about life careening out of control! The pediatrician is a regular entry in my datebook. I could argue, in fact, that the single biggest shock to new parents will be how sick their child is going to make them. If you ever want to invite disease into your house, simply plan an important meeting at work that you cannot miss. Nursing someone who is sick, being sick yourself, or recovering from being sick is a primary occupation of parenthood. If I ever find myself with too much money, I plan to buy stock in just one good antibiotic.

An irritating commercial for medicine starts out by reminding viewers that cold and flu season is upon us. I wonder why Madison Avenue believes Middle America needs to be told the obvious. I know everyone is sick. Everyone I know is sick. Nobody is immune. The one time I smugly assumed we had passed the age of ear infections was the time I got one. Likewise, for a few seconds this fall I foolishly harbored illusions my family might escape the current pestilence.

"We haven't been very sick this year," I pointed out brightly to my husband.

"*Shhh*, don't talk about it," he admonished superstitiously—as though germs are a form of verbal contamination.

They must be. We've been sick ever since I had to open my big mouth. It even works by telephone. I once talked to a friend in New York about her child's illness, and two days later my kids developed the same symptoms. I recently listened to a new mother of one say that she thinks it's unfair to take her baby out in public with a runny nose. If I subscribed to that theory, no one in my family would have left the house this month.

My children share their germs with a willingness unheard of when it comes to the last serving of cake. They would use a ruler in order to evenly divide a cookie, but they trade illnesses with unprecedented generosity. The fact that they are incapable of covering their mouths or voluntarily washing their hands may have something to do with it. My kids think hygiene is a dirty word. The fact that everyone is sick also may have something to do with it. In some circles, fevers are cool. Healthy kids can feel left out.

On a typical morning this month two kids woke up feverish—good thing I was home to take them to the doctor. Now I know that the pediatrician gives a price break for the second child in the same visit. In one day at bat I scored a triple: I ended up with three kids taking three different kinds of antibiotics. (At least the youngest, already taking medicine, wasn't getting any worse.)

An endearing aspect of coughs, colds, and flu season is the good grace with which my children accept illness. They hold me personally responsible for the medicines they are required to swallow and make sure I am apprised of every ache or sleepless night. Although it is a battle, I see to it that they get better quickly. We have only limited infirmary space in our house. One time the day the children went back to school was the day my husband got sick.

"I'm not feeling so hot," he said. "I'll stay home this morning and just finish up this report for work."

He sat, bundled under a blanket, in front of the computer I needed to use.

I asked: "Hungry?"

"Yes, actually I am," he replied, as though the thought had never entered his mind.

By the time he wolfed down breakfast and showered—and I had finished the dishes—he felt better. Good thing I had been home to take care of him. When I got sick, honesty compels me to admit, I did it on the weekend—almost as if I knew that otherwise there would be no one to take care of me.

I remember the spring I rejoiced because finally, at last, all of us were free of colds and there was nobody left to get the chicken pox. My oldest cut short my jubilation by coming down with the flu—all over the bedding and carpet in two separate rooms. When he was done, he wanted me to hold him. After I finished washing all his laundry, I waited for the other children to get sick. But I am savvy. While I waited, whenever we traveled in the car, I took along a bucket for insurance. I wouldn't leave home without it. Sounds like another commercial to me.

As you might suspect, over the years I have amassed a fair-sized collection of reasons why school secretaries have telephoned and told me to take my children home. My children have vomited on their friends, shoved strange objects inside assorted apertures, and broken out in evil-looking rashes. This year was, however, the first time I ever had to collect a child because of head lice.

We have had close calls before, of course. Lice epidemics have worked their way through several of their schools. Officials armed with cotton swabs, rubber gloves, and Popsicle sticks have prospected in their hair before, but this was the first time any of them had ever struck it rich.

My reaction was less than pure pleasure. I rated the news as somewhat better than dismemberment but far worse than an outbreak of chicken pox. My first reaction was that I immediately began to itch. My scalp itched, my shoulder itched, and I even had to scratch my elbows. My second reaction was annoyance at the thought of surgically cleaning my children and all the contents of the house. And my third reaction was embarrassment.

"It doesn't mean you're dirty," comforted another mother. "Think of it as dandruff with personality."

I know lice have as much to do with dirt as ants have to do with crumbs: Both come anyway. But that knowledge didn't help much. As I informed the parents of my daughter's playmates of her condition, I knew how it feels to have a social disease. Hearing tales of similar suffering from other mothers whose children are far cleaner than mine only helped a little. Walking into the drugstore, asking directions to the lice treatments, I would rather have shouted "Which way to the Trojans?" instead. I noticed even the cashier backed away from my money. And while I used to lust after stock in companies whose products treat ear infections, after checking out the lice-treatment prices, I have changed my mind. Fear impelled me to buy nearly every booster treatment on the shelf.

My daughter, initially thrilled at missing a day of school, soon changed her mind as I scrubbed her scalp and pored through her hair. Lice give a whole new meaning to the expression "head check." I now know the origin of the expression to "nitpick." (My husband is wrong; I had never done it before.) Gathering the nits from my daughter's hair, I pondered for a moment where to throw them. I settled upon the diaper pail, wishing them a horrible death by asphyxiation.

The afternoon she was diagnosed, my daughter became convinced that she was in reality Typhoid Mary. She worried about whether she should go outside to play.

"I don't know if I should play with anyone," she said. "I don't want to 'explode' the lice all over them." I reassured her. At that particular moment, I said, I could personally guarantee she would not "expose" anyone to anything. Nevertheless, that did not stop my children. Lice became a new item in their arsenal for warfare. Here is what I heard when my daughter and son had a fight:

"Stay away from me," she shouted at him, "or I'll give you lice." My son retaliated a few minutes later.

"Don't touch my toys," he ordered. "You have lice!"

My daughter played outside. That night when I rechecked her head, I was astounded to discover white spots the size of marbles. My first reaction was that she had some Miracle-Gro strain of lice. Then I realized she had been playing in the berry bushes. I knew I was hyper when I found sand in my son's hair and panicked again.

Life is getting back to normal now. My house and my daughter have never been so clean. My daughter's teacher still checks her head before she says good morning, but I think I have convinced my daughter that there is no shame in lice. I do not want her to feel any sort of stigma just because she had those disgusting things in her head. I, of course, know otherwise. The childhood curse of my brothers has come true: We have had the cooties.

5
Chronic Critique Syndrome

*They drive me crazy,
but I'm already nuts*

Thirty minutes remain before school starts. Real mothers begin the countdown with warnings:

a. "You need to pick out something for show and tell."
b. "You need to find your shoes."
c. "You have to clean up your room before we leave."

Pick one, any one. It doesn't matter. What matters is what doesn't happen: anything.

"We're leaving now," you say. "And you haven't:

a. picked anything to share,
b. found your shoes or,
c. cleaned up your room."

Whatever you say, the answer is as follows: "You never give me enough time to get ready!"

As a parent, most realities of the world become your fault. This is known as the Boomerang Effect. Whatever words you hurl at your children execute a U-turn and return to slap you in the face. They come in the form of a complaint. Children are champions at complaining. As a reflex action it ranks right up there with sucking a thumb. Apparently believing they are born with divine rights to a perfect world, most children are disappointed when life is not up to snuff.

In their attitude toward me, my children sometimes can be more taxing than the government. In my attitude toward them, my children undoubtedly think I am the same. The mother-and-child relationship can be summarized thus: You love each other every bit as much as you drive each other crazy.

The way my children talk drives me crazy. They do not talk so much as they complain. I tell my seven-year-old to turn off the television because it is time for him to go to school.

"Again?" he shouts, because, after all, he went to school only yesterday. "Why does school always start during my favorite show?"

Life for my five-year-old is "boring." It is "boring" to stay home and "boring" to go to playschool.

"There's nothing to do at school," she laments. "I had a really hard day today at school. Nobody played with me. I never got a turn on the tire swing."

I ask her teachers if she seems unhappy. They tell me that on a scale of 1 to 10, she's off the charts at 12. She has a ball.

Children find fault with nearly everything. Clothes are too scratchy; sleeves are too long. We go outside too late; we go to bed too early. We go out all the time; we stay home too much. It's too cold outside; it's too hot to play. One of their biggest complaints is that we adults never let them do things for themselves. Again, here is how it goes with my children:

Before heading upstairs to coax the youngest to sleep, I issue instructions to my five-year-old.

"If your brother comes home while I'm upstairs," I tell her, "please ask him to be quiet."

My daughter puffs up with self-importance. "I'll do it, Mom," she assures me.

She doesn't do it, however, because without thinking I deny her the chance. Having easily lulled my youngest to sleep, I am already downstairs when my oldest son comes home. Automatically I intercept him at the door and tell him to be quiet. My daughter throws a fit.

"I wanted to tell him to be quiet!" she shrieks. "It was my job! You never let me do anything!"

Momentarily, I am stunned by the blast of her explosion. I hadn't realized we were talking about anything important. In retrospect, I should have. Children spend their childhoods scrambling to grow up, and nowhere is this more evident than in the Mother, Please, I'd Rather Do It Myself Syndrome.

My three-year-old, for example, has assumed complete responsibility for closing up the house. He has to turn off the lights and slam shut the front door. Let someone else presume to do it and he goes berserk. I would never dream of helping him off with his coat or into his high chair without express permission. To do otherwise would be an affront to his dignity. Likewise, my seven-year-old will skin his knees scaling the kitchen cabinets rather than ask for help getting a cereal bowl. Once a child has decided he is capable of handling the job, he will tolerate no outside interference. Heaven help the bumbler who tells my five-year-old how to set the table.

Kids want to be in charge. They want to be in charge, for example, of their clothes. My children quickly learned how to take things off, more slowly how to put them on. So I have backed off. I let them pick their own outfits and never point to the pockets they have positioned in the rear.

In a world that renders them essentially powerless, children crave authority. And although I would like to give mine each absolute control over making their beds each day, this is not necessarily the direction in which they believe their talents lie. Young children concentrate on physical mastery, but older children are into emotional domination. Especially appealing to a child is the opportunity to tell another child what to do. ("You're not allowed to cross the street.") Better still is the chance to legitimately interrupt another child who is having fun. ("Mom said you have to come inside for dinner now.")

In their scramble to assume grown-up authority, my children end up being childish. After all, sometimes I would like to go to the grocery store without an escort. But do I scream and yell and throw a temper tantrum? Of course not. (If I thought it would work, however, that might be a different story.) Some days the house is not even large enough for three children each intent on doing everything for themselves. My three-year-old wants to turn off the television set before dinner. My five-year-old cries because she never gets a chance to turn it off. And my seven-year-old is angry because he does not want anyone to turn it off. At such times, occasionally I have been known to slam my way into the bathroom, desperate for privacy. Sometimes, when raucous children swarm after me, I am finally able to legitimately shout: "No thanks! I'll do it myself!"

Now I do not believe my children are the original grumps. Another mother once asked me if it is possible for a seven-year-old girl to be premenstrual. But I do suspect children are grumpier than they used to be. I do not remember having the courage to nag at my parents the way my kids complain to me. My children expect life to be a full-course meal; I remember being grateful for small scraps. I never would have complained that I "only" got to go on the merry-go-round two times.

I call my kids down to dinner while I exercise small motor skills cutting portions for three children. Observes my son with ill-concealed disgust:

"Oh, Mom, why did you call us when dinner isn't even on the table yet?"

And I wouldn't mind a few simple, declarative complaints so much. But complaining seems to come part and parcel with whining, a manner of speech I compare to driving with a worn-out brake shoe. Morning and night I hear a broken record: "Why do I have to brush my teeth?" "Why do I have to wash my hands?" Talking through their noses, they tell me that everything is too much effort.

Amidst such a torrent, however, some complaints tend to red-flag my attention more than others. I am particularly angered by two varieties my five-year-old tosses around. These start out either: "You always . . . " or "You never. . . . " I am "never" as nice to my daughter as to her brother. I "always" smile at him. I "never" let her sit in the front seat. I "always" let him sit in front. I love those absolutes. The world comes in only black or white—and my daughter remembers only the black.

It makes me see red. Some days, I just don't think I can take one more negative comment. My kids are always complaining. They never give me a minute's peace. They complain and complain and complain . . . And now they've got me doing it.

■   ■   ■

At its essence, I believe my children complain because I am in charge and they are not. A fundamental element of my relationship with my children is power. I am the boss and they are the workers. Mine is the authorized signature on the credit cards, and they are broke without me. Some days it seems as though from this fact all other truths descend.

My three children, you must understand, overwhelm me. So I spend a great deal of effort trying to prove to myself and to them that I am in control. My children complain to me, but I inevitably nag at them. Without even trying, toward my children I have become a combination policeman, prison guard, and boss.

On a typical afternoon, here is my soundtrack:

My son and his friend have removed every pillow from the family room couch and chairs in order to construct their fort. In addition, the two of them have spread all the magazines across the floor to form a "bridge" so they can avoid stepping in the "hot lava" that apparently flowed across the carpet when I wasn't looking. They see the mess as evidence of what a great time they are having. When I discover it, I see merely the mess.

"You two have to put all of that away when you're finished playing," I admonish them from a fundamental position of weakness since the damage already is done.

"We will," they chorus. But twenty minutes later, seized by the sudden inspiration to play outside, they don't.

No longer a mother, I am a traffic cop: Inside, pick those up, put those away. Grudgingly they comply. Released from servitude, they bolt to freedom in the backyard—and as they flee I notice they are carrying the contents of the toy doctor kit from upstairs.

"Those toys are supposed to stay inside," I remind my son.

"Aw, Mom," he sighs. "We won't lose them. We just want to play with them in the backyard."

Swayed by the pretense of humility in his tone, and conscious of my bad-guy image in front of his friend, I relent. Only a few minutes later I am sorry. Glancing casually out the kitchen window (What? Me spy?), I see my son flooding the yard with the hose as he tries to turn a pretend hypodermic needle into a water cannon. His friend attempts to catch ants with the pretend thermometer.

"Hey, guys," I shout in my most authoritative prison-guard voice. "Turn off the water and keep the toys out of the dirt. Remember, they have to go back inside the house."

The boys mumble what I am forced to conclude is an assent. I find out otherwise later, of course, when I begin negotiations over lunch. After pointing out the toys now impacted with dirt, I present the menu of nutritious options available to them. ("Hi, I'm Teryl and I'll be your waitress this afternoon . . . ") We discuss briefly why cheese alone does not qualify as sufficient lunch to earn an ice cream bar for dessert. We argue about how many slices of apple per plate are required to adequately flesh out a sandwich. Then, on the condition that they wash the doctor toys and wash their hands, I agree to provide yard service and feed them outside. I keep my end of the bargain; they do not.

"Pick up, guys," I admonish as my voice gradually escalates in pitch. "You got the toys filthy. That's the last time I let you bring them outside. And wash up!"

The other boy casts sympathetic glances at my son who must continually suffer under my regime, but at least he shows preliminary signs of response. Eventually the boys—recognizing that I am fed up—pick up, wash up, and eat up. As they bolt to the freezer for treats, I say nothing about the bread crusts or apple pieces left on their plates. They grab their ice cream and head for the living room.

"Eat at the table!" I shout, asserting myself as boss.

With the long-suffering looks of wild animals trapped into domestication, they comply. Clearly, they are sick of listening to me—and actually, on days like this one, so am I.

Some days I deliberately want to step out of character. I don't always want to come down hard on my kids. I don't want to forget what it's like to be young or to have fun. The day I caught myself arguing with my daughter about where in the closet her shoes must go, I had to remind myself these are children—not military inductees. No wonder my older children sometimes forget that on my hands and knees down on the rug, once upon a time, I was their first friend. Now they don't want to play with me. Instead of friendship, they offer me challenges— to my authority, to my sensibilities, to my sanity. I need to maintain control over my children, and I know this means that they will not always like me. But at least some of the time I hope that they do.

And so I have been trying to loosen up. Things have changed since I had to teach them not to touch a hot stove or to run out into the street. Those items are nonnegotiable, and I had no choice but to say "no." The issues we face today are more ambiguous, and sometimes the verdict is still out. Now that my children are entering the grade-school years and beginning to think for themselves, I try to understand their viewpoints and respect their judgments.

This can be difficult, however, when confronted with every passing fad my children decide to adopt as their own. My biggest challenge is not getting bent out of shape by everything my children throw at me. Every stage, I tell myself, is normal. This, too, shall pass, I repeat to myself in what has become my personal mantra.

Just as they vacillate between wanting to be dirty and never wanting to come out of the bathroom, so too they change their definition of what's "cool." While parents before me have had to cope with Darth Vader or the Prince of Power, I had to make my peace with the Teenage Mutant Ninja Turtles. When my oldest turned six, they were the rage. They were a fad that year, like slap bracelets and fanny packs. But at first I wasn't sure they were as harmless or unavoidable. I had to measure them against G.I. Joe, Barnyard Commandos, and He-Man and rate them on the scale of the offensive. I had to readjust my thinking. I started out, after all, believing that my boys never would litter, lie, or play at war.

In order to check out the turtles myself I took my children to see the first turtle movie. I remember standing in line, waiting for my turn to be relieved of my money. The reviews were irrelevant. For most parents in America, including me, choice was not an option. Our kids had to see the Teenage Mutant Ninja Turtles movie. Hence the line.

I wanted to see it, however. My kids were captivated by the characters and I wanted to understand why. After all, when they were infants I tasted their baby food in order to know what they were eating. So I go to the movies with my kids to monitor what they are seeing. (Since I became a parent and curtailed my lavish nightlife, mostly I see matinees. The only recent Academy Award winner I've seen at the theater was *The Little Mermaid*. Since having children, in fact, never have I seen so many movies starring animals.)

Ninja Turtles are unique. The cartoon show was the best thing to happen to turtles since the shell; they hadn't received this much publicity since that overrated race with a hare. (The Turtles, in turn, were the best thing to happen to pizza sales since home delivery.) In one way, I understood their appeal. The Turtles have a lot of personality. In a movie that made New York City appear slightly more depressing than a sewer, at least the Turtles knew how to have fun. The Turtles had class. They were named after Renaissance artists in an allusion totally lost upon my children. They fought a villain named Shredder, familiar to adults from the Watergate hearings—another allusion my children missed.

I realize that fads ebb and flow with a regular tide. My daughter has no interest in a Cabbage Patch doll and I suspect my youngest won't grow up to play with Ninja Turtles. But for a while, Turtles were hot. All the boys wanted their own army of warrior Turtles and their associates, each complete with an arsenal of tiny plastic weapons that got lost almost immediately. When the Turtles were really scalding, they were impossible to buy. I found it interesting that in most stores the good guys were sold out while the villains remained available. The

Turtles were relatively inexpensive, unless you were heavy into accessories. We were not. I have no interest in any vehicle that launches moving projectiles or any substance that bills itself as "ooze." But I know one mother whose son owns a Turtle upon which she spent $200. That's how much the plumber charged her to dig Raphael out of the toilet trap after her son tried to send him back to the sewers.

Yes, for a while, the mother of sons was hard pressed to avoid Turtles. And for my six-year-old's sake, I struggled to evaluate what I thought of them. Translation: I tried not to automatically reject or ban them entirely from our lives.

I guess Ninja Turtles serve the same imaginative purpose as G.I. Joe and Ghostbusters. They let boys feel powerful. As candidates for heroes, so what if turtles seem as unlikely as earthworms? They exercise a child's imagination. As role models, however, Ninja Turtles are not something I want to encourage. I figure the Turtles were pegged as teenagers because that's an obnoxious age only a six-year-old could admire. The heroes in a half-shell do nothing but eat pizza, crack jokes—and fight. I'm not sure how my kids can reconcile such actions with the advice I've always given them: "Use your words and share."

I'm concerned about moral values, of course. I asked my son if the boys who fight and steal for the Shredder are good guys or bad.

"They're bad guys," he answered with heart-warming assurance.

"How come?" I asked, shamelessly probing for a value judgment.

"Easy," he answered, with a neat sidestep. "They work for the bad guy."

The Turtle movie was heavy on the fighting, which troubled me most because it was made to look like a lot of fun. Only bad guys died and any bleeding was discreet. I explained my feelings to my kids as I quizzed them about the violence. It didn't bother them. It bothers me, which is why toy bombers and guns haven't been welcome in our house. But somehow my opposition isn't as effective as it once was. My son has no guns, but he's always fighting a bad guy with sticks or baseball bats.

Somehow I don't mind as much as I thought I would. I won't buy him the props to duplicate the TV show, but I don't mind if he wants to pretend his good guy is a Turtle. He knows it's no more real than

Star Wars. I've decided the kids don't take it seriously, so why am I? In other words, I didn't really mind shelling out for the movie.

So sometimes I deliberately try to just say "yes."

I remember the time my son was standing beside me, in an agony of anticipation, poised for flight.

"Please, Mom," he begged. "Can I climb up there, just one time?"

"Up there" was the top of our six-foot wooden fence. From there he would have a vantage point to see into our neighbor's yard and, more important, to talk to our neighbor's son. From there he also would be high enough that a good fall could splatter his internal organs all over the driveway below. I didn't want him to climb up there almost as much as he wanted to climb up there. As a mother, I have a vested interest in his survival; as a seven-year-old, he feels indestructible. He thinks he is a goat.

He knew the odds were good that I would not let him climb. I knew the odds were good that he would do it some other time when I was not looking. As an automatic denial formed in my mouth, I found myself choking it back.

"All right," I sighed, surprising even myself. "You can do it for just a minute. The instant I say so, you get down."

My son flashed me a look of pleased surprise, and then grinned as if to say: "See how neat my mom can be?"

And I stood there grinning, too. I was pleased with myself for conquering the automatic impulse to say "no." In the days since my hair dryer first became a pull toy, I've had that impulse a lot. One time my daughter wanted soda to drink, and I told her in no uncertain terms that she could have juice or nothing. As I walked away, I heard my son say sympathetically to his sister, "I know. She's tough, isn't she?"

I wasn't sure I was flattered. That is not exactly the reputation I desire or the stuff of which fond memories are made. As a child I remember beseeching my mother one morning not to send me to school because we were going to have a dippy substitute again.

"If you stay home, you'll have to help me around the house," my mother cautioned.

I agreed, and I remember helping her to make beds. But I also remember how proud I felt that she had listened to my evaluation of the situation and treated me as a grown-up. She had respected my feelings.

As a mother, one of my toughest and most unexpected challenges has been learning to go with the flow. It is not easy to jettison the assumption that I know more than my children about everything. I try to remind myself that their opinions count.

The expression, my kids would tell me, is to "chill out." And so I have been trying to refrigerate my feelings. I did this, for example, the day I brought home a box of Alpha-Bits cereal. When he found them, my son was in a state of shock. He couldn't have been more incredulous than if I had offered him a cigarette. He thought it was never going to happen. He's been with me at the grocery store before when I routinely deny him most cereals he wants to buy. By rote I veto any cereal whose claim to fame is that it's "frosted" or contains marshmallows. He's heard me explain at length how the better the prize pictured on the box, the worse the nutritional value of the cereal inside. So he never expected to find Alpha-Bits in his own house.

"Are we having company?" he asked, remembering that when his cousin visited I made an exception and allowed Froot Loops into our house because my sister-in-law said my nephew would absolutely starve without them.

"Nope," I answered. "I just suddenly remembered that I used to eat them for breakfast."

And it's true. I do not recall any battles that might have preceded it, but I do recall feasting on Sugar Frosted Flakes and Alpha-Bits regularly. And, obviously, my teeth didn't fall out and my brain didn't rot.

Alpha-Bits may be an oldie and a goodie, but they are still hot to the preschool set. They remain, after all, a big item in television commercials. My three-year-old, who had refused anything but Cheerios for over a year, pointed to the Alpha-Bits and demanded some immediately. My five-year-old was disappointed in the cereal, claiming that the letters don't look as big as they do on television. But she gobbled them down anyway.

On that first morning, my kids were amazed to find the cereal in our kitchen. It was like a celebrity in our house. They wanted to know why. I'm searching for an answer. All I can say is that a wave of nostalgia must have overcome me. I grew up in an innocent time when people didn't worry so much about doing everything right. I don't recall ever eating yogurt or granola as a child. As an adult, I am beginning to question whether I really need to deny my children every snack that claims to contain "10 percent fruit juice."

The same nostalgia grips me sometimes when I see Fred Flintstone. He is mindless like the other cartoons I try to discourage, but I don't feel threatened by him. He is familiar. It's hard for me to say that my kids can't watch the show when I long ago memorized its theme song.

Oh, sure, I understand that my parents' generation was easygoing in part through ignorance. You can skip through a minefield if nobody tells you bombs are out there. I know my mother did not abstain from alcohol or tobacco during four pregnancies. She delivered four healthy babies whom she nurtured with formula. I remember numerous spankings, but never do I recall being sentenced to "time out." I believe today we know how to do things better. But I also believe we take our task too seriously. We don't want good children; we want them new and improved.

Now I'm beginning to agree that less can be more: Once in a while I need to chill out. A little straying never hurt. Denial, after all, is what makes the forbidden tempting. For a long time I never allowed my children to taste chocolate milk. One swallow of that, I feared, and they forever would scorn milk that is merely white. But one day I weakened and let them try chocolate. Ironically, they didn't like it. Too sweet, they said. The same way with toys. I used to shop only at "educational" toy stores because I figured those toys are "good" for you. Now I've decided that something advertised in commercials isn't necessarily "bad."

So for a while we were busy at my house wolfing down that box of Alpha-Bits. I probably won't buy the cereal again, but that one time really didn't hurt. Alpha-Bits come in the shape of letters. I could always tell myself it's educational.

In courting my children as friends, I'm starting to learn not to sweat all the small stuff. Not every snack is going to be healthy; not every meal will balance perfectly. When my son was in kindergarten, for example, I used to worry about what he brought for show-and-tell. At first I thought it had to be educational or exceptional. Now I realize he should take anything that makes him feel proud, even if it is a Ninja Turtle. I'm also starting to realize there's a lot to be said for convenience. I guess I really wouldn't want a world without kids' meals or diaper wipes. Just because something is easy doesn't automatically make it morally wrong.

Likewise, I'm starting to accept that quality does not always count. I am fully prepared to trash inexpensive furniture now, in fact, so that eventually I can replace it with something good. When you have children, a certain amount of mud and destruction comes with the territory. I'm starting to understand there's no point in making life any harder than it already is. Fads will pass and take the Ninja Turtles along with them.

And so sometimes I try to stifle my impulses and remind myself that exercising better judgment is not always best. All of which is how I found myself sitting on the driveway, if you remember, standing by should it become necessary to catch my son, who was shouting to his buddy from the top of the fence. The mother next door was attracted by all the commotion. Invoking higher authority, somewhat sternly she asked my son, "Does your mother know you're way up there?"

And as my son answered, "Yep," I smiled to myself.

■ ■ ■
6
It's So Noisy I Can't Hear Myself Scream

Using their words

"Can you say thank you?" my husband asked our youngest. "When are you going to talk?" Our son, thirty months old at the time, used to conserve his energy for climbing on top of tables and dashing down the street. He wasn't talking and he wouldn't reveal the answer. It's not that he was mute; he was noisy. In addition to his grunts and groans and exclamations of excitement, he prattled and pantomimed. He simply was not ready to speak more than a few syllables of English. My husband and I told each other he spoke perfectly—in Dutch. But when he wanted something we understood him very well, nevertheless.

Obviously communication through any means is a key facet of the adult-child relationship. However, the very concept implies that children and adults actually understand what the other is talking about. This is not always true. Over the years I have discovered that children who speak do not always listen. And when children talk, their timing can be so lousy that adults may not want to listen.

So the fact that my youngest has been slow to talk has been fine with me. My two other children talk and argue and complain and issue orders quite well in English. I am not all that eager to add another voice to the chorus. One of the biggest changes in my household since the arrival of children has been the increased noise level. My children are loud. My ears are constantly assaulted with the sounds of fights, arguments, conversations, snatches of songs, and questions.

I believe verbal children fall into one of two categories: They either talk incessantly when you wish they wouldn't, or they say nothing at all when you wish they would. Sometimes the same child does both. To begin with, children who talk can have no sense of timing. They believe their voices offer them carte blanche to interrupt. My daughter can wield her voice like a battering ram. She uses it to bust up my attempts at adult conversation.

"Mommy, is green in the rainbow?" she has to know while I talk on the telephone.

Loudly she sings along with her favorite song or commercial. "Don't talk when I'm talking!" she screams at her brother as they jockey for verbal supremacy.

I have tried to teach her etiquette.

"You have to say 'excuse me,' " I tell her. "You can't just start talking to someone who is already having a conversation."

So now she doesn't just start talking. First she interrupts by repeatedly shouting: "Excuse me! Excuse me!"

Even when they aren't interrupting my words, children can interrupt my mood and derail my train of thought. They have lousy timing.

Damp with perspiration inspired by rank fear, I have emerged from beneath the dentist's drill to rejoin my children in the waiting room. My mouth is stretched from sitting for over an hour with both lips wrapped behind my ears, and the left side of my mouth drags down to my chin because of the anesthetic. With superhuman effort, I grimace in an attempt to smile reassuringly at my daughter so that she will never fear the dentist.

"Mommy, you're done," she chirps. "Now can you read me a story?"

My children are always a heartbeat too late or a moment too soon. If I have dinner ready now, they want to eat later. If I haven't defrosted a thing, they want to eat now. If I want to talk to them, they don't want to listen. If I am talking on the telephone, they want me to listen to them now. My daughter starts conversations while I am using the hair dryer.

I happen to believe that quite often timing is a critical element of communication. This also applies to the response. If I tell a child to get dressed, I like to see it happen during that same morning. If I hear screams and yells coming from the other room, I cope better if I am not ensconced in the shower. (I would never take a bath without hiring a baby-sitter.)

Children also believe timing can be everything. My children, who are most vocal when they are interrupting, expect to go to the head of the line when it comes to their own instant gratification. And sometimes they want to gratify themselves by not allowing anyone to wait. This happened one day when I picked up my daughter at preschool. Full of self-importance, she was bearing a present for Mom and Dad.

"I'll carry this present," she announced, handing me her lunchbox, backpack, the book she had brought to share, and three different colored-marker renderings of two girls dancing in a field of flowers beneath a rainbow—all of which I dutifully admired.

"I'll bet you want to know what's inside this bag," she hinted as I flagged down my eldest and tried to pick up the pieces to a train set my youngest had scattered across the classroom floor. "It's very delicate. I'll bet you can't wait to see." I assured her that I was dying to know, but added that I was also anxious to go home.

"This is a present for you and Daddy," she continued as I manhandled my youngest into his car seat and slammed the car doors to trap everyone inside. Through the windows I could see her mouth still working. All the way home—as my youngest howled in an expression of his indignity and as the tape player spewed out the lyrics requested by my eldest—my daughter blabbed about her secret. And as the car pulled into the garage she asked, "Don't you want to open it now?"

"Let's wait for Daddy," I suggested.

"No," she answered. "We don't have to."

"But it's for both of us," I responded.

"I want to show you now," she said.

"Can we go into the house?" I asked as I unpacked the car and realized her lunchbox had leaked.

"All right," she allowed. "But hurry up. This is important and you need to open it now."

I opened it. Now, I am not denying that a Rudolph the Red-Nosed Reindeer constructed out of a pine cone is important. I merely suggest it was not important at that precise moment. To me, the timing was wrong.

Children don't see my point, of course, which is why children and parents can be couplets out of rhyme. The other night, when my children were glued to some ridiculous movie about a mouse floating across the ocean in an old shoe, I tried to get them into the bathtub. I told them to get moving, but they wouldn't budge. I know what they were thinking. My timing was lousy.

Daily I see numerous examples of how a verbal child appears to hear nobody but himself and definitely listens to nobody but himself. My oldest son certainly contributes his share to the noise level in my house. He is like a dog, I joke, and needs to be run daily. A perpetual motion machine, he gyrates, bounces, and fidgets. No part of him is more active than his mouth. He emits animal noises and jungle sounds, chants meaningless words, and plumbs the potty for new interpretations. It's the sort of white noise that makes me see red.

"What kind of jelly do you want on your sandwich?" I ask. "Orange or red?"

"Red," he answers, his leg keeping the beat. "Red, red, red-d-d-d, red-d-d-d-d."

"Can't you be quiet? Can't you try to sit still?" I ask in exasperation.

"Mom," he replies with surprising candor, "I can't even stand still."

My children also excel at blabbing. Ask them at dinnertime to recount their day's activities, and frequently they will be stumped. But should they be privy to a secret, they will vomit every detail.

"Mom, we went to the store and brought you a surprise," my son tells me. "It's in the car in a brown bag but Dad bought paper and he's going to wrap the perfume and give it to you tomorrow."

Another time my daughter says, "I liked Daddy's friend at the jewelry store. When is it going to be your birthday?"

Conversely, sometimes my children's mouths do not flap in the breeze. Rather, they are welded shut.

I hear suspicious noises down the hall. "Who's in there?" I call to no avail.

I hear rustling in the kitchen. "What are you eating?" I ask a silent snitcher.

And sometimes, of course, they answer but they say nothing. Literally.

"What are you doing?" I ask my daughter as she attempts to sneak silently past me and down the stairs.

"Nothing," she answers. Later I discover she has been coloring a bracelet onto her arm with lipstick.

"Where did you go?" I ask my son after he had disappeared outside.

"Nowhere," he answers, leading me to suspect he sneaked across the street.

My daughter lays her stuffed Snoopy on the pillow and uses her hairbrush to give him a medical exam. She talks earnestly to him about his symptoms—until she observes me listening. Then, with an embarrassed smile, she stops. She clams up cold. When I was a child, of course, I was the same way. I also posted verbal "no trespassing" signs. I understand that "nothing" is code. Translated, it means: Grown-ups stay out. None of your business.

As usual I am of mixed emotions. I crave my own quiet time, yet I feel sad when my children quietly shut me out. All of which probably means I shouldn't complain. At least they give me something to talk about.

■ ■ ■

Not all that comes out of children's mouths, of course, are interruptions. Foul language—as in potty talk and profanity—is another way in which my children test me sorely. I suspect some of their behavior is orchestrated for shock effect, to underscore the difference between them and us. And, of course, it worked the time my daughter was four and I overheard her swear.

"Open the door," she ordered. Receiving no discernible response from her brother, she repeated, "Open the damn door."

My husband, who also overheard, was upset that our daughter could swear.

"Where does she hear language like that?" he asked me in an accusatory voice. If words could point, his would be an arrow directed at me. And rightly so. A few minutes later, however, I heard him explode.

"Damn it!" he shouted. "Can't you kids ever leave my tools alone?"

The point is not which one of us is guilty of teaching our children bad language. The point is how well they learn. My friend drove one foul-mouthed child home from school and said her children learned three objectionable phrases in under ten minutes. In my car pool on the way to religious school one Sunday, a four-year-old boy with the face of an angel began to chant, "Luck, suck, fuck." I once overheard my son utter a vulgarity that even I would never use.

"Where did you learn a word like that?" I asked him.

"Oh, some guys were watching our soccer team practice yesterday," he answered, "and they said it about us."

If my son remembered every new word the first time he heard it, his vocabulary would be so large his head would tilt. But, of course, he doesn't. Perhaps swear words stick because when we use them, we do so with a special emphasis. All of which makes children experts on every word we wish they could ignore. They have only to hear a naughty word or see a crude gesture once, and by the afternoon they have made it their own. They are connoisseurs of the gross.

I should know. My oldest especially is in his golden age of potty talk. When he was little, we used to make do with "private parts." This covered everything adequately, I thought. But not now. Now each organ has its own descriptive term to be whispered conspiratorially to buddies with a modicum of giggles. Somehow, at his age, no joke is funnier to him than the noises his own body makes. They are always good for a laugh.

To a certain extent we adults are drawn into it. My son decided his pediatrician was an OK guy when he looked up my son's nose and pronounced, "No goobers."

Most families have their potty jokes. The favorite in my household was when my husband was eating his vegetables and dropped a pea on the table.

"I pea-ed on the table," he admitted. It was a worth a laugh for weeks.

But some of the humor is strictly not-for-adults-only. One child has only to call the other "butt-face" and both break up into gales of laughter. A typical exchange that reduces them to hysterics might go like this:

My daughter to my son: "You farted eleven times."
My son: "Is that possible? [laughs] I won't tell you my secret."

It's going around the first grade. I heard one boy ask a girl the where-abouts of Susan.

"In the bathroom," she answered.
"Doing what?" he inquired, somewhat inanely I admit.
"Diarrhea," she answered.

For a time this jingle was in the Top Ten on my children's hit parade:

> *Jingle Bells*
> *Batman smells.*
> *Robin's in the hall.*
> *Joker's in the bathroom peeing on the wall.*

My friend's children have rewritten another familiar jingle:

> *Tom and Mary kissing in a tree*
> *First comes love, then comes marriage,*
> *Then comes Mary with a baby carriage . . .*
> *But that's not all, that's not all.*
> *Now they're drinking alcohol.*

In another variation on the theme, my son turns to his sister and says,

"Spell 'happy.' "
"H-a-p-p-y," she complies.
"You said a bad word," he chortles. "You said *pee-pee*."

During a first-grade spelling bee, the entire classroom broke up into gales of laughter when the teacher instructed my son, "Spell 'but.' "
The hot riddle in my household goes like this:

Question: What are the two smelliest letters in the alphabet?
Answer: *PU*.

Some of this behavior, I know, is for effect. Kids talk this way to push our buttons. The words themselves are probably not so important as how we adults respond to them. I can think of no other reason why children believe pretend vomit is cool. My three-year-old, who speaks so little English that he does not yet have a word for his sister's name, says one word with perfect clarity: "poopoo." He may not know why, but he always says it with an expectant smile. I can hardly wait until he can enunciate that concept more clearly.

That is, of course, the curse of siblings. Contamination not only stinks, it sinks. My five-year-old knows words my seven-year-old has just learned. What my seven-year-old is learning to spell, my five-year-old can define. I marvel. Was it just the other day I seriously debated whether *Snow White* was too scary a movie for my children to see?

In the car my oldest taught his sister this song:

There's a place in France where the naked ladies dance.
There's a hole in the wall where the men watch it all.

That ditty evidently topped the school hit parade. I'm willing to bet there was not a child in the first grade who had not heard it. Now it's also gone pre-K.

Children teach each other, obviously. I don't know which would upset me more: if my son learned something truly obnoxious from another kid, or got caught teaching it to somebody else. He came home from school the other day, wanting to make a spitball. Spitballs evidently had been a big topic of conversation among the boys. I was relieved to note that he crumpled an entire sheet of paper and then had no idea what to do with it next. I refused to show him.

I try not to overreact about all this. I tell my children I don't want to hear vulgar or crude talk. I tell them I'll try to stop and I expect the same of them. I am careful not to throw a conniption when they swear, or they will catch on that this is important to me. Lately I've begun to sense I've made an impression on my oldest. The other day my son became uncomfortable when I cut the nail on his middle finger.

"Are you sure you want to touch that finger?" he asked me.

"Why not?" I responded.

"Well, if you stick up your middle finger, it means you don't like someone," he said. "And if you stick it up two times, that means you really don't like them."

I thought that was a helluva note.

■ ■ ■

When children talk—or complain or swear, as the case may be—it is no wonder we adults do not always want to hear what they have to say. But there is blame enough for both. At least children are generally straightforward about saying what they mean. We grown-ups are not, and because honesty is out of fashion we don't always hear our children when they tell it like it is.

When my daughter finished her first swimming lesson, she wanted to know why they didn't teach her anything.

"We just put our heads under water to find the rings," she said. "We pretended our fingers were candles and we blew them out. See? We didn't learn to swim. We just played games."

By opening her eyes under water and learning to blow bubbles, she was in fact learning skills essential for swimming. But my daughter, with her tell-it-like-it-is mentality, didn't recognize that fact.

We grown-ups can be devious. The other day, when my children were warring mercilessly in the backyard, I asked them if they were interested in paid employment. I offered them each a dollar to clean and wash everything in the playhouse and all of the patio furniture. They were interested in the money. So they spent an industrious, cheerful hour during which they got wet and got along beautifully. At the price, I thought buying their cooperation was a bargain. They, of course, thought I was paying for their work—but I considered the clean furniture a bonus.

As an adult, I have learned that sometimes it is best to be tricky with children. I do not always tell them what I mean, and if I do, I do not always tell them all of it. I do not say, "Let's read that book while you lie on your bed because that makes it easier for me to put you to sleep." I doubt whether "Open your eyes under water" would work as well as "Find the ring in the pool." Likewise, when the school cafeteria wants to sell chicken pieces, it markets them as "Ninja nuggets." Hey, it works.

Unfortunately, because I sometimes go around the corner in order to get across the street, it is easy to forget that children travel in straight lines. They are more direct. When my three-year-old's class was baking bread, his teacher asked him to put the egg in the batter. He dropped it in, eggshell and all. She didn't, after all, tell him to crack it.

Oh, sure, children do cry wolf. My five-year-old daughter screams with convincing authenticity over just about any upset. I have learned to distinguish genuine anguish. But sometimes, when children tell it like it is, we grown-ups don't always hear them. A friend relates the story of how her little girl got all dressed for that first nerve-wracking day of school and then began complaining her tummy hurt.

"You're just nervous," her parents explained. "You'll feel better when you get there."

But their daughter disagreed. And again at lunch she complained about her stomach. When school was over, she changed her clothes to go play and announced that her stomach felt fine.

"See? I told you it was just nerves. You feel better now that the first day is over," crowed her mother.

"No, it wasn't school," answered the little girl. "Those new pants are too tight."

I might not have accepted that story, however, if I myself had not once ridden roughshod over what my son was telling me.

When he was three, I bought him a new pair of shoes. They fit him perfectly in the store, but the next morning he began to complain as soon as I put them on him.

"Shoes hurt. Don't want to wear them," he said.

"They're fine," I told him.

"Don't want them," he said.

"We don't waste shoes," I told him. "When we buy new shoes we wear them."

In the car going to preschool he complained piteously about his shoes. Finally, thoroughly exasperated, I said I would take the sneakers off and show him that the shoes were fine. So I did and they were fine. But they fit him a whole lot better once I took the tissue paper out of the toes.

■　　■　　■

Obviously parents are not the only ones who don't listen. But when children deign to listen, this does not mean they hear. Perhaps half of what we tell them flies over their heads as so much gibberish.

I have proof. According to published reports, all across America hundreds of patriotic second-graders stand together during assembly and sing, evidently, about the Mycon Tree. Apparently, they understand that it relates to a "sweet land of liberty," but that must be as far as their comprehension goes. Freedom, they must believe, is organically grown. When I first heard that anecdote years ago, I had no children and so I failed to grasp the real significance of it. Now that I have a daughter of my own who tells me she went shopping at "the swamp meet," I understand.

It's not so much that children are lazy listeners or that adults are sloppy speakers. Rather, what's remarkable is that when transmission and reception are so easily garbled, how do adults and children ever manage to communicate at all?

"I killed a window," my daughter proudly announced at age three. "You killed a 'window'?" I replied gingerly. "How did you do it?"

"I stepped on it," she answered. "I stepped on the black window spider."

We visited a new house to admire the rather extensive decorating. "It's just elephant," gasped my daughter in admiration.

At other times she has climbed on the bathroom scale and asked me, "How much do I wait?" She had a teacher, Valerie, whom for over a year she called "Balerie." My daughter had a friend named Monica, whose full name she believed to be Harmonica. She has pointed to the man in "Star Trek" with funny ears and asked me why they call him Spot. She has asked me if her new game comes with "destructions." She is the girl who had been fighting a cold and one morning announced, "Ah, now I can breathe through both nozzles of my nose."

My daughter is young, I tell myself, and it's only natural that she misconstrue some cues. I know other kids do it. A friend of hers came home from preschool to tell her mother the new boy in class was named Flake.

"Flake?" her mother questioned.

"Yes, Flake," she replied impatiently. "You know. Like corn flake."

My neighbor's four-year-old overheard her mother say she was going to make pot roast stew for dinner and announced to the neighborhood they were having cockroach stew for dinner.

My daughter is on a par with her older brother, who used to think we put groceries in the "refooderator." Likewise, he used to say we were going to barbecue hamburgers after we heated up the "chuckles." I know of a child who listened to the news about the U.S. showdown with Iraq during the Gulf crisis. He turned to his parents and asked why everyone was fighting so much with "a rock."

But then I begin to wonder. Eventually, don't children finally start to realize that something is amiss? Do they ever see the gap between their words and their meaning? After watching Peter Pan when he was five, my son went around the house singing the Darling children's bedtime song about a shepherd. "Tender cheddar," he warbled, sounding like a commercial for Kraft. What's the story got to do with cheese?

A friend tells the story of a four-year-old, whose mother found him after he scaled the living room shelves to play with her pewter collection.

"You can't play with my pewter collection. My pewter is not a toy for you," she reportedly admonished her son.

"Well, then I'll go play with Dad's," he retorted—and flounced down the hall to where his father keeps the computer.

Those make for humorous moments for mothers, but when the problem turns up in school, it ought to give teachers pause. A mother told me this story: The first-grade class had been preparing for Presidents Day, talking about the accomplishments of George Washington and Abraham Lincoln. Then each child was asked to draw pictures depicting something for which each president is famous. Sure enough, one kid produced a picture of a bearded man with reindeer and sleigh.

"We haven't been talking about Christmas," said the teacher. "Why did you draw a picture of Santa Claus?"

"That's Abraham Lincoln," responded the child. "You said he freed the sleighs."

I recently had this remarkable conversation with a seven-year-old girl.

"Know what I wanna be when I grow up?" she asked. "An electrician."

"Oh," I replied, scrambling for an appropriate response. "Well, that's great. You can make the lights come on."

The girl assessed me for signs of dementia. "No," she said with a lofty look. "I just love babies."

7
Getting Along When You Don't Get Along

▚▚▚▚▚▚▚

Who said we were friends, anyhow?

"L ook at what a good job your brother did on the potty! Isn't he terrific?" I ask my daughter, hoping for some positive reinforcement.

"So what?" she responds. "What's the big deal?"

If I think my relationship with my children is rough, I have only to observe how children treat each other to realize that I am wrong. Children are brutal to each other. They are rude to each other, they compete with each other, they copy each other, and they erect the foundations for their friendships upon shifting sands.

Among siblings, competition is the standard mode of operation. No discussion about childish behavior would be complete without mention of it. My daughter does not rate a gift by how much she likes it. The key factor, rather, is if it is "better" or "worse" than what her brothers received. I ask a child to wash. He refuses on the basis that nobody else has done it yet.

Eating lunch can be a competitive sport. Suddenly one child puts down his glass of juice and declares with a flourish, "There! I beat you. I finished first." Of course no contest, to my knowledge, had been declared. But it doesn't matter. No matter is too small or too big to be reduced to competition between my children. When I pick them up from school, they hold veritable shouting matches to see who gets to talk to me first. Sometimes I must be careful that while my conversation is directed at one child, my hands are busy stroking or hugging the other. Praise for one upsets the other.

Competition perhaps weighs most heavily upon my daughter. In many ways I understand. We are both children in the middle. I also competed when the oldest claimed all the attention due the first and the youngest claimed all the attention due the last. My daughter doesn't yet have homework for me to praise, and she no longer wakes up from a nap smelling musty for me to hug. She is finding her own way down the middle. Sometimes I think it is the hardest pathway of all.

One day while we played a record, she and her younger brother danced. They were both darling, but I admit there was something particularly adorable about watching my three-year-old attempt to boogie. My daughter noticed.

"Watch me," she demanded. "Your eyes weren't on me."

That is, of course, the complaint of any sibling. In translation it means: Look at me, give me more attention. Attention is the fundamental commodity for which all children compete. But while vying for attention crops up constantly in the form of daily squabbles, I did not expect it to be an underlying theme when the kids weren't even fighting. I found out otherwise when we were planning birthday parties. My son was going to be six and two months later my daughter was going to be four. I consider my daughter's behavior a classic:

I turn to my son, dangle a verbal worm on a hook, and ask the single question in the world most guaranteed to catch his complete attention: "Who do you want to invite to your birthday party?"

Enthusiastically, he bites and spews forth the names of his dearest buddies. I have never previously heard of several, but studiously I record his every utterance. The subject, however, fascinates more than just my oldest.

"What about my party?" demands my daughter, even though her birthday is not rapidly approaching. "Let's talk about my party."

"All right," I reply with equanimity. "Talk."

She sighs a moment in rapture and then begins. "I want a ballerina party," she states. "All my friends who take ballet can come in their ballerina costumes."

She rattles off a few of those accordingly selected. Wisely, I refrain from observing that she herself does not at this time study ballet. My son can be forgiven for smirking. No girls are to be seated around the Batman tablecloth at his party. Wisely, I refrain from observing that the tablecloth is as close to the movie as he is going to get. I steer the conversation back to my son. "Now, what kind of games do you want to play at your party?"

To a soon-to-be six-year-old, this question is second in importance only to what kinds of treats will be in the goodie bag. Earnestly we compare the merits of "Father, May I?" and "Duck, Duck, Goose."

"I want to have a tea party," interrupts my daughter.

"I'll remember that," I inform her solemnly.

A week later, we are in the bakery, awed by the endless possibilities for birthday cakes.

"Don't you want a Batman cake?" I ask my son, who regards me with astonishment for making such an outlandish assumption. Table-cloths, I had failed to realize, have nothing to do with what's served upon them.

"Baseball," he declares with satisfaction. "I want baseball because this year I am going to play baseball." Shrewdly, he wants to know how much whipped cream will adorn his cake and who will get to keep the plastic baseball players on the top.

"What about my cake?" demands my daughter. "Doesn't anybody want to talk about my cake?"

Of course I do, and she obliges.

"I want beautiful roses on my cake," she says. "Pink and red roses. Oh, no. I mean I want a rainbow on my cake, a beautiful rainbow. Maybe rainbows and roses. It will be so pretty."

Finally, the great day dawns—which is about how early both excited children are up and running about. My son devotes his usual thirty-seven seconds to wardrobe selection and personal grooming. My daughter is still begging to wear nail polish when the first guest arrives.

Determined to look her best, she changes into her tutu halfway through the party.

The party passes in a kaleidoscope of action. When it is over, I feel as though I have spent the afternoon on the inside of a garbage disposal. My sensibilities are shredded. My son has a ball. He rips open his presents, chows down every morsel of cake, and generally behaves like a crazed chimpanzee. My daughter hovers near the edges of his limelight. Too soon for him, too late for me, we find ourselves scraping frosting off chairs and picking pieces of popped balloons out of the bushes.

"Was it a good party?" I ask, never too proud to curry a little appreciation.

"It was terrific, Mom," my son assures me before running off to play with his new toys.

My daughter plaintively inquires whether he has to share. Then she casts a dispassionate eye at the birthday decorations.

"Time to take them down," she announces with flat finality. "His birthday is over. Doesn't anybody want to talk about mine?"

One time I mistakenly thought I could harness my children's competitive instincts to my own advantage. I thought that two highly competitive children might try to outdo each other by seeing who could behave better, but such was not the case. As I discovered instead, they will compete for attention even if they have to get it by being bad.

Standing on the bathroom scale one morning, I saw the solution to my problem. (No, not that problem.) The solution was trading stamps and the problem was my oldest son's surly attitude. Adults, he had been making it clear, are superfluous aggravations placed upon the planet to torture boys—even worse than sisters. My son did not consider doing as he was told a viable alternative to ignoring it. So the problem was how to encourage positive behavior in my son, and the solution was trading stamps. When I went to college, my mother sent me off with a bathroom scale she acquired by redeeming trading stamps. Today trading stamps have fallen from favor, as have the full-service gas stations where she used to get them. Nevertheless I still use the scale and I still see merit in the idea.

This is how I tried to repeal a law of human behavior. The law says that if not all of the children are good all of the time, then some of them must be bad some of the time. I failed. Instead I merely proved the Seesaw Theory of Child Behavior.

"Every time you are a good helper, I'll give you a sticker," I told my son and daughter. "Every five stickers on your chart means you get a prize. Get ready for bed without an argument, and you could get a sticker. Stickers will be your reward for outstanding behavior."

That did it. My son's eyes gleamed and he hasn't been the same since.

"Let me help you set the table for dinner," he says, charging eagerly into the kitchen.

"I wasn't in time out at all today," he shouts as I pick him up at school.

"I'm all ready for bath," he announces, before I even fill the tub.

"How come you're being so terrific?" I tease.

"Because I want those stickers," he answers, deadly earnest. Whenever he is near the refrigerator, he eyeballs his sticker chart the way an investor pores over the stock market closings. Since I've discovered what every kindergarten teacher already knew, my son hasn't been the same.

Neither, unfortunately, has my daughter. When her brother earned so much attention for behaving, she decided to swing the spotlight back—by misbehaving. Unfortunately, I had failed to realize that when one child garners attention for being good, the other will compete by being bad. Competition fuels their behavior up and down like a seesaw. True to the precepts of the seesaw theory, while my son had been a problem, his sister had not. He had been the one with whom everything was a fight. She was the one open to rational discussion. No longer. Once the sticker program started, she perfected new responses to everything. It was as if her mouth had a death wish.

"So what?" she would snip with an I-dare-you sort of look on her face.

"I don't have to if I don't want to," she would say, another one of my favorites.

Oh, she realized she was not doing as well as her brother in the sticker department. But instead of getting better, she got worse.

"Give me a sticker! He always gets them!" she snarled.

It was not easy awarding that first prize to my son and not to my daughter, but my credibility demanded it. Privately, however, I began grading on the curve. I lowered the standards my daughter had to meet to earn a sticker, just as I raised them to demand more of my son. I did not want one to pull too far ahead of the other.

But now I wonder if I have solved anything. Mathematically, I came out even. My son's behavior improved, but my daughter's is worse. As I said, once again the Seesaw Theory of Child Behavior held true. As they compete for attention my kids simply alternate going up and down. And that is why parents must always be up—on our toes.

■ ■ ■

Siblings compete constantly, but even within relationships outside the family kids can be tough as nails. They will cut each other cold with absolutely no sense of loyalty and talk about their birthday parties in front of children they have not invited. As they get older, however, children discover all that loyalty they formerly did not have and apply it to their peers. Then, wanting to go along with the gang becomes the equivalent of social survival. It can influence everything from the way children talk to what they wear. Just watching all this can be tough on a parent.

Pausing regally at the front door, she is a lady addressing her liege.

"Sorry, Julie," my daughter haughtily intones. "But I do not want to play today."

My heart aches at the sight of Julie's crestfallen face; my daughter seems impervious.

"Julie is your friend and you made her feel sad," I not-so-subtly reprimand my daughter.

"Sorry," she repeats. "But today I want to play with Kate."

For today, at least, Kate is the highly coveted prize in my child's goodie bag of friendships. But I cannot vouch for tomorrow. The shelf life of a child's loyalty is even shorter than his attention span. In the first few weeks of kindergarten, my son had three "best" buddies. They varied, I suspect, with respect to changes his teacher made in the classroom seating plan.

When it comes to first friendships, I am not nearly so tough as my children. I am more like Silly Putty, picking up impressions of hurts and slights from everywhere. I cannot help but agonize as my children blithely run through the minefield of making friends.

I know what I want. I want my children to be liked and to like others. I want them to mind their manners, share their toys, and play with the children I enjoy. That is not always what I get. Sometimes my children cannot share their toys, let alone a friend. I have watched them battle for possession of a visiting neighbor. When my son has a friend visiting, my daughter will play in a corner of the same room and then try through conversation to insinuate herself into their action. Usually the friend will not object, but her brother will. On other occasions my daughter ejects her brother or they both eject the three-year-old.

"They won't let me play with them!" my son complains.

"We don't have to!" shouts my daughter.

Two days later she is the aggrieved party, asking angrily why the boys never let her play with them.

At the playground I meet mothers I like and see children who strike me as adorable. It goes without saying that they usually bear no relationship to the kids my children select to bring home. (I do not know which is worse: when my children's friends drive me crazy or when the friends are not the problem but their parents are.) A friend and I were feeling triumphant the time we finally sent our sons, both seven, to camp together. At last they would get the chance to know each other. Turns out the two boys never played together at all.

What children lack in finesse they possess abundantly in bluntness. Routinely I see children callously jilt each other when a "better" friend comes along: "You can go home now; I'm playing with Mary today." I have seen a mooning girl hover dejectedly near the object of her desire—checking back every hour even after being told her friend does not wish to play.

Kids don't see the contradiction in their behavior. I remember when my daughter was so excited because her first friend from school was coming over to play. If I could have bottled her excitement, it would have been stronger than coffee.

"I'm so glad to have a friend," my daughter bubbled over to me. "All the other kids already are friends, but how did they start to be friends if they didn't get to know somebody new? You should be nice to friends."

While we were talking, her old friend from the neighborhood came over to ask her to play. My five-year-old gave her a coldly appraising glance and said, "No way."

I shudder with gratitude that I no longer must endure the social cruelties of children. I would rather fall down the garbage disposal than have my feelings ground up by their changing loyalties. It is bad enough to watch.

A friendship in full flower can be a beautiful sight. When my seven-year-old sees his buddy next door, he reacts like a thirsty flower when it's watered. He perks up all over. But kids' friendships are highly perishable. At their ages, friendships are made or broken on the basis of who gets to go first at Candy Land, who has possession of the ballerina Barbie, and who agrees to color instead of play dress-up. Two children panting to see one another sometimes can get along in each other's company for a total of twenty minutes. This is particularly irksome when it occurs at your house and the other mother won't be back for another hour. There is nothing like groveling to five-year-olds.

Coping can be hard on a parent. I think it is easier to carry on a conversation in the dentist's chair than to know with certainty what to do. A friend told me this story:

One day when her daughter Lisa was bored, they saw another girl, Courtney, with whom her friendship had cooled. But Lisa and Courtney agreed to play. Just then Pam, more highly desirable, came over wanting to play.

"You can't play with Pam. You're already playing with Courtney," her mother said, taking a stand against disposable commitments.

"Well then," huffed Lisa. "Then I don't want to play with Courtney."

So Courtney and Pam decided to play together, and the mother was left with Lisa—and left wondering exactly what principle it was that she had defended.

My seven-year-old has had equal difficulty charting his course through changing friendships. He is uncertain how to maintain old friendships while making new. He doesn't know whether they are strong enough to stretch beyond the boundaries of different classroom assignments. The plot can become rather Byzantine to follow. I know one boy who switched attention from his old friend to become buddies with somebody new—and then one day found his old friend and his new friend playing together without him. He reacted with all the composure of an outraged lover.

Frankly, in the face of all these heavy emotional entanglements, I find my three-year-old something of a relief. He has the emotional posture of a punching bag. Each day he's ready to start a relationship anew, with absolutely no recollection of injuries suffered the day before. Immune to subtleties, he's straightforward and direct. If he wants you to go away, he screams at you. If that doesn't work, he stomps on you. But I can deal with his behavior. With my youngest, at least, you know where you stand.

With the older kids, I am not so sure. They place parents in an awkward predicament. Do you get involved and fight your child's battles for him? Or do you hold back, knowing that eventually they all get as good as they give? The child who utters "get lost" eventually hears it himself.

I know two brothers who dislike each other's best friends. "For some reason they don't get along," says their mother with a shrug. "But I try to stay out of it."

I know she is right. I need to learn not to take their relationships so seriously—because the children do not. A child's spirits are made by

Rubbermaid. They bounce back from slights a lot faster than I get over my embarrassments. I have heard my oldest brutally castigate a guest, "You're no fun. You always have to have everything your way." But by the time I amble over to poke my head into the room, the boys are playing and the words are forgotten by everyone except me.

Intellectually I know that these things take care of themselves. What goes around comes around. And the day will come when my daughter will beg in vain for the favor of an old friend's company. Still, I am tempted to be my children's emotional bookkeeper. I debit and credit the tally of their friendships to see if they are well liked. I try to balance the books with mitigating words.

"She's feeling a little grumpy right now. I know that she would like to play with you another time," I soothe.

"You made Julie feel sad. You can have more than one friend and play with them at different times," I sermonize.

"You shouldn't talk to your friends like that; those words would hurt your feelings, too," I admonish.

But ultimately I know that my words do no good. Just as I cannot settle every scuffle, I cannot manage every friendship. It sounds brutal, but every child has to learn his lesson in the school of hard knocks. I just don't want to watch. And so, concerning my children's friendships, I'm trying to learn from my youngest. As a toddler, when he didn't want me to see him, he would close his eyes. I'm going to make myself try it.

When it comes to standing firm against peer pressure, however, I want to see exactly what's going on. Since there are times when somebody has to stand up to the group, I prefer my children to be firm like a stone wall than to have the posture of Silly Putty.

Peer pressure comes into play about the time children decide friendships are not disposable. Then they seek to make them permanent. Adrift on the stormy seas of kindergarten and first grade, many children cling to the buoy of friendships. They want to be accepted and see conformity as the key. They start to act alike and talk alike. Suddenly, your son sounds like the boy next door.

When my children were little, and still shredding their friendships, I did not realize how much I should appreciate their nonconformity. For a long time I wanted the child who would stay with the group. I remember at Mommy & Me class how the toddlers would straggle in a circle, clutching their tambourines and shaking their bells, trailing us mothers, who clapped out the beat. My two-year-old, however, was more interested in the ball across the room. He would slip out of formation and my grasp without a backward glance. And as I futilely attempted to entice him back, it never occurred to me that I should not totally despair at his nonconformity. I did not realize that the day would come when I would relish any such show of independence.

When it comes to conformity, older children become the original lemmings.

The kindergarten teacher is asking her students to draw pictures of what they want to be when they grow up. As a sample, she shows them another boy's depiction of himself as a policeman. Then she asks what they want to be. The girls are evenly divided between ballerinas and nurses. Nearly all of the boys (surprise) want to be policemen—including my son, who previously had never shown the slightest bit of interest.

The culprit is peer pressure. Kids want to conform. They want to be like their friends, act like their friends, and own the same things as their friends. They want to be stamped with cookie-cutter conformity so that they all look the same. The only time my daughter would ever wear pants, for example, was when she had a best friend who wore them. I wish I could harness the power of conformity for the times I could use it to my own advantage. Unfortunately, a two-year-old wearing diapers or a three-year-old sucking a pacifier has tremendous capacity to ignore the opinion of his peers.

But some time after age four, the child who has always turned to you for approval starts to turn away. This coincides with the time your child sees you more as a parent than a playmate. My youngest still sees me as a playmate. I am not his consolation prize for when nobody else is available to play. He considers me a first prize. His older brother and sister, by contrast, play better with their friends than they do with me. No wonder children come to value the opinion of other children with whom they play more than the opinion of their parents, with whom they do not.

Peer pressure is powerful. One time my seven-year-old received Mickey Mouse socks with bows sewn on them like bow ties. He loved the socks; the bows didn't bother him a bit. But he wore the socks once and then asked me to cut off the bows.

"The guys said they were sissy," he said.

"Do you like the bows?" I asked.

"Sort of," he answered. "But cut them off anyway."

I cut.

Children push hard for the items their friends have that they want their parents to buy. Patton would envy the campaign my daughter began to wage at age four over Barbie dolls. (I did not give in, but she received them as gifts anyway—making the issue moot.) Likewise, for a while I knew of no seven-year-old girl who didn't want a crimper for her hair.

"All it takes is one slumber party and they won't talk about anything else," said one mother shortly before her capitulation and her visit to the small appliance department.

My seven-year-old believes the Constitution grants each child cookies in his lunchbox and a Nintendo in his bedroom. I don't read it that way. And while I expected the pressure, I was not fully prepared for how hard it can be to resist. The impulse to give your children what they ask for is strong.

We wage a tug-of-war of wills. But over the years I have discovered that if I suddenly let go of my opposition, my child's obstinacy can collapse. Take ballet lessons as an example. Before she was barely four, my daughter had been wanting them for over a year. But at that age, she couldn't stick to anything for more than two minutes. I thought she was too young to start lessons. For a while, we parents maintained a unified front. Then one by one the defections started. Events began moving beyond my control when two of my daughter's best friends were enrolled for lessons. They flaunted their costumes and flayed my daughter's heart.

"I think ballet lessons are more work than you realize," I tried to reason with her.

"No, they aren't," she adamantly denied.

Then my neighbor had a stroke of genius. She hired an eight-year-old ballet student to give our daughters introductory lessons. They would get an idea what a real class would be like to see if they really wanted lessons. To me, the experience seemed perfect—and so did the price. The lessons, which we all took quite seriously, lasted three weeks. At that point, my daughter's form was as lukewarm as her interest.

"Let's stop," she finally confessed. "Ballet is too much work."

I didn't hear another word on the subject until a year later, about the time I would have brought it up by myself.

8
Why Boys Won't Wear Pink Tights

Who's modeling for this role, anyway?

When it rained the day of my daughter's birthday party, I did not panic. Had it rained the day of my son's party, I would have. Fundamentally, I believe a herd of rampaging boys could inflict far more damage upon my house than a gaggle of girls wearing party dresses. Years of experience have taught me that girls and boys are not alike; they are dangerous in different ways.

Childhood behavior cannot be divided only along the lines of acceptable or annoying. It also separates quite clearly along the fault line of boy versus girl. Children see their parents as role models. Like father, like son, we say. Like mother, like daughter. This is true in my household as well. Faster than ice cream melts, my Cleopatra of a daughter has frozen her gender identity into place. It is an aspect of behavior I have tried to change, with no luck. Gender is a blueprint for behavior. Anyone could tell you, it would be easier to reverse the flow of the Nile than to alter the nature of the imperious queen who floated down it.

On the face of it, giggling girls are easier to handle than stampeding boys. I can talk my daughter into going anywhere, for example, if I let her wear her party shoes. Sometimes, at the end of the day, her clothes are not even dirty. My daughter plays with blankets and tucks in her stuffed animals to sleep. My son builds Lego creations and then uses them to conduct bombing runs all over the house.

Let's start with boys. They just don't behave like girls. The boys I know are dirtier than the girls will ever be. Like the family pets, most boys belong in the backyard—otherwise they will track all over the carpet. When my son's nose is runny, for example, he wipes it with his hands. No detective work is required to figure this out. The evidence is smeared across his face, his hands, and his shirt. Dirty streaks decorating his face, deposited there by his encrusted hands, indicate that my seven-year-old tends to wipe his nose in an upward, saluting motion. Likewise, his T-shirt ripples from repeated stretching—evidence that he also uses it for a quick wipe. (A scholarly note: The practice of preferring clothes to handkerchiefs is evidently age-old. Legend has it that Napoleon tried to break his soldiers of the same habit. He had sharp buttons sewn on the sleeves of their uniforms, making it painful to wipe one's nose with one's sleeve. I rest my case.)

In keeping with historical tradition, my son rarely uses a tissue. During allergy season, when his sneezes erupt in rapid-fire succession, my husband and I foist tissues upon him faster than his nose can reload. We still lose the race. I find those tissues later, used once, stashed under his bed.

My son, other mothers inform me, is not unique. Other boys misplace their underwear, eat with their mouths open, and play with their chewing gum. Boys commonly employ their fingers to rummage around in their noses. More than one mother reports having to chisel off the walls what their sons have found up there. Once upon a time I used to think the most disgusting parts of parenting were solved by potty training. Now I know better. I can hardly wait for the day when my son fights for his turn in the bathroom.

I expect toddlers to behave like barbarians. They are to be excused for squishing what they do not eat and throwing what they cannot squish. When my son was a toddler I expected his high chair to be ringed by the debris from every meal. But I also used to expect improvement with age. I can see now that expectation, like natural childbirth, is somewhat overrated. I have seen my oldest wipe his nose on the carpeting. I have watched him watch television picking his toes as instinctively as my youngest sucks his thumb.

Nothing helps. Each night I give my son a bath, and then I wonder why he always looks dirty. His knees and his neck never look clean and his hair never remains combed. His personal hygiene, in short, cannot be tamed any more than his cowlicks. I watch him and wonder how I could have produced a kid incapable of closing a door by holding the doorknob. His fingerprints adorn every painted surface in the house. I know he is mine, however, because after dinner he still leaves a circle of debris around his chair.

My son bears small resemblance to the child of my fantasies—the one who was always clean, well behaved, and dressed in adorable outfits. That mythical child would happily wear whatever clothes I picked. Immediately after learning to walk, he would learn how to blow his nose. That child would never dig for bugs beneath the patio rocks, just as he would never dig through his drawer to find the obnoxious shirt I had hidden at the bottom. After such a child walked through a room, I would never be able to tell that he had been there.

Now I will not unequivocally state that my son's behavior is a genetically sex-linked trait. It is not conclusive that my son's drawers resemble the aftermath of a rummage sale and my daughter's drawers are organized with military precision. Gender need not be destiny. Just as there are boys who never rip the knees of their jeans, there are girls who do not beg to wear party shoes. But I have noticed that more often it is a boy who seems incapable of remembering to flush.

In other ways, boys at this age seem to finish second to girls. Take school, for example. My son has some wonderful attributes. Unfortunately, they are not always those talents a teacher can appreciate. Girls seem faster to master the skills so highly prized by teachers: sitting still, standing in line, and concentrating. Kindergarten demonstrated to me that such abilities do not come easily to boys.

I remember one time watching when the kindergarten teacher, sitting at the front of the rug, was explaining how to count money. My son, sitting at the back of the rug, was volleying fuzz balls with his buddy. They pitched the balls back and forth, until my son's attention turned to his knee socks. He concentrated upon rolling them down evenly to form a tube around his ankle. Then he did the same for his friend. The teacher asked what was going on.

"I was just rolling down Tyson's socks," answered my son affably.

"Well, let him do it himself," she replied with far less exasperation than I would have displayed. It was obvious why she had changed his seat assignment on the rug three times since school began.

The lesson completed, the class moved from the rug to the tables. One child was chosen to pass out the paste pots while everyone else started their worksheets. My son engaged in a prolonged search to locate his neighbor's missing black crayon. At the end of class, as she did each day, the teacher selected students to receive Good Citizenship Awards. Although my son came up in rotation that year to earn several, I wish he had qualified more often.

I believe his fate was sealed at birth. Even as a baby he followed his own agenda. He would never eat when I was hungry or take a nap because I was tired. He did everything in his own time. He was always a handful, always on the go, and always messy. He hasn't changed.

Boys will be boys, people say. These same people say my son is all boy. But I wonder if they are speaking in code. I wonder if that is their polite way of hinting that society should remand animals to the zoo. Occasionally I find myself wondering: Why can't my boy be more like a girl? No, I do not want him to kiss his teacher good-bye as some girls do. But I would not mind an improved ability to sit still, to pay attention, and to take school seriously. In kindergarten, especially, girls seem to score better on this.

My son's attitude toward homework is typical. I see it as a learning experience; he sees it as a race. How fast can he cross the finish line? When he brought his kindergarten homework to school, twice he forgot it under the slide. And when he brought it home, he frequently had folded it into a microscopic square I had to read between the pleats.

As a mother, I do not seek perfection. I recognize that when my son is interested in something, he is very, very interested. But when he was in kindergarten, I wondered how it would feel to have a child who cared about using an eraser or earning gold stars for his chart. My son did not.

He is, in short, up to his old tricks instead. He does not care about something just because I believe it is important; he will not study just because I want him to learn. From afar the girls seem more eager to please, more eager for the approval of others. My "boy's boy" remains singularly unaware that the world is judging his performance.

I must admit, I don't think I would be happy at the other extreme. I do not want my child to brownnose the teacher or tattle on everybody else. I'll take a kid with spunk any day over a Goody-Two Shoes. But sometimes, as I watch my son gyrate to the beat of a drummer only he can hear, I feel a mild regret. Once in a while I wouldn't mind if he were the child chosen to pass out the paste pots.

My daughter, I already can tell, would like that job next year in kindergarten and probably will get it. She can sit still and raise her hand quietly. But while girls remain cleaner and inflict substantially less property damage than boys, they are not necessarily easier to handle. They are less physically destructive and more decorous, but emotionally they can exact a heavier toll.

The boys at my son's birthday party would not sit still; the girls at my daughter's party would not sit next to each other. When the kids began to crowd closer during the flannel board story, the girls dueled it out with their elbows. Girls strike me as less straightforward than boys, which can be another way of saying they are more devious. When my son is angry, he strikes out with his fists. When my daughter is angry, she doesn't lift a hand. But she can lob a zinger like a hand grenade. She can cut you down to size without a knife.

"You're never happy at me!" she shouts. "The baby gets all your smiles!"

Girls have faster mouths and sharper tongues than boys. When my son doesn't know the answer, he clowns around or ignores the question. My daughter improvises.

"What's this shape?" I ask her, pointing at a rectangle.

She hesitates a long moment and then asserts, "It's a door."

At times my son has a hard time sitting still to listen; my daughter is a student of language.

"What's for dinner?" she inquires hours ahead of schedule.

"Shoulder steaks," I respond—not because I know what this means but because the butcher does.

An hour later my (starving) daughter asks, "Did you say we were having elbow steaks?"

Another time she comes sobbing to me about her brother: "He called me a greedy little brat."

"Do you know what 'greedy' means?" I ask.

"No," she blubbers.

"Greedy means that you want everything for yourself."

A few days later my daughter's friend runs sobbing from the room. "What's the matter?" I ask.

"She used a bad word," comes the answer. "She said I was greedy."

My son, who wanted to know if warm water comes from the warm part of the ocean, has a literal mind. But my daughter is more shrewd.

"You better not go to Stacy's," I tell my daughter. "Her mother says she has the grumpies."

"Well," she responds defensively, "did she catch them from me?"

If toughness is what it takes, my daughter will make it. When there is a war over who gets to sit in the front seat (otherwise known as "front-sies"), I put my money on her. Of my three children, she screams the loudest and carries a grudge the longest. ("I won't talk to you," she says. "That's your punishment.") She is my only child ever to pack a suitcase (with her bunny rabbit slippers and stuffed lamb) and announce she was leaving home because I made her get dressed.

She knows her own mind. One time she was chasing her brother's friends, playing on the floor, and making a tremendous racket.

"Get out from under the chair and act like a lady," I admonished her.

"Well, I'm not a lady," she answered without missing a beat.

She is a cactus, this daughter of mine. Tough on the outside, but if you get past all the prickles she is sweet on the inside. Once when we were talking quietly, I told her that sometimes I wished she would stop growing up so quickly and be my little girl for longer. My daughter patted me on the hand and sighed.

"I know, Mommy. It's sad," she said. " 'Cause when I grow up I go to live with another family."

Sometimes I admire her toughness, even though I take pains not to encourage it. She came home from preschool one day to describe for me the battle of the paste pot. To me, it is a classic story from a girl, four going on five, who always wants the last word.

"I asked for the paste," my daughter said. "Karen wouldn't let me have it. We argued about it. Then she scribbled on my picture; she said my girl wasn't very good. So I scribbled on her picture.

"Then Karen took the paste and moved it across the table. So I took the paste cap and put it on her head. I told her: 'Nice hat.' "

I thought of all this recently after my daughter told me that she wants to be Snow White when she grows up. I bit my tongue rather than tell her that, for a girl like her, I think the job holds no future.

I have thought a lot about this gender gap: why it's there and how to cross it. Everywhere I see evidence of how children have taken gender stereotypes and adopted them as their own. And I have some theories about why this is so.

"I don't like it at school when I have to hold hands with boys when we say the blessing at snacktime," my daughter informs me.

"Why not?" I inquire, ever the straight man.

"I don't like boys," she says. "They're different than girls."

Speaking as the mother who wanted one of each, it's safe to say I have noticed. I noticed at Halloween when I watched an endless parade of brides, princesses, and cheerleaders alternate with Ninja Turtles, Draculas, and pirates. You don't need much analysis to figure out that princesses get rescued while pirates are powerful. I notice that my daughter draws pictures of rainbows, butterflies, flowers, and smiling people. My son draws elaborate pictures of heroes fighting with weapons amidst urban landscapes of tall buildings. My daughter's aspirations are definitely unlike my son's.

During science in first grade the teacher calls upon Joseph to explain why the plant has begun to turn yellow. It is his turn to play plant doctor.

"Come on up, Dr. Joseph," she says.

A few minutes later it is Emily's turn to expound her theory.

"Come on up, Dr. Emily," she says.

"Doctor Emily?" the class hoots. "It's Nurse Emily."

Not so, the teacher explains. Girls can study to be doctors every bit as much as boys.

"Now, Emily. Do you want to be called a nurse or a doctor?" she asks after completing a rather impassioned defense of women's liberation.

"Nurse Emily," the girl replies without hesitation.

I once asked my children to flip through a toy catalogue and give me birthday ideas by circling whatever they liked. I have no doubts they took the job seriously. Literally everything that my daughter circled was pink or purple.

"How about these building toys?" I asked, pointing to red, blue, and white pieces I never previously had viewed as sexist.

"I don't like to build," she answered.

"How about these building toys?" I asked, pointing to pink and purple pieces that can build a doll house.

"Those would be all right," she allowed, only complicating my impressions. Doesn't she like to build, I wondered? Or does she think girls shouldn't build—or does she think they should only build girl things?

"Did anyone touch my fairy wand in the car?" my daughter demands by way of greeting as I pick her up from preschool. She is voicing, I am beginning to suspect, the key issue confronting her generation. I have no illusions about what to expect from my youngest son. The pattern is set all too clearly before him, and he will follow his big brother into the land of macho skyscrapers, noisy trucks, and pretend battles.

But where did my oldest son and my daughter learn so well? Why is one child rehearsing for a lead and the other a supporting role? Who taught one to choose soccer and the other ballet?

I suppose, in part, I did. I started by dressing my daughter in pink and my sons in blue. Of course infant boys and girls get to share a few nonsexist animals such as giraffes or teddy bears on their coveralls. But as they got older and the animals were divided, my sons got lions and my daughter got kittens. I dressed my daughter in ribbons and bows and my sons in shorts. All too soon the boys are relegated to dressing either like an infielder or in something covered with cars and trucks. This explains why as boys become men they find the advertisements for tires on the sports pages.

True, my husband and I are also teaching new, subtle lessons about how women can be more than mothers, or about how men can do more than work. But sometimes I fear we sabotage the lessons we are trying to teach with the messages we subconsciously send. Actions can shout while words whisper. My daughter copies me as I cook, garden, and shop. My son sees his father fix the car, work with tools, and step on spiders. We, in turn, copied our parents the same way. I probably would sew if my mother had. (No doubt my daughter probably also will tape her hems.) We buy no toy guns, but my husband watches war movies. I tell my daughter appearance isn't everything, and then she sees me apply lipstick to go grocery shopping.

I think television also has taught my children. They absorb the stereotypes in cartoons and commercials. Commercials have not yet discovered gender liberation. You don't see boys playing with Barbies or girls racing cars. And although it is not destructive for my daughter to aspire to comb her pony's hair, it is not productive, either. April, who pals around with the Ninja Turtles, has a television career of her own—but her real job on the cartoon show is getting rescued. Even Miss Piggy, who certainly is a Muppet star, has nothing more serious on her mind than how she looks and where her next date is coming from.

But most of all I think nonsexist, liberated parenting stands a very slim chance. You can no more sway a boy against guns than you can change the way a child sleeps. Nobody forces boys to play with guns or girls to feed their baby dolls. Some children are always neatly under the covers and some have always flung them aside. The best you can do is cover them up after they fall asleep and hope they will stay warm.

Gender is not destiny, but it certainly counts. Why else do little girls hurt feelings while little boys hurt with their hands? Why else does my daughter neatly set the table while my son gladly would eat without silverware? Why does she love clothes, enjoy shopping, and prefer salads—and he does not? Why else can both of them play outside for an hour and only one of them require a bath? Boys are different from girls because they are born that way.

■   ■   ■

It is only logical, therefore, that my daughter takes after me. My daughter may look a great deal like her father, but in her attitudes and behavior she resembles me. Children are always watching and evaluating their parents, and nine times out of ten getting ready to either copy them or make sure they will never resemble them again. An astonishing part of the relationship between parent and child is the shock of looking at your children and recognizing the ways in which they have become just like you.

My five-year-old daughter is a case in point. She not only resembles how I act as her mother, but also how I acted as a child.

"Let me give you a full report," she announces in the morning after the baby-sitter is gone. And she does, omitting no transgression large or small, real or imagined, committed by anyone in the house except for her. My daughter has her application in for sainthood.

"The boys took food in the family room," she gleefully informs me, clearly relishing her role as unpaid informant. "They didn't want to brush their teeth. I brushed my teeth when I was told."

She demands perfection, this child who regularly organizes and inventories her stuffed animals. I cringe some nights when she sets the table. Carefully she selects which silverware each child shall receive, and then she folds the napkins and aligns them perfectly straight. The napkins are her donnybrook. She becomes hysterical if anyone messes them up. Sometimes her big brother inflicts intentional torture: He moves his napkin.

My daughter at five already is a microcosm of the woman she will become, so I anticipate trouble. I can say this because she reminds me of myself.

It is not raining, but my daughter arrives back at my door absolutely soaking wet.

"Before you go in the sprinklers you must always ask me if it's all right to get wet," I admonish her.

"Why should I ask you first?" she responds. "You'd just say no."

Did I ever talk to my mother that way? She probably thinks so. Daughters have a way of putting mothers in their places. The other day as we pulled up at her school, my daughter realized she had forgotten her lunchbox on the kitchen counter.

"Mommy, where did you leave my lunch?" she asked, neatly transferring the burden of guilt.

My daughter walks across the room, trips and stumbles over her brother, who is lying on the floor watching television.

"Why do you have to be there?" she complains indignantly.

In a family otherwise composed of males, we are similar, my daughter and I. My husband tells me I, too, am adept at twisting an argument to place the blame anywhere but upon myself. As a child I, too, chewed on my hair. It turns out we have the same mother. Even as I speak the words, I, too, remember my mother ordering me to "get that hair" out of my face or to wear some dress I absolutely loathed.

My daughter looks to me for female understanding. We go out for tea and talk about clothes together. Fortunately, I am not so old I cannot remember how special it felt to wear party shoes without straps. I can understand the importance of a dress that twirls. We both understand, for example, the critical nature of hair. My daughter's haircut is adorable. Layered short, it allows her natural curls to frame her face. It is an effortless look I could achieve only with a perm, hair dryer, mousse, and a full hour in front of the mirror. It is a look that all my life I have wanted to have.

"I hate it!" she explodes, staring at herself in front of the mirror. "It's all puffy on top. How can I go to school like this? All the kids will laugh at me."

My five-year-old daughter deplores her curls. She wants her hair long and straight. "Like a princess," she tells me. She is close to tears, trying to flatten every curl that frames her face so cutely. With soothing words and a wet brush, I try to smooth out the fluff I had instructed the stylist to cut in.

All women, I suspect, are never satisfied with their thighs or their hair. It's just that we imagine we can do more to improve our hair. I have a wave that I detest and a flip on one side that drives me crazy. In my quest for the perfect do, at times I have worn my hair long like Alice in Wonderland and short like Little Orphan Annie. I am never satisfied.

Age entitles me to my vanities. I was surprised, however, to discover that hair also is important to a five-year-old. I know that my daughter has strong feelings against party shoes with hearts and in favor of those with bows. But I had not imagined hair would be such a big deal for her until junior high. A friend tells me otherwise. She says already her eight-year-old is nearly late for school most mornings because she won't leave the bathroom until she "gets her bangs right." Those words suddenly evoked my own desperate childhood sessions with a wet comb in front of the mirror.

I did not cut my daughter's hair in order to torture her. She wears her hair short because she refused to comb it when she wore it long.

"Get that hair out of your face," I would admonish, as did my mother before me. "If you won't comb it, then I'm going to cut it."

One day she told me to go ahead.

The battle, I suspect, is eternal. My mother used to say the same words to my sister. To this day, my sister refuses to wear her hair short the way our mother once made her. And to this day my mother still tells me how much cuter my sister would look if only she would cut her hair.

Men, I gather, cannot understand this female thing about hair. My husband tends to lay low whenever I am fussing.

"Do you like my haircut?" I inquire after a radical change.

"Yes, I like it short," he says from atop the fence. "But sometimes I also like it long."

Men don't understand the supreme importance of hair. Their hairstyles are essentially generic. They don't understand the trauma of telling the stylist exactly what you want, and then not getting it. They do not know the humiliation of waiting in public for your perm to relax. A woman's hairstyle is one of the most critical fashion statements she can make, involving fundamental decisions such as long or short. Anyone who has ever grown out her layers knows how lasting the consequences can be.

I have to smile at my daughter, however. She rants and raves against her hair when it looks absolutely perfect. She says she wishes her hair were straight like mine, but she doesn't know what she's talking about. Now I, on the other hand, have serious troubles. I wish my hair were curly like hers. Now I'm trying to coax a curl into the right side on the bottom, and it just wants to flip. I don't see how I could possibly leave the house looking like this.

It is definitely uncanny how my daughter and I sound alike. I do not enjoy conversation first thing in the morning. Nevertheless, as I stumble downstairs bleary-eyed at dawn, my husband smiles, tells me what he has to do that day, and asks me how I'm feeling.

"I don't know yet," I snap, completely overwhelmed. "I just got up."

A bit later my daughter stumbles downstairs bleary-eyed at dawn. Awake now, I smile at her and talk about the day. She doesn't respond.

"What's the matter?" I ask.

"Mom!" she mutters. "I just got up."

Sometimes when I hear my daughter, my words from my *own* precious childhood seem to be coming out of her mouth.

"Bedtime. Brush your teeth," I tell my daughter.

"Well, nobody else has," she drawls as if that justifies perfectly why she is not moving.

"Please pick up your laundry," I tell her another time.

"I don't have to," she answers with a defiant sniff. "The boys didn't pick up theirs."

My five-year-old cannot yet multiply or divide, but she is an accountant. When it comes to chores, she keeps score on everybody else.

She tallies her brothers' performances and privileges and ranks them against her own. For every request served at her, she lobs back a question of her own. Why should she make her bed if her brother didn't? Why can't she stay up when everybody else is? Reasonable questions—from her perspective, of course. And familiar questions as well.

As a child I remember that I, too, excelled at peripheral vision. I, too, was always looking sideways to see who had gotten excused from dinner without finishing their peas. I, too, delighted in being the bearer of bad news about somebody else. As a child I, too, wanted to worry about everybody else but myself. Keeping my siblings in line was always so much more interesting than toeing the mark myself. But now that I am a mother, now that I have to do it, I have concluded that watching out for everyone else is not much fun. I would love to get dressed in the morning without worrying about whether everyone else did, too.

Try telling that to my daughter and she won't listen. She can't hear me over the sound of her own rallying cry.

"It's not fair. It's not fair," she protests endlessly and repeatedly every day—as though fair treatment means identical treatment.

"It's not fair," she complains when her older brother gets new pajamas that she does not need.

"It's not fair," goes her refrain when her younger brother stays up later after he has taken a three-hour nap.

Who ever said it would be fair? I did, of course. As a child I sang verses to the same song. If he gets one, then so do I. If I have to, then so does she.

Even as an adult, knowing better doesn't always help. I still heard the litany like background music recently when I chose presents to bring back from a trip for my three children. The temptation to buy three-of-a-kind items was overwhelming. I knew there was not one thing all three of them needed, but I also knew that at least three gifts the same would be "fair." (I opted for different presents and endured a few tense moments while each child opened his gift with one eye watching to see what the other kids got.)

But I know a great deal now that I also did not believe as a child—such as why I sound like my mother.

"Worry about yourself," I now tell my daughter when she is the one who needs a bath.

"You're not your brother. He eats all of his dinner," I tell my daughter when I explain why she cannot have any more snack.

"You get up the earliest," I tell my daughter when I explain why she has to go to bed first.

Now I know that fairness does not mean sameness. I know this, but I also know there is no way I can convince my daughter. She won't believe me until she's a mother herself. Meantime, she's going to trip eventually as she walks along looking to see where everybody else is going.

Some days I can only marvel at this daughter of mine, five years old going on fifty. I wonder how she knows so early what skills will be expected of her later as a mother.

A veritable bloodhound, she is relentless on the trail of her own desires. The white leather sandals I bought her have a tiny dirt spot.

"I can take that out with cleaner sometime. It's easy to do," I tell her in an attempt to calm her fretting.

"Can you do it now?" she asks.

"It's really not that dirty," I answer. "I'll get to it in a little while."

"Well, maybe I can get out the cleaner for you," she replies.

"It's upstairs and I'll get it later," I reiterate.

A short while later I make the mistake of going upstairs.

"Is this where you keep the cleaner, Mommy?" she asks ingenuously.

"Yes."

"Well, don't forget you said you would clean my sandals when you have time," she reminds me.

How could I forget with my daughter on the job? At the grocery store, she is more helpful than a list. When I am away, I know that having her at home is the next best thing to being there. I can rely upon her to represent me in my absence and to show the flag for all the rules my husband is tempted to sweep under the rug. She keeps the family in line.

"Daddy didn't feed the fish the way you do," she complains to me after I have been away. "He didn't save any of the old water to pour into the new. I told him that was wrong. I told him you don't do it that way."

There is something familiar about my single-minded and relentless daughter. She reminds me of myself when I harass the kids to pick up their laundry or harangue my husband to clean out the garage. She has learned from a master. This does not mean, however, that my daughter is a perfect joy to have around.

"The fish water is dirty," she informs me one morning as I stumble to consciousness. "You said yesterday you would change it. I think you better do it right now."

Obviously, I wouldn't know what to do if my daughter didn't tell me. I couldn't possibly manage without her instructions. She has to tell me everything. And because of her, now I understand perfectly how my husband feels.

9

Get a Life; Or, What Have Children Done to Mine?

Nothing lasts forever—my body, myself

Before I had children, I don't remember ever taking the time to talk to anyone in front of whom I had to kneel to make eye contact. Children were simply not of immediate interest. I had few friends who were mothers, and I remember having little sympathy for the harried-looking women I saw trying to cram groceries into their carts and keep their children out of trouble.

Now I am one of those women. The other day at the grocery store I noticed that the food inside my basket was piled well above flood level. Idly I wondered what happens when one cart is no longer big enough to hold the weekly shopping. My youngest was trying to gnaw through a sealed package of gum, and my daughter was swinging the chain to the checkout line Ninja-style. And then it hit me. Nobody wants to get in the checkout line behind me. I have become the woman other shoppers avoid—and the portion of my mind that remembers going out to dinner after work on weeknights is embarrassed. To perfect strangers, something inside me feels the urge to blurt: Hey. I didn't always used to be like this.

I thought about how I have changed the day I received a call from the office at my son's kindergarten. It wasn't of the usual come-and-get-him garden variety telephone call.

"You'd better come get your son," said the school secretary, without preamble. "He has a bean stuck in his ear."

My mind, already in overdrive contemplating illness or possible acts of destruction, slammed on the brakes and began to spin its wheels.

"He what?" I answered with my usual eloquence.

"He has an orange bean stuck in his ear, or maybe it's a vitamin pill," she replied.

"Well, I didn't give him a vitamin this morning," I answered irrelevantly. "Can you take it out? Did you stand him on his head and shake him?"

Across the telephone wires the secretary made it clear she saw no humor in the situation, although I, of course, had not been joking.

"Oh no, I wouldn't try that," she admonished. "It could go down even further into the ear canal and require an operation. You might want to take him to his doctor. They have special tools."

"Is this an emergency?" I asked, being the kind of person who takes some comfort from labels. "I just put the baby to sleep."

A moment of slightly miffed silence. "Well," she answered. "I can send him back to his classroom and tell his teacher to keep him quiet."

Apparently the bean is already stuck, I thought to myself, as I nevertheless promised to fetch my son as quickly as possible.

No sooner had I hung up the telephone than it rang again.

"I can't really talk now," I told my friend. "I have to call the doctor. My son put a bean in his ear."

She laughed. Involuntarily I laughed too, and I found myself thinking of the song in which mama says not to put beans in your ears. It's probably my fault, I mentally giggled. I don't believe I ever told him not to put beans in his ears or, for that matter, not to put stones up his nose. Hanging up, I called my pediatrician's office, where a sensible, seen-it-all nurse told me to take tweezers and give it a try myself before scheduling surgery.

And as I waited for a reasonable hour to wake my youngest and arm myself with the tweezers, I found myself smiling at myself. When did my life become the chorus of a silly song? When did I start to feel like the straight man in a standup routine? Children have changed my life.

They have had an impact upon my life like a three-car pileup. They have sabotaged the way I feel about myself and what I am willing to believe about others. Sometimes I feel like the opening gambit at a potted-fern bar. I find myself thinking to myself: What's a nice girl like me doing in a place like this? I am surprised by how completely I have adopted the lifestyle and attitudes of a mother.

A lot of these thoughts seem to hit me in the grocery checkout line. I think I total up the changes in my life along with the price of my purchases. Just as I never used to buy gallon jugs of juice, I never would have expected some of my current attitudes. Some things that I believe as a mother I never would have believed before. One time, waiting my turn in line, I idly scanned the tabloid headlines:

WOMAN GIVES BIRTH TO HER FATHER.

SIAMESE TWINS WED.

FLYING SAUCER GETS PARKING TICKET.

I didn't believe a word.

My daughter, originally standing by my side, began hopping frantically around me. Despite my entreaties to confess before I unloaded my cart, she denied adamantly that she had to potty. Again, I didn't believe a word. As a mother, sometimes I think my reliability record would rival an airlines'. I'm correct more often then I'm wrong, and it turns out I was right about the potty. I can't be positive about the headlines, however, because once in a while the unbelievable is true. Here are some entries from a mother's believe it or not:

I never would have believed that if your kids are driving you crazy, the solution can be more kids. When I'm at my wit's end with my own children, it always helps to invite over the neighbor's brood. The other kids not only help keep my kids in line, but me as well. I would never throttle my own children in front of witnesses.

I never would have believed that a mere child could defy a grown-up. Now I know what the mouse said to the elephant. It was a loose translation of "So what!" (The mouse probably wanted to wear her new party shoes to school, and the elephant tried to stop her.) Some children are slender reeds that will not snap.

I used to believe a child could be trained to do anything; now I believe in equal measure it is the parents who are trained to live with anything. Likewise, I used to believe a child is largely the product of his environment. Now I know that in the womb there are infants fully prepared to hate peas or to turn Popsicle sticks into guns. Some children are simply incapable of sleeping late, going to bed early, or eating at mealtimes. I also used to believe not all little girls want to dress like ballerinas, wear lipstick, or color rainbows. I still want to believe this is true—even though I haven't met any girls who don't.

A few years ago I never would have believed that given a free hour with none of my children home, I would become totally paralyzed and incapable of doing anything. Other mothers also tell me they are so intoxicated by the unfamiliar ability to choose, that they dash from chore to chore unable to decide what to do next. We only succeed in settling down to the most urgent matter at hand minutes before we are due to pick up the children.

Likewise, seven years ago I never would have believed that my previously open-minded perspective would shrink to tunnel vision. Tantalized by a new recipe in a magazine, I decide not to clip it after I ask myself: Would a three-year-old eat that? Noticing a new teenager in the neighborhood, before I ask her name, I ask her, "Do you baby-sit?" When confronted with an activity that requires an output of effort after 8 P.M., I ask myself: Is it more important than sleeping?

Since becoming a parent I am amazed by my own inconsistencies and inadequacies. I deny my children sugar-coated cereals yet allow them to douse their pancakes in syrup. I lose a game of Concentration to my seven-year-old because I can't pay attention long enough to win. I realize I have forgotten how to function without interruption.

Parenthood, in short, has taught me how little I know. So when I see those unbelievable headlines at the grocery store, I do not believe a word—but I do not entirely rule out their possibility. They say truth can be stranger than fiction. Lately, I haven't had much time for reading.

_____

I am, clearly, married with children. You are either familiar with the species or you aren't. We recently got new neighbors. To my disappointment, they have no children—which means I won't get to know them nearly so well. More so, they won't get to know me nearly so well. They won't fully understand why I am the way I have become.

"They have no children," I informed my daughter.

"I know that, Mommy," she chided me. "They have no kid bikes in their garage."

You can't say that about mine. Three bicycles (two with training wheels I trip over), two tricycles, one scooter, a plastic car, red wagon, and fire engine are jammed inside my garage. It is not always easy to park the car. Hey, I want to explain: My garage didn't always used to be like this any more than my furniture had all those nicks.

But back to the bean. Laughing at my son, and laughing at myself, I went off to check out his ear. As an excavation site, I decided, the ear was preferable to the nose. Approaching my son warily, I grabbed his head. Ruthlessly, using the nail of my little finger, I scooped out not a bean at all but an orange plastic bead of the sort used for stringing.

"How did that get in your ear?" I demanded sternly.

My son played me like the straight man I have become.

"I saw it on the playground and kicked it," he answered. "Then it flew up and got stuck in my ear."

■ ■ ■

Children also have changed my life by adjusting my expectations. Now mine are lower. Before I had children, nobody ever said raising a family would be easy. I believed they would be a challenge, but I never anticipated how much. Now that I have kids, I always believe the worst. When it comes to daily life, I always see apocalypse now. I see trouble ahead as plainly as the crumbs on my kitchen floor. I take personally the portions of school forms that ask for "others to call in the event of an emergency." When my son greets me by asking, "Guess what happened to me today?"—frequently I would rather not.

Some families are seated at the restaurant just as the children complain they are starving. I take it for granted mine still will be home trying to agree on where to go. Likewise, when the gate comes down because the merry-go-round is full, I expect us to be the ones who get to go first—next time. I see further evidence of my pessimistic outlook those nights when I try to convince my daughter to potty before bed because I am sure that she has to go.

I have come to believe that if for others life is easy, for me it will be hard. Other people pick up their cars on time, as promised. When I show up with three cranky children in tow, mine requires a part on order for two weeks. Other women take a chance on a blouse, and when they get home it matches their skirt perfectly. These are the kind of women whose checkbooks also balance. Choosing a blouse while chasing after my daughter, I buy the wrong shade of blue. And my checkbook is always wrong.

Likewise, I used to believe in toys. I started out buying toys under the erroneous assumption that if I only found the right toy my children magically would play happily for hours. Now I realize that nothing can make them play happily for hours. I would be grateful for twenty minutes. In a recent week the brakes on my car went out, the washing machine flooded, the oven failed, and the garage door opener developed hiccups. If machines can fail me, why not my own flesh and blood?

Children can humble your expectations. I believe a realistic outlook spares disappointment. It's insurance, like spreading out newspaper before the children watercolor. As a realist I am not surprised when the doctor examines my son's rash and says, "Gee, I haven't seen this for a long time."

When we put new carpet in the living room, I expected it to get dirty. My husband had assumed it would remain clean.

"Look at those spots," he frets. "Look how dirty it's getting. Everybody out. Nobody walks in here anymore."

When my son comes shouting that his brother cut his eye and has blood all over his face, I believe him. That way I am relieved to discover the "blood" is only jelly. In the same way, I am not surprised to find that my children have left footprints in my refrigerator or decided it was fun to tape the toilet lid shut.

I have become an expert at anticipating, especially the worst. Here is how my sense of foreboding can slip into overdrive on a busy morning:

My adrenaline is pumping high as I propel myself out of bed intent on heading for the shower. I am thinking about an important luncheon that day with an out-of-town editor. Before heading for the bathroom, however, I reconnoiter the children. My husband is out of town and unavailable for crowd control. As usual, two kids are parked downstairs in front of the television. Knowing that fights are more likely to break out during commercials, I want to synchronize their television show with my shower.

Then I look for my third child. Most mornings he warms up by running in circles around my bedroom chair. This morning, however, he has wrapped himself in his blankie and lies listlessly on the carpet. The only sign of vigor is the speed with which he sucks his thumb. Aware of my attention, he stumbles to my side, clings to my knees and cries piteously for me to pick him up. Trying to brush my teeth with one hand and balance my toddler with the other, I also try to cheer him up. I offer him his toothbrush, his breakfast, and his favorite truck. He rejects them all.

Never one to miss a clue, no matter how subtle, it occurs to me that my son might not be feeling well. Failing to detect any visible signs of a rash, a fever, or the plague, I decide it is safe to take my shower. I pry my son loose, inwardly apologizing as I pacify him with the upstairs television.

In the shower, my mind switches to fast-forward. First, I reject the obvious. I do not want to cancel my meeting and I do not want to bring a cranky child with me. So I am going to have to stifle my pangs of conscience and go anyway. Then I set to work mentally readjusting my schedule so that I can put my son to sleep before the sitter arrives. I rationalize that he will wake up feeling better than he does now.

He's going to run a fever, I decide as I lather up, and it probably will spike in the afternoon while the baby-sitter is here. I calculate backward the four-hour intervals for Tylenol to see when I should start to ensure maximum comfort and a good nap while I am gone.

He must be coming down with something, I tell myself, and it's just getting started at 7 in the morning. On the chance that something horrendous develops, I'd better find a neighbor who will be at home to back up the baby-sitter. It's silly to make a late-afternoon doctor appointment now, I think, rejecting the idea even as I reach for the cream rinse. Better to wait and see how he sleeps tonight.

My mind darts ahead to tomorrow. Mentally, I review my schedule to see when I could fit in a visit to the pediatrician's for the earache he probably has. Then I remember the flu reportedly working its way around, and I strain to remember the symptoms. As I rinse, I try to recall how much my son ate for dinner the night before.

Toweling off in the bathroom, I tell myself to calm down. If he gets really ill before I leave, I sigh to myself, well, then I guess I could cancel the meeting. What kind of a mother would abandon a sick child? Stepping back into the bedroom, I curse the fate that conspires against me and wonder whether the editor will be in town another day. Shaking wet hair out of my eyes, I go to check on my son. He isn't where I left him.

I patrol the rooms upstairs, my ears straining for his moans. I don't hear them. On my way downstairs I stop to get the phone number for my editor's hotel. Then I head into the family room. My toddler is there all right—laughing merrily and running in circles around the couch.

Sometimes the only thing more active than my son is my imagination. After a while I begin to wonder if I am not being realistic—just pessimistic. Recently, I spent half a morning looking for the missing mate to my daughter's sandal. I looked under the bed, in the laundry, and behind the toilet—places I would not be surprised to find it. I found the sandal, finally, in the closet where the shoes are kept.

Another time I went looking for my son, who had been outside playing. I screamed for him up and down the street and quizzed his friends. No luck. I tried to squelch the niggling feeling of unease building in the pit of my stomach. I found my son, finally, at home in the family room talking to his father.

You'd think I would learn, but of course I have not. I remember a stretch of weeks when my son's lunchbox regularly was returning from school half full.

"How come you didn't drink your milk?" I queried, concerned by the sudden loss of appetite.

"Didn't want to drink it," he answered.

"How come you didn't eat your fruit?" I asked, wondering what disease was going around.

"Didn't want to," he said.

"Why didn't you want to?" I prodded.

"I didn't have time. I wanted to get the green shovel first," he answered with a trace of impatience. His mother is dense.

"What's so important about the green shovel?"

He fixed me with an exasperated gaze. "The green shovel," he answered impatiently, "digs the best."

■ ■ ■

Not only have my children led (or misled) me in ways I never would have expected, but so has my body. Since children, my attitudes are no longer the same. Neither are my looks. In changing, my body has betrayed me. Subconsciously I always expected that I would bounce back from three pregnancies none the worse for wear. I expected that I, unlike other mothers, would never visibly age. Since I've had children, of course, that is exactly what I have done. I never expected it would come down to a desperate matter of exercise classes and makeup, but that's exactly what it has become.

With some smugness I used to smirk at those willing to pay big bucks for a stair-climbing machine. For much less money, I would allow strangers to fetch and carry in my house any morning when I am trying to clean up the kitchen plus get three kids dressed, downstairs, and out the door. For years, in fact, I have maintained that mothers automatically get their exercise. After all, we bench-press babies and jog after toddlers, so we ought to be in shape.

But as I have gotten older and gotten into carpooling, I have begun to think otherwise. Inadvertently, my children have begun to point it out to me. My daughter longs to do cartwheels, something I will never again attempt in this lifetime. While he was learning to ride, my son was eager for me to help him with his two-wheeler. I can no longer run down the block bent at a ninety-degree angle more than two times in rapid succession.

Standing in the shadow of forty, I am suddenly concerned with two things I previously had taken for granted: acting young at heart and looking it. First, I wonder whether I ever again can look good—partly because now I automatically don't. Rolling out of bed I am as likely to look ravished as ravishing. Although I would like to think I can stay in shape without any particular effort, this year it has hit me that the kind of effortless beauty I desire requires a lot of work. Suddenly I no longer smirk at women who refuse to leave the house before they've "done their face." Now I am doing mine. Suddenly I have become aware of exercise and makeup, both of which I had always previously ignored. Now the truth has dawned: I need them both.

A twelve-year-old in my neighborhood recently told me I look pretty good. Then he handicapped my score by adding: especially for having three kids. I was humiliated. I want no-excuse admiration. Instead, I realize that I need help. The nutritional breakdown on the back of a package of cookies, for example, is useless for me. It defines a serving as one cookie; for me it is more often the entire box. The section of my closet devoted to clothes that no longer zip is larger than the section devoted to clothes that do. I have been losing and gaining the same five pounds for the last two years.

Lately I have become concerned because I have begun to meet moms who are tough competition. Several of them wear mascara and lipstick before 8 A.M. Several of them are younger and several are in far better shape than I. I saw one mother vault over the chin-high fence around the playground. I cannot even lift my three-year-old over that fence.

So I have started to do aerobics—but secretly, at home. This spares me the mortification of having to appear publicly in costume looking like a sausage wearing a belt. And this way nobody but me knows that I am incapable of touching heel to toe while snapping my fingers and smiling.

I attempted urban renewal on the slum of my body once before. Seven years ago, when my eldest was newborn, we exercised at a Mommy & Me class. I used to pray that my son, dozing snugly in his carrier, would cry and give me an excuse to stop. I was tempted not to nurse him before we went so that his howling would give me a break before I suffered a heart attack. After three months, I dropped out of class. The instructor kept changing the routine just when I got the hang of it. On my last day the instructor "congratulated" me. "You couldn't do anything at the beginning," she said. Today I wouldn't damn my own children with such faint praise.

I do not enjoy close encounters with full-length mirrors and I do not enjoy exercise. (As proof of my integrity, I have never worn a warm-up suit to the grocery store.) Vanity, however, is a great motivator. And I do not want my thighs to keep moving after my legs have stopped. So despite that teacher and her hips that I can never hope to have, I am trying again. I have bought a beginner's video, and I have actually used it. It is depressing to imitate a woman who must have inspired the Barbie doll. After several months of practice, I think I have mastered the warm-up.

"If that tape's not hard enough for you," offered a friend, "I can lend you something else." I graciously declined.

I wish I could say I suffer my humiliation in total privacy, but that isn't the case. I have children in the peanut gallery. I tried to entice my five-year-old into joining me. She was thrilled when I allowed her to wear her ballerina costume, but she lost interest fast after the first ten minutes. When I asked her how I was doing she told me, "You look much better today, Mommy."

I tried exercising once when the three-year-old was home. The first time he thought it was funny to sit on my head while I did sit-ups. The second time he perceived it as a marvelous opportunity to play inside the medicine cabinet.

The other day I was hard at it when a seven-year-old neighbor wandered over, saw me in front of the TV, and joined right in. I worked extra hard to impress her. When we were finished, I noticed that I was panting and she was not.

"The guy on the television in the morning is harder," she informed me. Oh yeah?

"Next time, you should try doing it with me from the beginning," I found myself saying. "After all, I'm in pretty good shape for having had three kids."

I don't want to hide behind disclaimers, of course. I want to return to the thrilling days of yesteryear when bartenders would ask me to prove my age. I want to return to the times when strangers would ask me if all those children were mine—because I didn't look old enough to be their mother. I want, of course, to take for granted what is no longer mine.

I recently had my first facial and found that what I want bears small relationship to what I have. As the attendant wrapped me and swabbed me, I secretly hoped she would ask me if I was married. Then, after I confessed to a family, I fantasized she would gasp in astonishment and tell me that I look fantastic. She didn't.

"Your skin is congested," she announced, evidently confusing my face with a freeway. She muttered about toxins and bringing my skin into balance. Then she asked what I use in my morning beauty routine.

"Nothing special," I mumbled, since I don't have one. How to explain that some mornings I skip a shower in order to make the beds? "I'm under a lot of stress." I added this by way of all-purpose excuse. Then I tried to relax in the dark while she globbed my face with what felt like varying degrees of hot motor oil. As my son would say, I was slimed. It didn't do much for my face or my ego to discover that my fantasy was a hallucination.

I retain great faith in the cosmetics industry, however. So if I cannot be in great shape, perhaps I can use makeup to pretend that I am glowingly healthy. A while ago I went with my mother to a cosmetics counter. Perched on a stool at the makeup counter, my faced tipped at an impossible angle, I tried not to blink as a stranger applied mascara to my eyelashes. Mentally I closed my eyes and hoped that I would turn out to look more normal than the slightly garish sales clerk. But my feelings of foolishness were assuaged by the fact that nearly every counter in the cosmetics department was packed. Not only were they packed, but they were filled with women my age—all of whom had decided it was time they learned how to apply makeup.

"It's time you learned how to do all this," my mother had chided earlier, while she gently implied that at my age a dab of lipstick no longer will suffice. Clearly, she thought I was beyond girlish beauty. I wouldn't have let her talk me into it, however, if I hadn't tended to agree. Once I started buying moisturizers, I think I always knew it would come to this. I cannot say whether I am at the age where I find makeup appealing because it colors my face or because it covers up the lines. I only know that for me the natural look no longer suffices— unless I've worked hours to achieve it.

For my husband's benefit, of course, I try to pretend that it does. He believes clowns wear makeup. He also believes my face looks great so long as he cannot tell that I am wearing anything over it. But men, of course, do not (pardon the pun) face the same problem. Often their appearance improves with age. This means that in high school and college when we women looked great, some of them looked pretty silly. We closed our eyes and married them on faith. They have grown up to look distinguished, not old. Now they may be concerned with hair loss, but definitely not crow's feet.

I am interested in makeup, however, not so men will think I look good, but because I hope it will make me feel great. A make-over provides the same therapeutic value as a new haircut. I advise all new mothers to do one or the other shortly after having a baby. Both entail a relaxing interlude when you place your fate in the hands of someone else and come away looking different. Both are a harmless form of self-indulgence. I do not mean to imply that only mothers spend their time doing things for everyone else instead of taking care of themselves. I do not mean to imply that the birth of children is the kiss of death to a woman's attractiveness. But I do mean that on bad days, to some mothers, it can feel this way.

Hence the makeup.

After my make-over, the woman who stared back at me from the mirror was not myself. Not only was she wearing lipstick, but she had found the time to apply eyeliner, mascara and four different shades of eye shadow. She looked stylized and infinitely more exotic than an everyday mom. I did not feel totally comfortable with the way she looked, but I suspect she represented an improvement over the regular version.

With the exception of my daughter, my family was not so sure. My husband suggested the makeup looked a little heavy, but that perhaps I would look better in a darkened room. My seven-year-old also was nonplussed.

"How come your face doesn't look the same as when you left home?" he asked suspiciously.

The answer, of course, is because I didn't want it to. I expect makeup to make me look different and, more important, feel different. If I am a reclamation project, makeup implies there is still hope. But in a larger sense, the makeup I bought is an investment in fantasy. I expect to put it on and feel one step closer to glamorous. I expect to put it on and forget that I am leaning over the diaper pail. And I expect to put it on and forget how much money I paid for it.

The problem, of course, is that not only is my body getting older, but also my mind. Not only am I having to work harder at looking young, but also at thinking young. Before I became a parent, I figured I would be different. I would always stay young at heart. I would always be fun to be around and I would never forget what it was like to be a child. Before I became a parent I wouldn't have believed otherwise. Now I know the truth.

When I was a child, my teachers constantly would change my seat, reporting to my parents that I talked too much with my neighbors. I don't recall ever being concerned by these reports when I was a child. But I feel different now that I am getting those reports about my son. I wonder why I am concerned but he is not. Doesn't he realize his future is at stake? My perspective has changed. Let's face it; I no longer buy my clothes in the junior department. I went to see *The Little Mermaid.* After watching Ariel rebel against her upbringing and her father, I identified with King Triton. It will not be easy to relinquish *my* daughter to marriage, either.

I know, of course, that adults and children are not the same. Our biological clocks are set to different time zones. My children want to eat lunch at the time I used to rouse myself for brunch. They want to eat dinner before I have even decided what to cook. They like to skip naps and stay up late. I love to doze in the afternoons and go to bed early.

Clearly, as an adult, I am on the other side of a great divide from childhood. So why does it trouble me when children also perceive it? Recently my husband and I visited cousins who put us in our numerical place. The adults had fifteen years seniority on us; their children were about fifteen years younger than us. Socially speaking, we could have gone either way. I like to think I am as contemporary to the children as I am to their parents. So it bothered me when these college-aged children didn't feel contemporary with me. Home for a summer of close quarters with their parents, they did not feel they had anything to say to somebody else's mother.

Sometimes, when I deliberately try to bridge the gap, it doesn't work. I remember once spending hours squatting on the ground, surrounded by black Legos, searching for a gray Lego with three bumps. If I had wanted to build a castle out of Legos, I would have set aside an entire afternoon to do so. But I hadn't planned on it. Why my son was given a kit clearly labeled nine to twelve years old, I will never know. But I do know that is why at the last minute I was drafted to help.

After a while, I began to get into it. I did not begin to get good at it. If Legos were important to me, I consoled myself, I would excel. But they are important to my son, and so I gave it my best shot—even though my primary motivation was to get the pieces off the floor to reduce the likelihood that my youngest would swallow one of them. In the end I was confounded by the directions and much too slow. Where my gray wall met the green corner, I was off kilter by one bump. When I drafted a neighborhood twelve-year-old to act as consultant, the first thing he did was rip apart everything I felt I had accomplished. I watched him, trying not to show that my feelings were hurt. I wondered why parents aren't good at the same things as kids, and why we aren't given credit when at least we try.

I had never realized that I would value the opinion of children. When the kids congregate in front of my house, I like to think it's because they know I won't bug them—not because we have the thickest lawn for somersaults. When I wear new sneakers, I am absurdly pleased because a ten-year-old tells me they look great. When I crack a joke, I have had children stare at me as if to say: I didn't know you could laugh. When my son's kindergarten friend visited, he did not know what to call me. I was surprised when he settled on "Mom." I had not realized that I have become a generic.

My husband joins the neighborhood kids as they pass the football. He bows out after a minute, but I wonder how they would react if he stayed in for a game. Can parents be participants with children or are we forever consigned to be only referees? I used to think that if I felt young at heart—even as a mother—I would be. Now it turns out children are the judges of that.

■ ■ ■

10
Getting Away from Them All

*I'd never left them before,
but I plan to do it again*

I remember one time talking to a friend, a single mother who was interviewing for a roommate.

"This guy didn't want the apartment, but he asked me out," she complained. "I'm not looking for a date; I'm looking for a roommate."

I recognized that our situations are reversed. As a married mother, I have a roommate. Lately I have been looking for a date. Basically, the passion of my love life burns with a slow but steady flame. But occasionally I feel the need to check the pilot light. Because of the children, my husband and I have limited opportunity for romance. One recent afternoon, for example, we believed we were alone. Our toddler was napping, our son was at a friend's, and our daughter was playing down the street. No sooner did we even contemplate snuggling on the couch than our daughter, the homing device, returned. Snuggling time was over. Clearly, if we retain any interest in privacy, my husband and I need to get away. Alone.

Eventually most parents decide to have no more children. Eventually most parents also decide to escape from the ones they have. In other words, while an afternoon off can be liberating, several days and nights off would be even better. Getting away is essential to staying home

— — — — — — — — — — — — — — — — — — — —

happily the rest of the time. If you love 'em, once in a while you must leave 'em.

When you bring each child home from the hospital, you also bring home a 24-hour-a day job. Three children means a 504-hour-a-week job. Eventually you will acknowledge the need for a coffee break. This realization may hit first during a day when you have been hard pressed to squeeze in your morning shower, or perhaps after you and the children have been held prisoner an entire week by unrelenting snow. You will respond to this realization by prevailing upon relatives or baby-sitters. You will buy yourself a few hours' peace. But eventually, after the first flush of baby love has faded and weaning is complete, you will crave more. You will want, as the children say, to go away on a sleep-over. You will want real time, especially with your husband.

Although we knew we needed to get away alone together, my husband and I waited six years before taking action. Although we have celebrated numerous birthdays and anniversaries over the years that provided ample excuses, we did not use them. We never had the right combination of children old enough and someone young enough, capable enough, and willing enough to watch them. Finally, for our fifteenth wedding anniversary, when our oldest was six and our youngest was two, my husband and I went away for a weekend.

We fantasized about two weeks in Hawaii; we settled for two days down the coast. Realistically, we weren't ready to leave our children for any longer than that. And the place, we decided, wasn't nearly so important as the time alone together. So for our anniversary we checked into a nearby resort, defining "far away" as any place where the children could not find us. We were intent upon pampering ourselves and talking to each other—occupations neglected for the previous six years.

It was a weekend of rediscoveries. The first thing I noticed was that if we both stopped talking, our hotel room was quiet. If we had so desired, we could have heard every word of the evening news. Then I noticed that if we did not have to hold hands with our children, our hands were suddenly free for each other. Meals became peaceful oases, no longer playing fields for shouting matches. My husband and I both ate warm food while we were sitting down. I ordered nothing I have ever cooked before and nothing my children will ever let me eat again. I even ate a salad that resembled the groundcover I am trying to pull out of my garden—something nobody would eat at home.

In addition to the obvious, we did other things we cannot do with children around. Desiring to be pampered, I treated myself to a facial and a leisurely bath. My husband indulged himself by also doing something else impossible with children. We stopped at a special hardware store offering 50 percent discounts. He spent nearly an hour considering the relative merits of various cordless tools. He stood calmly in the aisle and carefully pondered his selections. Ordinarily our youngest would have given him ten seconds to decide before he began to rearrange the drill bits. Like newly exchanged prisoners of war, we gloried in the freedom to do what we wanted, when we wanted, the way we wanted. We want to do it again every year.

Understand, I am not saying we slipped out the door and slipped back into the way we were before we had children. We called home, shopped for presents, and talked nonstop about the kids as we headed home on Sunday. But going away was worth it. When we got home, at least a full twenty minutes elapsed before I felt as though we had never left.

■ ■ ■

Getting away does not only mean with your husband. Sometimes the best company to have is nobody but yourself. Mothers need time to themselves. During the last year I have gone away twice on business trips. These solo ventures included the first time I ever left both my husband and my children overnight. Because these absences were not entirely by choice, I found them to be a curious mixture of relief and regret.

On my maiden voyage alone, the family drove me to a nearby city for the opening swing on a publicity tour to promote my first book. When we said good-bye in the driveway of my hotel, it wasn't as easy as I expected. I had been so concerned with leaving, I had never considered being alone.

It seemed a role reversal that my husband was staying home with the kids and I was not. Despite my detailed flow chart of daily duties, I was worried about how things might go—especially after my husband asked me what time school started. He seemed startled when I reminded him to pack lunches and wash a load of laundry. I gave a lot of instructions to my daughter on the theory that, unlike her Daddy, she knows the location of most things in the house. She, in turn, knew that I was nervous and reassured me that I would do just fine.

"It will be OK, Mommy," she said. "Even if you spill your milk."

As we exchanged surprisingly soggy good-byes, I recognized the irony of going away on tour in order to talk about the family I was leaving behind.

"This is the first time I've left you," my daughter cried as my family began to drive away. It was also the first time I'd ever left them all. Walking back to my room, I discovered my son's diaper bag still slung over my shoulder. I had forgotten to stow it in the car. Hanging on me, it seemed a fitting metaphor for my life.

In the days that followed I cannot deny a sense of liberation, of relief. It is far easier to propel one person out the door at an appointed time than my usual four or five. Getting showered and dressed was a luxury. With children in the house, it had been years since I had been able to lay out my clothes across my bed. Somebody would either jump on them or take them. At breakfast one morning I watched a nearby family coping with their toddler. He kicked over his juice, he kicked off his socks, and he sat there bawling while his father ineffectually squeezed a plastic elephant in his face. I sat there in my silk suit and mentally rejoiced that the child was not mine.

It is far easier to talk lovingly and humorously about your children when they are not around to annoy you. Mine were not around to annoy me; they were not around at all. So I also missed them. In addition to relief, I also felt loneliness being away from home. I had needed some time to myself, it is true, but perhaps not as much as I got. A solitary hotel room is spacious, but it's also nearly empty. I called home frequently during my trip, conversing more lovingly with my husband by telephone than I do in person. I was amazed by how small my children's voices sounded across telephone wires. Across a room their shouts send my eardrums into cardiac arrest. We all felt a keen emotional tug during my absence. Distance had disrupted the rituals of our lives. I telephoned one afternoon when I would be unable to call that night. My daughter mourned: "But how will I tell you good night?"

After only four nights, of course, she was able to do that in person. And when they picked me up at the airport, my children stroked me constantly as if to satisfy themselves that I was really back. My youngest grabbed my hand from his car seat and tried to reel me in from the front seat like a fish. My husband also was glad to see me. He greeted me with flowers and later he downed with gusto his first home-cooked meal in a week. He said it was great to be with the children but admitted to having had his moments. His voice was a tad testy as he asked them to quiet down; I recognized his tone.

It took me time to adjust to being home. I felt like a swimmer who, once having climbed out of the pool, needs to get used to the water all over again. I had to take my household and once again make it my own. I threw out rotting raw vegetables and replenished the supply of frozen foods. I washed the party dresses my daughter had convinced her Daddy she could wear to school. But I did not comment. How many other husbands would cover for a wife who regularly lambastes them in print? I was glad and grateful to see my husband; he had pitched in like a trouper. As I walked in the door, I swear he breathed a sigh of relief that I was back. But then so did I.

The next time I left my children, I was on a freelance writing assignment during which I was supposed to relax and write about how it felt to get away. I went to a weekend camp for mothers only in California's San Bernardino Mountains. I found out that although relaxing isn't quite as easy as it sounds, travel can have unexpected benefits.

The timing for the assignment was perfect. It came during the dog days of summer after camp had ended but before school started, and I was ready for a break. I had savored my first sips of summer like the first cup of coffee in the morning. But by late August my resources and enthusiasm were down to the dregs. So I didn't hesitate to accept an assignment that involved the "hardship" of going away alone by myself.

"Think of it as a business trip," I told my husband, who about once a week comes home from work after the children are asleep or leaves before they are awake. Although I felt fully entitled to go, I nevertheless worried how he would manage. I worried that he would leave all the laundry for me; he worried that I would leave skid marks off the side of a mountain road.

"You forget that I drive in rush-hour traffic while three kids fight World War II in the back seat," I glibly reminded him. What else did I expect, I thought to myself, from a man who knew me before I could drive? Then, paying my dues to the guilt department, I shopped, cleaned, and washed before I left. I worked so hard, in fact, that had I stayed home for the weekend I would have had no chores to do.

That was, of course, the attraction of the trip. I relished the notion of nothing to do. As I packed my sleazy paperback I realized that I hadn't had such high hopes since the first time I started potty training. Thrilled at the prospect of spending two hours alone in the car, I pulled away listening to a Raffi tape—until I realized that for once I could pick something else. After driving about an hour I conceded that my husband had a point. I know less about the insides of the car than I do about the car seat and I couldn't understand the instruction manual for that, either. I would be inept in a crisis. As I started 6,700 feet up the mountain with only Carly Simon for company, I fought the urge to look down and indulged my maternal instinct to hug the yellow line. I made it, however, just fine.

Big Bear Lake is pristine, beautiful, and a wonderful spot for a family vacation—a thought that I squelched immediately. Lately I have been spending more time at the playground than the wilderness, but I can appreciate natural beauty. "Unspoiled" refers to any place without diaper wipes—and some places should be kept that way. With that in mind, I called home to announce (a tad triumphantly) my safe arrival. I had to call twice. The first time my three-year-old answered and hung up. As an article of faith I told myself that my husband had everything under control.

The biggest rule at camp, the counselors told me, is never to pick up after yourself. They said the idea is to relax—which is not as easy as it sounds. I spent the weekend trying to do it. After eating on picnic tables in the homey atmosphere, I had to fight an impulse to clear my dishes. But I appreciated eating a meal without getting up once to pour juice. At camp I had a modest room to myself. But since I define privacy as going solo to the grocery store, it felt luxurious. I used the shower often and the television not at all. My room was quiet, and I lusted after the prospect of going to bed with a book.

We mothers spent Friday afternoon settling in, comparing notes on the drive and getting acquainted around the fireplace at the main lodge. A bit defensively, we all explained the reasons why we felt entitled to a weekend vacation alone. Talking about the mountain drive led to a debate about whether it is easier to be the passenger in the car who must control the children or the driver. The consensus seemed to be that we would rather drive.

Then some women headed to the hot tubs. I headed to bed early to be alone with my book, which I expected to be a definite improvement over the night before, when I had slept with my three-year-old's feet in my back. But when I snuggled under the covers, I couldn't sleep. I realized I was waiting for someone to kiss me good night.

The next morning I woke up at 6:45 A.M., the time my five-year-old always goes to the bathroom. I took a cup of coffee from the camp office back to bed and suddenly realized: I had nothing to do all day but take care of myself. It felt like a great gift. I had time for a walk before breakfast to clear my head and work off some of the cheesecake from dinner. I walked briskly, the way you cannot move with a child in tow. Looking forward to the day ahead, I began to appreciate the possibilities.

Viewing the weekend as my own personal Outward Bound program, I agreed to go horseback riding—even though the closest I had come to a horse in thirty years had been a merry-go-round. The idea was to break out of my routine. I set out slowly up a gentle hill on Smokey, trying not to communicate my anxiety through my knees. We were supposed to walk, but he wanted to trot. We ended up in a contest of wills. I knew without being told that I hadn't completely gotten away from two-year-olds.

By lunchtime I guessed at least half the mothers had called home to satisfy themselves that things were under control. But not me. Sure I missed my children, and I wanted to know what they were doing. I am used to orchestrating every detail of the day. But if I called, I was afraid I would start telling them what to do. Then I might start worrying about whether they were doing it. Back in my room again I decided I must be relaxing a little. I had begun piling my clothes on a chair instead of hanging them up—a trait of my husband's that drives me crazy.

Next our counselors took us on a motorboat ride. One mother jokingly suggested a sing-along, but we decided against a rousing rendition of "Five Little Monkeys Jumping on the Bed." Instead, we talked about our families. We also talked about whether a weekend is adequate time to relax. Just to ensure that it was, I signed up for a massage that afternoon. As I lay self-consciously naked under a sheet in my darkened room, my masseuse gave me the bad news. She told me my left shoulder is higher than my right (from carrying kids) and that I am tight in the buttocks (from holding back anger). She urged me to relax while she pushed and rubbed. I couldn't help thinking about how my thighs were jiggling. Most men, she told me, fall asleep during a massage. Like most women, I could not relax to that degree. But afterward I did manage to lounge around the swimming pool for an hour.

On Saturday night the camp atmosphere—which had felt at times like a baby shower—suddenly seemed more like a slumber party. We spruced up our clothes and makeup. I felt slightly giddy myself. Maybe it was the wine, but freedom from baby-sitters can be a heady influence. I hopped into the car and went to see *Ghost,* my first movie since *The Jungle Book.* When I opened my purse to pay for my ticket, a raisin box fell out. Afterward I sat in one of the cabins for more conversation. We talked about whether we have all grown up to be everything we didn't plan on becoming. Acknowledging ruefully but unashamedly that I had, I went back to my cabin feeling thoughtful and relaxed, and I slept just fine.

Sunday morning I again woke up early. I jumped up with a jolt and immediately thought: Today I have to go home. But not yet, I told myself, settling back into bed. There was no rush; I had nobody to pack but myself. I took another brisk walk and stopped at the edge of the lake. I wanted to remember how it felt to stand alone in a place so quiet that the only sounds besides lapping waves were the footsteps of squirrels. I wanted to bottle the tranquility and take it home.

At the closing brunch we mothers reassured each other that we hadn't really missed our families all that much. I sat at the pool one last time and watched another mother float sleepily on a raft. Already thinking about getting home, suddenly I couldn't sit still. In early afternoon I said my good-byes, packed my stuff, and headed back down the mountain. The two-hour drive home seemed faster.

Pulling into my driveway and seeing my family again, I immediately saw things that were not the way I like them. My daughter was playing outside barefoot with my husband, and my sons were watching afternoon television. I found laundry still in the dryer and piles to pick up in every room. Unable to stand it, I spent the remainder of the afternoon washing, straightening, and putting away. Pretty soon the house looked as if I had never left.

When it came to my family, however, that is not how I felt. My time away had extra benefits. Despite his shortcomings in the laundry department, my husband had given me a weekend without complaint. Likewise, there was something wonderfully therapeutic about missing my children. I reached for them eagerly. Seeing them after an absence, I rediscovered all the ways in which they are so cute, the sweetness I tend to overlook in the daily rush. The rest of the day I had renewed patience for their interruptions and their quarrels. Somehow I was able to mentally uncork the tranquility I had felt up at the lake and take a soothing sniff.

Getting away provides perspective on life. I may not always be able to escape to a mountaintop, but I shouldn't need one in order to look down and see that most of my problems are small. Every day I try to hold on to that thought—for at least an hour.

11

My Mother Never Thought He Was Good Enough

The man I married, after the fact

At the front door I fish for my house key a few moments longer than strictly necessary. Mentally, I am bracing myself for reentry. Let's talk about emotional roller coasters. Very little matches the exhilarating high of leaving the house totally unencumbered by children—or the sobering low of walking back into the house to reassume responsibility after an absence. It is like comparing the way you feel after an illness with the way you felt while you were sick. It is the contrast between the finished product after two months of remodeling and the mess that preceded it.

In this case I had gone out alone to an office party. (To be quite honest, I would have gone to a dog fight if it would have gotten me away from everyone for a few hours.) Now I had to pay the piper. Maybe your luck with baby-sitters is better than mine. But I have found that the price I pay for an evening out is not only the money I fork over to the sitter. I have left sitters (supposedly) in charge who let the children stay up late when I specifically wanted them in bed early, or who take phone messages beautifully but forget to administer the medicine my child is supposed to receive. Before I go out, I hustle to get absolutely everything ready ahead of time. And when I get home, I hustle to pick up absolutely everything.

So sleuthlike, I begin downstairs to surmise what transpired in my absence. Clues are everywhere. Two toy trucks, a teddy bear, and a stuffed frog lie at the foot of the stairs, so I know the children enjoyed themselves by shelling the entryway. In the kitchen, dirty dishes are piled high in the sink. That is better, I tell myself, than finding them still on the table. Instead, on the table I find sticky wooden sticks. Like fossil remains, they are all that is left of three frozen-yogurt bars. A complete trajectory of drip marks on the dirty high chair tray indicates where my youngest must have eaten. I take a few seconds to wipe the table and counters, taking care not to drip onto my skirt.

Mounting the stairs without attracting the slightest bit of attention, I wonder fleetingly what anyone would do if I were an ax murderer. In the children's room, where my two oldest are sleeping, I begin to pick up the laundry they have strewn hurricane fashion across the room. When I am home, they know they cannot get away with this. I return discarded shoes to the closet, I deposit stuffed animals on their shelves, I dump the toy cars back in the proper bin, and close my son's dresser drawers, which have been left gaping open. Making excuses, I tell myself it is tough to pick up a room when you have no idea where anything goes. In passing, I fill the diaper holder, which I notice has been left totally empty. I grab the pajamas for my youngest as I wonder where he is, what he's wearing, and why he hasn't already been changed for bed.

My sense of annoyance bubbles to the surface like the fizz in a soda, and the good feelings from my evening out begin to fall flat. I tell myself it's no big deal. It has taken me less than fifteen minutes to clean up. In all probability the kids had great fun—something they undoubtedly would not have had with someone who made them pick up and clean up. (Someone like a grumpy mother.) If I wanted everything done the way I would do it, I tell myself, then I should stay home and do it. Even so, as I take a deep breath and press on to my bedroom, I grumble to myself that it would be nice just one time to come home to a house even neater than I left it.

Once again, I brace myself and then open the door to my bedroom. There, fully clothed on my bed, lies my youngest son. He is sound asleep. Lying next to him, also sound asleep, is my baby-sitter, my husband.

So let's talk about husbands, my husband in particular, and the ways they can drive their wives crazy. Their most important fault, I would have to say, is that men fail to do things the way women do. Men, in other words, do them wrong:

The two husbands are watching the two two-year-olds, and I cannot resist watching them watch. The men are having an involved conversation concerning the merits of two different computer systems. Their sons are roaming the street. Ours is brandishing a sharp stick of the sort I would never allow; theirs is halfway down the block chasing a dog. I watch, biting my tongue, to see how long it will be before the men attend to the children. I envy them their train of thought. When we wives are on duty, we never seem to complete our sentences. The children derail our attempts at normal dialogue. After five or six minutes, however, the men complete their conversation and then take a look around for their children. They find them. Nobody gets hurt, nobody gets lost.

So I guess nobody cares but me. I am vexed sometimes by how nonchalant a father can be. A man can fall asleep putting a child down for his nap. A man will watch his children while he also watches television. Worse, he thinks he is doing an adequate job.

Unlike mothers, fathers do not have their children on a leash. Men are not attached to their children's every moves as are we women. We mothers think that this leash helps us keep track of our children's whereabouts, but it also has a drawback. If our children are attached to us by a leash, then we also are attached to them. We are like paddle balls. Our sense of responsibility yanks us back to our duties and limits our own freedom to relax.

I am, of course, partly jealous. Intuitively I think my way is more conscientious, but I think a man's way is more fun. I think it's a function of very different management styles. Women are expedient; men are in it for the sport. Men don't want the first parking space; they will circle like a hawk searching for the best parking space. If a man wants to know whether January 26 falls on a Friday, he will remain on the couch and perform mental gymnastics to calculate the answer. A woman will get up and consult a calendar. Women keep the children on a schedule; men don't even realize there is one.

Consequently, fathers don't stay on top of details the way mothers do. Men are 50 percent more likely to forget to close the diaper wipes container. Quite often if a child gets cranky at noontime, the father will have no idea what's the matter. He is amazed when a mother reminds him that all living creatures must eat. A father is oblivious to social nuances. To him, a kid is a kid. If two children blatantly cannot stand each other, only an oblivious father would blithely suggest the two play together.

Only a father expects children to get ready for school with any kind of efficiency just because he tells them. He does not realize mornings are carefully orchestrated campaigns with the front door as their objective. My husband and children can be up for hours, but when it is time for us to go, then suddenly I am late getting them dressed because he has to leave.

Men must not feel the weight of their obligations as heavily as women.

"Bathtime is a special time for my son. My husband always gives him his bath," my friend tells me. She sighs. "I just wish he would play with him, though. He usually throws him into the tub and then goes to watch the news."

One morning at dawn, as my husband prepared to leave early for work, I asked him to please hang around while I took a shower.

"I'll be fast," I told him. "I'd just feel better if you would watch the kids while I'm under water."

I emerged from the shower to the sound of screams from our youngest, who wanted somebody to give him breakfast. I checked around for the whereabouts of my husband. Sure enough, he had waited for me to get out before leaving the house. He was downstairs in the den with the door closed so that he could hear while he was on the telephone with the office.

There are other occasions when I can contemplate my husband and forget exactly what it was that attracted me in the first place. It can be difficult to rely upon a husband to see things rationally. Not only doesn't he take his fatherly duties seriously enough, but too often he takes after his children. The story of my family's electric train will illustrate.

When Grandma recently came to visit, she made us an offer my husband couldn't refuse. She put up half the equity for us to invest in a railroad—nothing too fancy, just a decent span of track, an engine, and a few switches. Enough to make my husband feel like a transportation mogul. With his mother's encouragement, he hauled down from the attic his old Lionel train cars to go with the new track and unpacked the frustrated ambitions he had saved since his childhood.

I was against the idea. The notion of investing in one expensive toy predicated upon the theory that everyone in the family can share it epitomizes to me parental torture testing. I am, after all, talking about my children, who once quarreled all day over canceled movie tickets. The only time they willingly decide to share is when the possession they all coveted has been intrinsically devalued so that it has become worthless. Translation: It has become boring or it is broken.

So whenever my husband had broached the subject of setting up a sophisticated model electric train, I had been against it. I have no idea how I would walk around it or vacuum around it, and no idea how the children would all play in harmony around it. Laying track is something best not accomplished by committee. Every train has only one engineer and I did not think my kids would share.

I had no idea how right, and how wrong, I was. When we set up the train, what followed was nothing but war. Here is how it went:

"Let's make the track go this way," said one child, grabbing some pieces.

"Don't hook it up yet," my husband said.

"No, it's going to go this way," said somebody else, fitting the pieces to his satisfaction.

"Don't hook it up yet!" my husband shouted. "I told you we're just plotting the track. I told you to wait."

My youngest grabbed the boxcar as my husband shouted at him to put it down. Too late—I heard a shower of pieces fall to the floor.

"All right, everybody out," my husband ordered. "Just let me get this thing set up."

After dinner it began all over again. My husband strung two tiny wires from the switch on the table down to the track on the floor.

"Don't bump the wires. They're very delicate," he cautioned everyone seconds before our youngest stepped on them.

"Out of here!" he shouted, and the three-year-old became the first child to stalk from the room.

"I want to drive," my daughter whined.

"Give it gas! Give it gas!" my husband shouted.

My oldest ran the controls.

"Flip the switch! Flip the switch!" my husband shouted as derailment seemed imminent.

"Turn it off! Turn it off!" he yelled at our daughter. "When the train goes off the track, you have to turn off the power. You're asleep at the switch."

She, too, stomped from the room in an angry huff. The youngest came back and ran over to commandeer the controls.

"Don't touch that!" shouted my husband. "I have to help you. You can't run the train alone."

That night, for a while, the children played with the train while their father oversaw their every move. Then he decided to expand the track and install a new switch. He told everyone to stop playing so that he could work on it.

"But I liked it fine the way it was," disagreed our oldest.

"This will be better," his father outvoted him.

My husband fussed with the train while my son came to me crying. "Why can't we just have fun with the train?" he asked.

That's a good question and one I cannot answer. As I said, when children have a new toy, it can be difficult for them to share. I know that eventually my husband is going to let everyone have a turn. I only hope it's before the train gets broken.

The point—in case it didn't already stick you—is that men can be the youngest children in the family.

Take illness, for example. When colds rampage through my family the worst sufferer of all is the baby. By this I mean my husband. Every woman knows that when her husband gets sick he complains more frequently about feeling more miserable than she ever could. The higher they stand, I believe, the farther they fall.

One morning my husband and I both woke up with raging sore throats that blossomed into colds like the children had. But somehow his was much worse. For two days he stayed home from work. I stayed home and worked. I would rather march zombielike through my day than lie in bed and imagine the chaos ensuing elsewhere. And so in addition to taking care of the household, my work was complicated by having to step over the inert body of my husband lying helpless in front of the television.

On a day when my husband stays home ailing, the first symptoms of his presence become evident in the kitchen. The previously clear counter in my kitchen features all the debris of a recent meal. With an exasperated sigh, I rinse, stack, and wipe for what feels like the two hundredth time that day—and it's not even lunchtime.

During convalescence, my husband adheres to the old axiom about feeding a cold. (This has no medical basis; he also feeds a fever.) A plague of locusts, stranded in a Nebraska wheatfield, could not wreak more havoc than he does upon my kitchen. His throat may hurt horribly, but swallowing apparently makes it feel better. While my husband pillages, carefully hoarded leftovers vanish, lunch supplies for the kids evaporate, and my entire supply of canned soup is wiped out.

It's tough being home with four kids. The day usually starts with a blow-by-blow description of the progress of his cold: It's pushing on the ears; it's pounding in the head. Even counting football season, never has one man revealed so much on a subject about which I have no desire to learn.

"My throat is really sore. My ears are burning. You can't imagine how miserable I'm feeling," my husband will say after staggering from the chair to the couch.

Yes, I can.

I've heard wives say that after their husbands retired and began hanging around the house they faced the biggest adjustments of their marriages. Now I understand. A grown man is rather large to have underfoot; he's not as easy to step over as a two-year-old. Whatever bed I wanted to make, whatever couch I wanted to straighten, somehow his body would always be sprawled there first. It wasn't that I had to wait on him. I had to wait for him—to get out of the way.

The last time he was home sick my husband wandered about like a vacationer inadvertently separated from his tour group.

"What time do these kids go to school?" he asked with a note of desperation one morning as the regular car pool gang was destroying the house after breakfast. He's usually gone before the kids leave.

"There sure is a lot of stuff in this garage," he commented one afternoon as we spent forty-five minutes rounding up everything necessary to close the door in order to come inside. It's usually picked up before he comes home.

When he was feeling his worst, my husband would pass out in front of the television set. The kids would sneak into the room to watch, attracted by the normally forbidden fruit. As he started to feel better, my husband's body would remain home but mentally he would become plugged into the office by telephone and computer. The entire time he was home, in short, he was either watching a movie and trying to doze, or fielding phone calls at command central. In either case, he was shouting at everyone else to be quiet.

I cannot put my finger on how one man so easily manages to derail a previously efficient routine. The days my husband is home, dinner and bath are never on time and we barely make it to school in the mornings.

Part of my aggravation, I think, is because when he is around I keep waiting for my husband to help out. He stays home for the opportunity to rest; I see it as a chance for free labor. When three kids need baths or five people are all starving at the same time, I cannot help but expect any ambulatory adult in the same room to pitch in. My husband, quite rightfully, views himself as disabled. While he doesn't want me to wait on him, he certainly doesn't want to wait on anyone else.

Eventually the point becomes moot, of course. After every illness my husband goes back to work—never again to appear during the daylight hours until dinnertime. When this happens the kids miss him, of course. They think it is simply wonderful having him around.

Sometimes, honesty compels me to admit, my husband is not the only full-sized child in the house. Sometimes he and I vie with each other to see who can behave more like a baby. When neither of us wants to take charge, then division of labor becomes another problem in our household.

One time, for example, my husband was angry with me because when he got up in the morning the dirty dinner dishes in the kitchen were covered with ants. I was smugly silent. Eloquently, my silence shouted: It would have been easier to wash them the night before, wouldn't it?

"I thought I was putting the kids to bed and you were doing the dishes," my husband said as he glared at me. But my argument rests on firm ground. Every night I cook and he cleans. Normally we both put the children to bed, but I did it alone the night before because immediately after dinner he had fallen asleep across the bed with his feet on my pillow. I never agreed to anything since he already owed me.

Oh, but who's keeping score? Both of us, actually. And since we became parents I have found that we rack up points against each other with a vengeance. I do not know who established the unspoken rules for our contest of wills. But I do know that we both follow them exactly. The contest, like the rules, is silent and officially unacknowledged. We do not nag each other to take turns with the children; we wage a standoff. We wait to see who can hold out longer.

Maybe you play, also. The game originates when that first baby cries in the night and each parent feigns sleep in bed waiting for the other to stir. It is refined when the baby has a ripe diaper both parents pointedly ignore waiting for each other to change it. It is sort of like when the telephone rings and nobody rushes to answer it. My husband—who used to dash upstairs to greet the children upon arriving home from work—now hides out downstairs to read the mail and watch the news before shouting hello. Other times, when the kids are fighting, neither of us makes a move off the couch to see what's the matter. We wait each other out. We have become experts. (Please note, however, that in our maneuverings I enjoy an advantage of moral superiority because I take care of the children during the week.)

Here is an example of how the game goes: We once spent most of the day with the children at a museum. We came home exhausted and ready to rest; the children were ready to play. They needed an adult to open the garage and to watch them outside. My husband stonewalled by immediately lying down on the bed. I countered by reading the paper. The kids upped the ante by running out the front door. I increased the pressure by asking my husband if he believed they were safe outside alone. (The words were innocent but the tone was not.) I can't remember who won that particular round; it would depend on how quickly my husband was able to fall asleep.

Sometimes, when my husband is too slow on the uptake, I issue instructions by talking to my children. I am talking to my children, but my husband is supposed to be listening.

"Would you like to play outside?" I ask. "Daddy will go with you."

"Daddy will read that to you," I say, "after he gives you a bath."

Baths and bedtimes offer other prime examples of how we play. I give baths during the week; my husband takes charge on weekends. No matter how filthy our children become, I will not fill the bathtub on a Saturday. We have joint custody of bedtimes, but once again we fight a war of avoidance. I know that if I linger long enough downstairs packing lunches, my husband should have teeth brushing well under way. In turn he knows that if he goes upstairs and switches TV channels long enough, eventually I will start the faucet.

So that's how we play the game at my house. As our children battle to the death over who gets to go first, my husband and I angle furiously for the right to be last. Just goes to show you how petty children can be.

■ ■ ■

Men may think they are in charge of their household, but many of them are not really qualified to run it. Sometimes, it can only be a woman. She captains the ship on a day-to-day basis. By virtue of his performance the man is not always a help, and never as big a help as the woman would like him to be.

Household chores can rub at the relationship between husband and wife. They can create a lot of friction. As a woman working at home, it is inevitable that I should shoulder more of the day-to-day responsibility for the children. My husband simply isn't around. But if I could pick somebody to stick around to help me, I would choose a mother and not a father. Mothers have a better sense of how to make themselves useful.

Here is the view from the kitchen sink:

Dashing off to work in the morning, he informs me that he may be late and instructs me to go ahead and serve dinner if he's not home by 6:30. Mentally substituting tuna salad for the roast, I watch my husband kiss the children good-bye and run out the door. For the millionth time since I've begun working at home, I wonder if my husband appreciates how lucky he is to have good help. I run the household and care for our children with cool efficiency. I don't do windows, but I make beds, cook, fold laundry, and on any given Thursday I know the nature of our weekend plans. My husband does not.

To put it another way, I do not know of any husbands who wish they had another man in the house; I know numerous women who wish they had a wife. If you want to get a job done, ask the woman. In most cases she is the one who has ordered school pictures, collected for the paper drive, and organized her day around the soccer schedule. If it is something she cannot do, she will see that her husband does it. I have always suspected this female primacy, but the feeling has intensified since I've been working at home. I watch our children play with friends my husband has never met while they wear clothes he has never seen.

Understand, my husband is no worse than most. Conversely, this means he is better than some. He spends time with his children. He is a good sport and a good provider. He does not believe retirement planning consists of buying a lottery ticket. But he has his faults. He is typical of his species. He is the sort of man who leaves a coffee cup in the bedroom and the shift lock on at the computer. He is willing to do his share of the routine chores—so long as I tell him what they are.

Unfortunately, from my perspective, he is the sort of man strangers assume must make a wonderful husband and father. The one time in two years he accompanies us to the pediatrician's, the receptionist comes out from behind her desk to tell me how much our children look like their father. Those times he would take our children to pre-school, the teachers would rave the next day about what a great job he did—prompting me to wonder what the other fathers do. Throw their kids into the classroom from a moving car?

If I sound grouchy, I suppose I am. A lot of it is because I have waited in vain for someone to tell me what a great job I do. Since I am home all day in the company of children, of course nobody does. I used to have performance reviews, a paycheck, and an organized desk to call my own. Now I file my papers on top of the microwave.

I realize, of course, I'm also discontented simply because I'm getting older and so is my marriage. I'm at the age when everyone is talking about what's wrong with their backs. I'm at the age when my clothes have begun to leave dents in my body. My marriage is at the age when the love is still there, but the initial reverence is not. This is bound to happen when you launder a man's underwear on a regular basis. Plus, having three children in four years has had the same soothing effect on our relationship as remodeling a kitchen.

But the same old things in our relationship that have bugged me for years now are starting to bug me more. Ten years ago if you had asked why I am annoyed, I would have given a vague, general answer. Now if you ask me why I am annoyed, I can pinpoint it precisely. My husband, I realize, is never going to be quite like me. I will always open and deal with the mail each day as it comes. My husband will always pile it up and deal with it later. He is man, I am woman, and we are not the same. Let me explain.

When my husband and I returned recently from visiting another city, I noticed that he had brought with him the hotel TV guide. Not only did it contain information inherently useless back home, but especially so since my husband is a confirmed channel switcher. He would no more select a show before turning on the television set than he would take the first parking space he passes or look at the map before he starts driving.

He and I are different. These thoughts occurred to me the other day when I decided that some of the most significant differences between the sexes have nothing to do with reproduction. It was one of those mornings when my gross national product includes enough aggravation to export. Specifically, I was wondering why my husband cannot wash his face without giving the mirror a bath. But, actually, I was still smarting over an exchange from the day before.

We had taken the kids to a festival, where we stood in an endless line in relentless heat waiting for a turn to make cardboard hats. The kids decided to go to the puppet show instead, but my husband—engrossed in conversation with the stranger standing behind him—was not ready to leave.

"Let's go," I said to my husband as two kids tugged my hands and a cranky toddler cried.

"Be with you in a few minutes," answered my husband, oblivious to my irritation.

"Sure," I snapped. "Come when it's convenient."

Later, my husband asked why I was rude.

"Because I wanted you to come with us," I told him.

My husband gave me a look reserved for the hopelessly dense and answered, "Why didn't you just say so?"

And that, I believe, is the significant difference between the sexes. A man wants a woman to come right out with it; a woman feels she shouldn't have to. She wants a man to anticipate her needs. In other words, a woman wants a man who will empty the dishwasher without being reminded. When my mother or my sister come for a visit, they do not wait to be told. One look at me trying to stretch from the telephone into the refrigerator for the juice and automatically they get up to help pour. My husband does not.

So at times I have come right out with it. Recently, while my husband read and I talked on the phone as two kids held a shouting match between my knees, I did ask my husband to take them away. And he did.

But I want him to show some initiative. You see, once I start telling him what to do, then it's a short step before I am telling him how to do it. Once or twice a month, if I wave it in front of his face, my husband will help fold the laundry. I fold my son's shirts three times and his underwear once. This is the way they fit into his drawer. This is the way everything inside the drawer already is folded. My husband, however, folds the shirts twice and the underwear not at all.

"Fold them like this," I say.

"What's the big deal?" he says, folding them his way.

"If it's no big deal," I answer, "then please fold them my way."

We haggle like this all the time. A therapist would call it poor communication skills; we women call it annoying. I think it is eternal. The other night, after my husband opened the dishwasher and blocked my access to the counter where I was making lunches, I snapped at him once again.

He snapped back, "Did I ever tell you how much it bugs me that you never run the disposal after you make a salad?"

"Gee," I thought to myself, "how does he expect me to know if he doesn't come right out and say so?"

■ ■ ■

But at other times, I must admit, a husband ranks right up there at the top of the family flow chart. My husband is bigger than I, hence inspiring more fear and respect in the children. He is more handy than I. Our children automatically accord him the elevated status of somebody who is able to fix things—very important in a household where the destruction rate runs high. He is more rarely around than I, and as a less common commodity he enjoys a certain amount of celebrity. One morning he ran off to work so quickly I had to call his office answering machine so our three-year-old could tell him good-bye. When he comes home, he is appreciated by our children, who stampede to the door to greet him—if they are still awake, that is.

Most men—who have scant idea where their children are supposed to be at any given time—have two advantages as fathers because they don't know what's going on.

First, ignorance allows them to be tough. They can make choices a mother would find suicidal. A father finds it easy to come home, flip the channel, and interrupt "Hey, Dude" for the football game. Likewise, a father will turn off Wee Sing on the car cassette player in order to bring himself the news. My husband will spread all his tools out in the backyard and then order his children not to touch them. A mother would not. In other words, sometimes a father will lay down the law a mother would never want the headache of enforcing.

Second, fathers can be soft—which makes them more fun. Fathers play harder because they are never conscious of dirt or bedtime. A father is apt to excuse any magnitude of mess because the kids "had such a great time" making it. Men find it easier to go with the flow. My husband is handing the kids quarters for the pinball machines just seconds after I tell them they are not going to play anymore. My husband is passing them the bread just after I told them they had to wait until they ate all their dinner. A parent tends to spoil more when he is around less. In other words, sometimes the only way a man will lay down the law is after his wife tells him what it is.

"Daddy isn't as mean as you are. He doesn't make us do things," my daughter says to me.

"Why do you suppose that is?" I ask her.

"Because he's lazy," she replies.

In the interest of fairness, I once asked another husband how often men complain about their wives.

"We don't complain about our wives," he answered.

That surprised me—until I realized that this is probably because they have nothing to say.

I, of course, have said quite a bit. And having fired such a salvo I leave myself open to the criticism of being too hard on my husband. For the record let me state that, I am not trying to be a husband basher. Mine is a wonderful husband and father, and I love him very much. But I base my observations upon years of being his wife.

He deserves praise, obviously, for his good sense of humor and the ability to admit when I am right. He deserves criticism, obviously, for not doing everything my way. Having thus made it clear why my worthless husband knows nothing and does less, you will understand how I feel when he proves otherwise.

One time our youngest began waking at night, crying irritably every few hours.

"I'll bet he's cold," opined my husband.

I had the doctor check for fluid in his ears. He had none.

"I'll bet he's cold," maintained my husband.

I rubbed gel on his gums and gave him Tylenol for teething. Our son still cried.

"He's cold," repeated my husband.

So I bundled him up in his blanket sleeper. I'm sorry to say it worked like a charm.

12
I Never Thought I Was Good Enough

Convicted by a jury of my peers

When I was having little luck trying to wean my youngest, I once asked a pediatrician for advice. After two years of nursing, I was more ready to wean my son than my son was willing to be weaned. I was having problems.

"When I skip a feeding, he gets so angry I find it hard not to give in," I told the doctor.

"He certainly doesn't need to nurse for nutritional reasons," the doctor admonished me sternly, as if his attitude could bolster my resolve.

"I know that. The child eats like a horse. But he wants to nurse. He climbs out of his crib and screams at me," I replied.

"If he can climb out of his crib, then he shouldn't be in one. Put him in a regular bed," the doctor answered.

"How will that help?" I asked, unwilling to confess that my son sleeps in my bedroom. He not only has no bed, he has no room.

"Put him in his room at night and tell him to stay there," the doctor said. "If he refuses, put a gate across the doorway and lock him in. Let him scream."

I thanked the doctor for his advice, knowing before I tried it that I couldn't take it. Even if I had the bed and the room and the gate, I wouldn't do it. I paused for a moment to laugh at myself. It makes no sense to ask an expert for his advice if you're not going to follow it. Yet I believe we do it all the time. As parents we receive more advice than baby gifts. Sometimes we reject it, sometimes we accept it, and sometimes we use it to torture ourselves with guilty visions of what we ought to have done. I am an expert on guilty visions.

Mothers do the same thing: We rear children. But we do it in different ways. As a mother, I play pinball: bouncing between the teachings of my parents, of my peers, and of the authorities. In different ways, they are all experts. Some parts of their advice I keep; some I dump. Always I feel guilty that the way I have done it does not measure up to some golden ideal.

Very often guilt is what comes when we cannot meet the standards we have set for ourselves—and nobody sets standards for others better than experts. The experts with credentials tend to cause me the most anxiety. By talking authoritatively about how things should be, often they emphasize how things aren't.

Sometimes I am actually strong enough to just reject their advice out of hand without feeling guilty. With my third child I am less likely to do things by the book. More relaxed, I am ready to let him rise like water to his own level. I am not nearly so iconoclastic about his eating and sleeping habits as I was with my first. I know my kids will eat when they are hungry and sleep when they are tired.

But more often I accord a certain automatic respect to the experts. Impressed by somebody whose credentials are more established than mine, I will try to follow expert advice even when my instinct tells me it is wrong. When my hysterical son needed stitches in his forehead, the doctor bundled him up in a straitjacket so he couldn't move and told me it would be better if my son couldn't see me. Against my better judgment, ignoring my arms aching to give comfort, I stepped out of my son's line of vision. My terrified two-year-old howled and screamed and even managed to slip one arm loose while the surgeon tried to stitch. Unable to stand it anymore, I ran back to my son and rested my head on his chest, murmuring incoherent words of comfort—which is what I should have done in the first place. My son quieted down.

Other times I recognize the truth in advice but simply cannot comply with it. This makes me feel the most guilty. I regularly feel this way when the dental hygienist instructs me on proper care for my children's teeth and describes a daily regimen of brushing and flossing for each one. I nod in agreement, but I think to myself that I would be lucky to accomplish all that once a week. I feel this way when I read what the experts have to say about sleep. Once again, I know what I should do but I have difficulty doing it. I believe the books, for example, when they advise that a child needs to learn to put himself to sleep in his own bed. I also know that sometimes a ride in the car can be more expedient. Or we parents cheat in other ways.

"I've been letting him fall asleep in our bed and then moving him into his own," a friend confessed in a lowered voice. She knew she shouldn't do it, but she knew it worked.

"We just wait until he passes out on the floor," said another mother. "It's easier than fighting."

Likewise, I know a mother who does not require one more person in the world to advise her that her four-year-old must give up his bottle.

"I know it's time," she said. "He even asked for a coaster the other night before he put his bottle down on the table! But I tried skipping his bottle one night . . . and after about twenty minutes I couldn't stand his crying. I just can't do it."

I have a hard time taking the experts' advice about shouting. I don't know anybody who recommends it, including me, but that doesn't seem to stop me from raising my voice. Sometimes it seems to be the only thing that works.

On a typical morning we have a ten-minute walk to school and we are five minutes late getting out the door. In terms of leaving the house, my children are long past the two-minute warning.

"Let's go!" I bellow down the hallway in the direction of my son, who appears to be in a deep hypnotic trance induced by overexposure to "The Flintstones." The response is immediate. My husband, working down the same hallway, nearly suffers heart failure. He throws me a look that asks: Why did I marry a woman who shouts? That I cannot answer, but I do know that he should find my shouting no surprise. In a way it is genetic. My mother shouted and so do I. It is something I inherited along with her thighs. I could no more stop my shouting than I could select my frozen foods before my produce. There are households, I am told, where the parents never raise their voices. My neighbor says that when she gets angry her voice sinks lower and lower—just as her mother's voice used to do. If my mother had whispered, I am sure I would too. But when it comes to parenting, we do best what we know best.

I recently heard a psychologist discuss the best ways for parents to communicate with children. She spoke for an hour and never mentioned the word "shouting." The parents in the audience were not combative, but feisty. We didn't dispute the theories she presented, but essentially we asked: What if that doesn't work? A lot of these theories remind me of the walkie-talkies I bought my son. They work fine as long as you shout.

As parents we are on intimate terms with the chasm between theory and reality—and the rack upon which we stretch ourselves trying to bridge the two. We know what we ought to do, and we know what we do. And we know that if you get down in the trenches every day, you're bound to get dirty. I know I would be a better mother if I never became angry out of frustration nor disciplined in anger. I would also be a saint. Likewise, I know shouting can be counterproductive and ineffective. I have seen teachers silence an entire classroom using low, measured tones. When I talk softly to my children, however, they never notice.

And so, despite my best intentions, I will perpetuate my mother's practice—knowing intellectually that it is bankrupt but emotionally that it is satisfying. And for me, usually it is effective. My daughter, I am starting to notice, shouts in anger. I am neither upset nor surprised. She's going to take after her mother.

I confess to doing not much better when it comes to my children's squabbles. Sometimes they manage to drag me into it; sometimes they do not. But I never believe that I respond with the maturity to which in theory I aspire. I handle none of it correctly.

Here is how it goes: From the sounds of it, they are fighting a war to the death. Their argument—punctuated by screams, shouts, and tears—appears to center upon who has custody of the toy piano. The issue is clouded by the fact that my seven-year-old son got it out, but my five-year-old daughter got it next when he put it down. Now he wants it back. Although the noise is deafening, and my daughter's cries certainly sound realistic enough to indicate that her brother has clobbered her, I am not swayed to get involved. If I were to take any action at all, in fact, I might be tempted to close the door to their room to cut down on the noise.

Several years ago I used to intervene readily when my children were hurting each other. Now I try to avoid it. One time my five-year-old and three-year-old were going tooth and nail over who got to put pretend gasoline into the toy car. Just as I was ready to throw myself into the fray and negotiate a truce, the telephone rang. By the time I came back, the quarrel was settled and forgotten and they were taking turns.

Sometimes, however, my children will not leave me out of it. Shrieking and angry, my children insist upon turning to me as a court of the last appeal, running to me for a ruling. They seek justice. Several years ago I might have sought the same thing. Back in those days I used to employ a timer constantly. I would scrupulously keep track of who got to play with the piano for how long.

"Whose toy is it?" I might have asked.

"Who got it out?" I might have inquired.

"Did you hit her?" I would have demanded.

Several years ago I was interested in justice, too. But now I just want peace. I want to settle it by stopping it. Frequently I do this by shouting. Unraveling who is right or wrong sometimes feels like the least of my concerns. I am ashamed to admit with what alacrity I seize upon any expedience and improvise creatively on the spot. My daughter is insisting that she wants a turn to sleep on the top bunk bed.

"It's against the law," I tell her. "The bed came with a tag that said only seven-year-olds are allowed to sleep up there."

My son wants to ride his bicycle alone to school.

"You can't," I tell him flatly. "The school won't allow it until you're in third grade."

In other words, I used to have principles. I always punished children who hit and I was obsessed with finding out "who started it." Now I recognize that nothing is so simple. My son won't let his sister have a turn with the frying pan that came from the playhouse. I make him. He complies by throwing the pan at her as he stalks away. She screams and refuses to take her turn. Do I let him take it back? Do I force her to use it? Does anyone really care about the pan at this point? Sometimes I just throw both kids on their beds for quiet time. Sometimes I just shout at them until they are more afraid of me than of each other. I opt for expedience, and I am sure the experts would disapprove.

One time my children were fighting in the back seat while I was driving the car. As I negotiated my way through traffic they were hitting, biting, kicking, and screaming behind my back. As we pulled into the parking lot, my nerves snapped.

"OK! So you want to fight," I shouted. "Well, let's really fight. I'll give you five minutes. Go ahead and kick, fight, and scream. I won't stop you and I won't care. Just get it out of your systems and do it now, and then leave each other alone the rest of the day. Go ahead!"

Nobody budged. Once I told them to do it, they wouldn't touch each other. I don't believe the experts would endorse that tactic, and neither would I. But I couldn't help it.

When it comes to practice, lately I have been throwing theory out the window. I don't know what has happened to me. I used to be on top of everything. I never used to mix the red Play-Doh with the blue. I used to think children had to have baths every night. But I was a different mother back in the days when the comb marks showed for hours in my son's hair. Those were the days when I decided what my children would eat.

As a parent I remember that I used to negotiate settlements and take pride in the democratic process. (How many want chicken for dinner?) Now I see the advantages of dictatorship. (Good. We'll have chicken anyway.) When it comes to forcing a settlement, now I know how to lean upon the weak link. I know which child will knuckle under to intimidation, which one is susceptible to reason, and which one responds to bribes. I also know which one is liable to fly off the handle, refuse to listen, and scream just to get his way . . . other than me, of course.

Parents-to-be—whose idealism has not yet melted in the fires of reality—are most likely to take expert advice to heart. They still believe that doing it the "right" way is as important as getting it done. Some days, juggling three children, I am heavy into task completion. I consider myself something of a fallen angel. Likewise, I have lots of friends embarrassed to admit that their children play with toy guns or eat cereals copied after television shows. The only people capable of going by the book with children, in fact, are often the baby-sitters. The less emotionally involved you are, the easier it is to hang tough—which leads me to wonder whether people without children would make the best parents.

We all must make compromises with reality. I can feel mine coming on whenever the doctor issues instructions such as "Don't let him scratch." But experts also need to get more in touch with reality. I know a doctor who used to routinely advise bed rest for children with mild illnesses. Then he became a father and tried to administer his own advice. Now he tells parents just to try to keep the patient indoors.

Whatever my reasons, I always feel at least a little bit guilty for ignoring the advice of experts—until I remember that I ignore my own. I am, after all, a mother who can devour an entire box of Teddy Grahams after telling my children to eat fruit.

■ ■ ■

At times, however, I cannot even blame the experts for my guilt. I heap it upon myself in full-course servings. It is with great shame, for example, that I admit my son's seventh birthday party was not held at home. We joined thousands of other parents who preferred to leave the noise, the mess, and the clean-up somewhere else. We paid by the head for mediocre pizza and lots of token-operated games. The tremendous quantities of noise and commotion were free. The guests, who ran around like loonies, had a great time. My son had a great time. In my mortification at becoming just like everybody else, I did not.

At a birthday party, I have always contended, children should play together—not rush by one another in a mad dash to play video games. At a birthday party, children should talk to one another—not shout inside a room in which it is impossible to hear. Worse, a birthday party is the mom's job. She's supposed to decorate the house, lead games, and bake a cake. Everybody knows this. And for years I have done this. But this year I felt an overwhelming fatigue at the thought of ten first-grade boys rampaging through my house.

"So have it at a park," my husband suggested.

"Good idea," I answered. "I'll pick the park, pack the food, and buy the prizes. Can I count on you to organize games for a couple of hours?"

And that is how we opted for the pizza parlor.

I remember when I first jumped aboard the birthday party merry-go-round, the year my oldest turned four and parties blossomed on every weekend. We saw clowns, magicians, and even ponies. At my house we were not nearly so elaborate. The closest we came to a pony was Pin the Tail on the Donkey. But I felt virtuous. I invested my effort, rather than my cash.

This year I can make no such claim. Yet I have to admit that my guilt during the party was equaled by my relief afterward. It was over, it was done with, and my son was happy. He can't tell and doesn't care if his cake comes from a store or my oven.

That's a lesson my Type-A personality has been slow to learn. After all, I make the beds every day and balance my checkbook every month. I just cannot let things slide. After two years of picking up Barbie doll shoes from the floor, for example, I am just now starting to throw them away. But I still feel a twinge of guilt those rare times my daughter notices the shoes are missing.

When I mentioned my birthday party ambivalence to other mothers, I was surprised that they didn't all agree. They understood my relief but not my guilt.

"Wait until you try bowling parties," said one mother. "The kids love it. They bowl; they eat hot dogs and they never set foot inside your house."

I, of course, remain somewhat unconvinced. I feel guilty over store-bought costumes, bakery cupcakes, or anything that does not measure up to the perfect ideal I have no idea where I acquired but to which I subscribe wholeheartedly. I am, in short, an intimate acquaintance of guilt. I know all about it because I am the expert about what I am doing wrong.

The guilt comes most often concerning the matter of time: whether I waste it and how I divide it. I worry that I don't spend enough time with all of my children. I worry that I don't spend enough time with each of my children. I worry that I give unequal attention to my children, that I am not nice enough to my children, and I worry that I worry too much. I think that about covers it.

I worry that I am slighting my youngest child:

Grasping their crayons like daggers, the toddlers take a stab at coloring. My son actually manages to scribble in one corner of his page. It is art time at Mommy & Me class. I watch my youngest and casually glance at the creations around me. Then I notice. Every mother but me has marked the date on her child's drawing. Every mother but me, evidently, intends to save that drawing. I, quite honestly, never considered it.

Frantically, I cast my mind backward like a net, hoping to land a recollection. When was the last time I saved every piece of artwork my children produced? But I cannot remember. All I know is that now, instead of saving pictures, I wait for opportunities to sneak some of them into the garbage. When you add school and weekend creations together—and multiply that by three children—I figure the gross national product for artwork in my household has to be a conservative twenty pieces per week. Even worse, some of them consist of macaroni and glitter and other materials that tend to decay all over the carpet. I tell myself that by tossing out pictures I am merely being practical, not callous. But I wonder.

When it comes to my involvement, I am not the mother I used to be back when I would patiently watch my babies for hours waiting to catch their smiles. The pile of mementos I have preserved from my firstborn is deeper than the pile from my third. I charted the progress of each new tooth in my firstborn's mouth. My third child sprouted most of his without fanfare.

The amount of undiluted time I spent with my firstborn was greater than I spend with my third. I used to sit on the floor and play with my oldest; now my youngest plays with his brother and sister. I used to read books constantly to my oldest, but now I am training him to read to his little brother. I used to change diapers every hour, just as I also used to believe that when my child was awake he deserved my undivided attention. Now, with three children, I deal only in fractions.

As a mother, I want to be as fresh for my third as I was for my first. But my commitment has wilted slightly, along with my dedication to reading books on child development. I feel guilty that I do not do better. I know there are reasons. Two of my children are older. Like a good steak they require no sauce; they do not always need to be smothered with attention. My youngest, used to a crowd, happily tags after his siblings. Likewise, three children diminish my resources—so we piggyback a lot. Sometimes the only reason my youngest goes to the park is to attend soccer practice for my oldest. I tell myself what counts is that he gets there.

Yet my two older children also need their time with me. While they do not crave constant attention, they would like at times to escape the crowd. My daughter is not always delighted to go to the park because her big brother must.

"Why do I have to go to soccer practice again?" my daughter demands.

And, of course, she has a point. For someone who doesn't play soccer, she has been to an awful lot of practices. What counts to her is getting to stay home. Yet there are many days when I must drag three children to a lesson, to practice, or to the doctor when I really require the presence of only one. And sometimes on those days I feel as though

I meet the individual needs of no one. In retrospect, I marvel at my ignorance or my arrogance that persuaded me I could be a good mother to three children.

If I neglect my youngest, I also rarely get one-on-one time with my two oldest. I worry that I don't spend enough time individually with my three children. It is a difficult puzzle, finding pieces of time to give my full attention to each of them. Some days, as I dance the Virginia Reel with each child in turn, I wish we could slow the tempo—or maybe even sit one out. Some days I can concentrate upon no one.

I pick up two children at their preschool. The teacher informs me my youngest has bitten another boy.

"Did you get angry and bite?" I ask my son.

"Mommy, we saw a play today about the Three Billy Goats Gruff," my daughter interrupts.

"Great. Just a minute. Let me talk to your brother. Biting is a bad thing to do," I tell him.

"Mommy, the big billy goat came and ate up the troll," she tells me.

"You need to use your words if you are angry," I tell my son.

"The little billy goat was so cute," my relentless daughter says.

I try to talk to my son. The entire time my daughter, refusing to be deterred, recounts for me the plot to the story. I doubt that I carry on a meaningful conversation with either child.

The other day when his school was closed, I was home alone with my oldest son. The event is noteworthy, I believe, because it happens so seldom. My oldest son is alone with me only on the rare days when he stays home but everyone else does not. Sometimes, when he wants to talk, we have closed the door to the bedroom my children normally share and demanded privacy. But more often where my oldest goes, so go his sister and little brother. He is not always happy about it and neither are they. But, then, neither am I.

My daughter is alone with me each day for about an hour. That's the time when her younger brother naps and her older brother has not yet gotten home from school. My youngest son is alone with me some days when the others are in school.

"No fair!" one will protest upon discovering the other got to stay home. ("No fair," I sometimes think myself on those days when I have a lot of work to do.)

I have no idea whether I divide my attention evenly, and I worry about it a lot. Are my kids getting enough of me? Are there conversations we need to have, but haven't? Those times I have a one-on-one session I am always amazed at the feelings that pour out.

My daughter and I are driving home alone together from the grocery store.

"Mom, I'm having troubles at school," my five-year-old says. "I never get a turn on the tire swing at the playground. Sometimes I feel like I have no friends at all. And when I come to school and my teacher hugs me, I get embarrassed."

All of that in four blocks.

My daughter is at a friend's house, my youngest is asleep, and my seven-year-old and I have a few minutes alone at the dining room table.

"Those guys wrecked my sand castles again today and I got so angry," my son says. "Also, Peter keeps bugging me to play with him. I tell him no, but he won't leave me alone."

He swallows some juice.

"Mom, what would you do if a boy, not me—but you were his mother—got in trouble at school?" he asks.

"I guess I would want to know why," I reply.

"Well, it was me and I got in trouble for talking too much. It's only happened once and you really aren't angry, are you?"

All of that in ten minutes.

Even my taciturn three-year-old knows enough to point to his chest and grunt when there is action in the air. "Don't forget me. Don't leave me out," he is always saying.

I don't want to forget anyone. I don't want to leave anyone out. But some days it's a challenge counting everyone in. Whenever I feel good about which child I have taken care of, I also worry about which other child I have neglected. Some days I feel like a Lazy Susan: My kids spin me and help themselves. I tell myself that a buffet style of parenting is not necessarily wrong. I hope it means each child is taking enough of what he needs.

■ ■ ■

Obviously, life has got my number. I know that worrying begets worry. And while I know worrying doesn't make things better, that knowledge doesn't seem to help. If there is a place for guilt or worry, I will find it. Lincoln and Douglas were amateurs compared to the internal debates I have hosted over the matter of preschool: Which one should my children attend? How often should they go? And, most important, what if they don't like it? Always I question whether I am doing the right thing for them and for me.

My youngest clings to my hand and my heart with a strength I never knew he possessed.

"Momma," he bleats pathetically, every time I make a move toward the classroom door.

The child who started the first week of school without a backward glance has executed a total about-face. He has contracted a major case of separation anxiety. I have exhausted all my options. The day before, we talked in positive terms about his new school. I told him it would be a lot of fun. He agreed with me yesterday, but not today. I have tried distraction: "Let's work with this Play-Doh together." I have tried reason: "You know Mommy always gets you after lunch. I always come. I never forget." I have tried to be a tough guy: "Say good-bye. I have to go—*now*." Nothing seems to work. Finally, I pry my hysterical son from my neck, hand him to his preschool teacher, and flee to my car.

"Separation anxiety," I explain to a friend in passing as I don't stop to chat.

"You have to be fast and tough," she shouts after me.

Well, I used to be. When my daughter was my son's age, I bundled her off to preschool every morning and whipped out the door, down the freeway, and to my office without any prolonged trauma. I had to get to work. Now, when I have to get home, I wonder why leaving seems so tough. I never used to have much sympathy for mothers whose children were clinging to their knees. Suddenly, I understand—now that my child is clinging to mine.

Sometimes the luxury of having options threatens to paralyze me. My daughter still goes to preschool, but suddenly I felt guilty about planning to send her every morning. I wondered if I ought to keep her home more. But some days when they are home, my children complain it's no fun because I have to work. Then I feel guilty that my writing time comes at the expense of their time.

Like a scale, I try to weigh their needs against mine. I try to balance my time as an individual against my time as a mother. I come to all my daughter's school programs, for example, and help in her classroom when I can. One day her class is having a special luncheon.

"Are you coming?" the teacher asks.

"Are parents supposed to come?" I ask, knowing that I have a lot of work to do.

"It's up to you. You don't have to," she answers.

I work at home that morning, and when I pick up my daughter it is clear that I was missed.

"Hundreds and hundreds of mothers were there," my daughter says quietly. "But I know. Your work is more important than me."

I kneel down to softly deny and explain, but her hard words cut like a knife.

My children don't know how good they have it, and sometimes I forget. Some mothers must go to their jobs all day, every day. But rare is any mother who has time for everything. Obviously, it is an unmistakable luxury to be able to work at home and fit my hours around my children's schedules. I get to say leisurely good-byes in the mornings, and I get to be home to say enthusiastic hellos in the afternoons. When my youngest gets up from his nap, I get to be the one who cuddles him back to full consciousness.

But because I have the opportunity, suddenly I am making too much of things. Cross words with my children stay on my mind long after they have forgotten the conversation. I drill for oil in a sandbox. I believe guilt expands to fill time available. I have the luxury of being able to magnify my worries, but I'm not always sure it is good. I can see what's bothering me more clearly, but that's because I have made it bigger than necessary.

Like the way my son sometimes carries on when I leave him at preschool. At home, while he is at school, I sit at the computer trying to write. But I cannot concentrate. I have my youngest son on my mind, not my work. He is static, interfering with my reception so that I cannot think about anything else. Did he try to run down the hallway after me? Is he still crying? Is he taking his anger out on the other children?

I call the school, nonchalantly I hope, to see how he is doing.

"He's just fine," the teacher tells me. "He stopped crying the minute you left."

■ ■ ■

Earthworms, I think, have perfected the regeneration to which I aspire. Literally, I would tear myself into pieces and give one to each child. Then each of them could have their own complete mother. On really bad days I feel guilty that my entire family gets a low priority. I don't always know how to fit them in with the chores of the day, and when the chores are done I don't always save enough of myself for my family.

I think sometimes I can be nicer to strangers than to my own family. I seem to reserve my anger and impatience for the people I love. I remember as a child I always tried to call my mother while she was at work when I had to ask a favor. She seemed nicer on the telephone than when she got home. Now I realize I would not treat the people I work with the same way I treat my children. If someone spilled coffee on my desk, I would not lose my temper. Yet when my seven-year-old pours more milk than the cereal bowl could ever hold, I have not always been the picture of patience. I am even harder on my husband than my children. With my children, I try to tiptoe softly around their tender self-esteem. With my husband, I do not care if his feelings bruise easily. Against him I carry a grudge.

Preschool teachers have infinite patience with my children—but of course they are not related to them. I, too, am nicer to other people's children than to my own. I do not shout at somebody else's child. One morning when a boy in my car pool forgot his backpack, I did not even break stride as I drove back to get it. A few weeks later when my son forgot his lunchbox, I got angry. My five-year-old asked me once, "If our friends did something wrong, would you talk mean to them the way you do to me?" ("No," I told her. "I would send them home and let their mothers do it.")

In some ways we are simply more honest with our families. When acquaintances ask how we feel, we never tell them the truth. If my husband asks, I tell him about every ache and pain. It's like the child who does fine all day at the sitter's and then falls to pieces when his Mommy comes to take him home. We know we can relax among family because they will love us unconditionally—even if we are rude. So sometimes we deplete our resources of patience and consideration, using them up on strangers. Sometimes we don't save much for the end of the day.

Understanding, however, does not excuse. I feel guilty reserving my worst for the people I love best. The day can seem like an exercise in failed expectations. It tends to get worse by the minute. My daughter shows a lot more perception about this than I ever expected. One morning, after she stumbled downstairs still smelling sweetly of sleep, I hugged her tight.

"Boy, Mommy," she said. "We all seem to have the most love in the morning."

Often only the presence of witnesses can be required to make us mend our ways. One time as I drove five rambunctious kids home from the park, another mother marveled at how I was able to keep my cool.

"That's only because you're here," I told her truthfully.

Likewise, no matter how dreadful my children's behavior, I have yet to lose my temper in the doctor's waiting room, where the eyes of other mothers are upon me.

Sometimes improvement comes with a change of scenery. When my oldest goes to school, he touchingly embraces his brother good-bye in the playground. When he comes home, he doesn't want to be bothered. When my daughter and son go to preschool together, they do not fight. They are friends. At home it can be the opposite. Once, when my daughter came home from school, she dropped her paper. My youngest bent to get it. She screamed at him to leave it alone. He retrieved it anyway. She hit him; he threw his lunchbox at her. They had been together less than two minutes.

"We seem to get along better at school," my daughter explains.

It must be akin to the camaraderie that develops among Americans who accidentally meet abroad. Out of the usual surroundings, the familiar can be comforting. At home it can be annoying.

Once when I was feeling particularly ashamed of my end-of-the-day behavior, I confided in my daughter.

"Sometimes I'm not sure I'm always a good mother," I confessed.

"Oh, yes, you are," my five-year-old answered. "But sometimes when you're angry at me, I don't think you love me anymore."

I always remember that when the guilt comes.

The guilt comes some afternoons when it seems as though my children and I play tag: I promise a game of Candy Land; they try to catch me and hold me to my word. On those afternoons I worry that I do not do enough for my children. Other afternoons I want them to know I cannot do everything for them. In my heart I put them first, but in my daily life sometimes I end up putting them last. I meet myself coming and going.

"Let me just wash the dishes," I say before Candy Land. "One minute more; I just have to fold the laundry."

And so they wait, more resigned than patient, for me to sit down and play. Finally, nearly half an hour after I promised them, we begin to play. And the telephone rings.

"Can you talk?" asks a childless acquaintance who does not want to interrupt my writing.

"I just sat down to play Candy Land with the kids," I answer.

"Good," she replies. "I'm glad you're not busy."

When some people take mental census, evidently kids don't count. I have even seen parents who apparently believe children are invisible, not entitled to the full courtesies accorded a grown-up. At the preschool once a woman was holding her toddler who dropped his ball. My son chased it and returned it to the mother. She took the ball and went right on with her conversation. Her toddler dropped it again; my son retrieved it again. Three times my son handed her back the ball. Not once did she thank him.

Before parenthood, I used to be vaguely annoyed by friends who would put me on telephone hold while they dealt with their children. Now I not only think otherwise, but I understand perfectly. When I walk into a room, I greet the child as well as his parent. Children are like stacking rings. By teaching parents to pile demands in the right order—usually with the biggest rings first—they help us to clarify priorities. Obviously my kids count—and sometimes more than adults.

But it is a fine line. My children cannot take precedence over everything all of the time. When two daughters want an audience as they play ballerina, must their mothers sacrifice indefinitely all attempts at conversation in order to watch them? When I want to sit down alone with a book, aren't I ever justified in telling my children I do not want to read to them? I still see child rearing as a great adventure, but sometimes I would like a break from travel. I know that after every vacation there are always loads of dirty laundry.

I was outside the other day, watching my children play, and I couldn't help thinking about the chores I needed to do inside. And I felt guilty.

"Don't you ever feel a little crazy, spending hours standing around?" I asked another mother. "I have so many other things to do."

The other mother smiled contentedly. "Not really," she answered. "If my daughter has a good day, then so do I."

I thought about her answer all day, wondering why it isn't true anymore for me. Certainly when my children are happy, I am glad. But their happiness alone is no longer enough to make my day. I feel discomfited that now their happiness is not always the same as mine. I used to interrupt everything to talk to my kids; now I also try to teach them not to interrupt me.

Children, who live for the moment, are not big on deferred gratification. One time I manned the prize booth at a carnival. By saving their tickets, the children could redeem more of them for better prizes. Most of the kids, however, could not hang on to their tickets long enough to save them up. They traded them in right away.

It is not simple to put children in their place, taking into account both your needs and theirs. To children it can seem their place is always last. My daughter once asked me to sew her teddy bear.

"I'll get to it later today," I told her as I raced around the house.

"I know," she sighed without rancor. "You always do the things for me last."

I never want to put my children last, but sometimes I cannot get to them first. This bothers me, of course, even though I tell myself that worrying doesn't help. Nevertheless I fuss about it, much the way I spend twenty minutes trying to angle the sprinkler so it waters the corners of the lawn but not the sidewalk. I try to remind myself that even when the sprinkler isn't lined up perfectly, the grass thrives.

■ ■ ■

13

It's Not Easy Being Green

Getting serious

Her child-care provider, the woman who has wiped, fed, and hugged her children for nearly a year, has quit, giving two days' notice. The mother is totally absorbed in the crisis over arrangements. But I am shocked anew by a crisis in faith.

You see, I have always clung to my belief that the women who have watched my children have at least liked them. I know they do it for money, but taking care of children is more than a job. I choose to believe it is something of a calling. You don't sit on the babies, you love them. Yet if you care, how can you give a mere two days' notice before walking out of their lives? And if you don't care, what mother would want you to watch her children?

When I worked full-time, my children spent mornings at a child-care center. All of the workers were great, although I always knew which ones were my children's favorites. I felt nothing but gratitude for the times they cuddled my children, and I took care to let them know it. Yet the workers' pay was poor and the turnover high. To me, the hardest part of child care was telling my children every few months why that lady they loved was gone. I like to think saying good-bye was also hard on the women who left.

I have a difficult time accepting callous relationships, but then in thinking about my friend's problem, I realized that I am guilty of the sin myself. So many of our relationships are based upon proximity. I remember the people I got to know at work simply because their desks were close to mine. Sometimes, when our seats were changed, our conversations dwindled. I also can think of the mothers I have come to know because of my children. As we would stand daily patrol watching our children play, we would talk. But then, as some of the children grew old enough to stay outside without supervision, their mothers began to stay inside. We began to meet only in passing as one of us was coming out, the other going in. The confidences would dwindle.

Sometimes, of course, friendship transcends circumstance. I have friends from work who remain friends outside the office. I have neighbors who are friends regardless of our children. But more often than not, we fade in and out of each other's lives.

None of this troubled me quite so much, of course, until my children got older. Once again, wanting them to see only positive examples, now I am concerned about setting one. Now that they see more than they say, I don't want them to think relationships are disposable just because they become inconvenient. I want them to see only the best. For as long as possible, I want them to think everybody loves them. For them, I want the world to be perfect and safe. This is about those times when it is not.

When they were younger, I saw my job exclusively as sheltering my children. I would be an umbrella to protect them from anything ugly, bad, or painful. A parent's greatest fear is that he will not take good enough care of his child, that he will slip up on something critical. And so we worry—about everything we let them do and don't let them do. We ask questions so that the answers can reassure us.

"You won't let them play outside by themselves, will you?" asked the mother whose daughter was coming over to play at my house.

"You'll stay with the group, won't you?" I asked my seven-year-old when he was invited to attend a concert a freeway drive away from home. I worried about his going so far without me. I cautioned him about staying with his hostess, I gave him money for emergencies and a card with his name, address, and telephone number. I told him what to do if he got lost and warned him about strangers. But that night I was tormented by the taste of how it would be if something happened to him. My stomach clenched as I imagined the thought of life without him.

We try to cover every contingency, but of course we cannot. Gut-wrenching moments have a way of ambushing parents in our own backyards, bringing us face to face with our insecurities and fears. Everything can be sunny and bright, and then suddenly it's dark. This happened one day when my children came to tell me that they had misplaced their friend.

"She was playing right here and then she was gone," my seven-year-old explained.

"We've looked everywhere in the house and can't find her," my five-year-old added.

"Did you have a fight? Did she go home angry?" I asked. They shook their heads no.

Then, believing them but not yet taking them seriously, I went shouting through the house myself. I poked my head into every room, calling their playmate's name. No answer. I checked outside, half expecting to see a little girl who had decided abruptly to go home and was walking around the corner without saying good-bye. Nobody. Then, taking my children more seriously, I went back to every room, shouting again as I searched. No answer.

I called the girl's mother, not so much to say that her daughter was lost but to inquire whether her daughter was already found. I figured she had gone home without my knowing it. She hadn't. I shouted to my husband, we shouted to neighbors, and we all shouted the girl's name. I began searching places in the house where a child might possibly be trapped or injured. I also began to seriously worry. The girl's mother was beginning to panic. She ran crying, pounding on doors all up and down our street.

So when that four-year-old girl uncurled herself from under the stuffed animals on our top bunk bed and decided to come down, I was more relieved than angry. I didn't want anything to have happened to her and I didn't want it to happen at my house. As her mother cried, hugging her hysterically, the child honestly didn't understand what all the fuss was about.

You have to be a parent to understand. All parents wrestle with a monster hiding in the closet: It's the anxiety that something horrible will happen to our children. We shine flashlights of common sense to prove to ourselves that in most cases nothing hides in the shadows— but some nights we are convinced otherwise.

I invite a little girl over to play with my daughter.

"Fine," says her mother. "As long as you don't have a swimming pool. I had a daughter who drowned."

We all know the story of the child snatched on his way home, the child who had never opened that gate before or the child left alone in the bathtub for less than a minute. Sometimes we knew the child. "Freak accident" are two of the saddest words in the world.

Like children huddled around a camp fire, we tell each other these scary stories. At the beach one summer my youngest decided he could swim. While I was unpacking the towels, he marched into the water and did not utter a sound as he lost his footing and started to slip under. He had his first mouthful of ocean by the time I yanked him up just as the lifeguard arrived.

Those are the sorts of close-call anecdotes we recite around the dinner table as we piously sermonize to our children about being careful. As parents we develop an internal radar to monitor our children. Without looking, from any room in my house, I have a pretty good idea where my kids are. But nothing is 100 percent reliable.

As parents we all take chances. We gamble for the highest stakes as we try to locate the fine line between being overprotective and being prudent. All of us have run inside just to answer the phone. All of us have turned our backs for just a minute. The only difference, says a friend, is that once in a great while some of us get caught.

■ ■ ■

Sheltering our children is not always possible, of course. We cannot protect them from everything. In their relationships or on the playground, their feelings get bruised as well as their knees. They get hurt despite our best intentions. Their world cannot always be perfect and safe. I wanted to protect my children from physical pain, for example, but life decided otherwise.

Twice now, before he was even three years old, my youngest required surgery. My role became handing him over to strange doctors. Once he required hernia surgery and once, because of an accident, he required extensive stitches. Both times I felt crushing anxiety and both times I struggled to convince myself that even a parent who does everything right cannot always protect a child from pain. I have not fully accepted what I know to be the truth.

The hardest part about having a child who faces surgery, I now realize, is not the operation. In the case of an accident, it is the miscalculation that caused it. In the case of scheduled surgery, surrendering your starving, thirsty, disoriented youngster at the hospital is hardest. In both cases you must totally relinquish his well-being to the hands of others. I felt as though my son would blame me for the pain, the discomfort, and the fear. I felt as though he would think I failed.

"Is it serious?" I asked the doctor before the hernia surgery.

"Not to the surgeon," he replied.

A hernia requires the surgical equivalent of filling a cavity. A routine procedure, it seems, for everyone but the parents.

"What will the surgeon do?" my mother wanted to know.

"Well, he'll go in and fix the hernia," I answered.

My mother wanted to know more: How many incisions, how long, where will they be? She wasn't satisfied with my vague answers.

"You don't seem to know a lot of the details," she said.

"I don't want to," I answered about something over which we had no choice. When we remodeled the kitchen, I wanted to know the location of every inch of cabinet space. When doctors remodeled my toddler's intestines, I did not want to know details. I am uncomfortable in the presence of raw chicken livers. I saw no reason to visualize the surgery in the screening room of my mind.

I was more concerned with the presurgery instructions. These involved nothing more difficult than starving my son prior to the operation to prepare him for anesthesia. Somehow, he kept expecting breakfast. So I did what any self-respecting mother would do. We went for a walk to get his mind off food. I discovered our street has an amazing amount of activity at 7 A.M.

At fifteen months my son was a little late for the appearance of a hernia. But he also was a little early for the traditional means of coping with a child's hospital fears. He was too little to read a comforting story: "Baby Bear Goes to Surgery and Has a Swell Time." He was unimpressed by the stuffed Snoopy wearing surgical garb who greeted him on the gurney, upon which the cooperative patient traditionally is wheeled away.

As the nurse carried him away, a blue surgical hat slipping lopsided over one ear, he gave me a piercing look before he vanished around the corner and I heard his screams begin. He sounded angry. He knew he had been betrayed. I've seen that look before, of course. When my eldest received his first immunization shot, I'll never forget the disbelief in his eyes when he looked at me. "I trusted you," he seemed to say in the instant before he screamed. "How could you let them hurt me?"

And that, obviously, is the hard part of childhood surgery. To a young child's mind—and sometimes your own—you have relinquished your role of protecting him. You know the discomfort is for your child's own good; he knows he is scared and hurt. And he knows that you allowed it to happen. I understand why the nurses who administer immunization shots always grab my children for a hug before they turn them back over to me.

If your child has to undergo surgery, consider yourself lucky if you can opt for something speedy. Waiting rooms can be lovely places, but you prefer not to linger. Sitting there I could think of other fun things I would rather be doing, such as installing safety latches on the kitchen cabinets.

My son's surgery, as predicted, was routine. Afterward, my husband and I vied with each other for the privilege of holding his limp body in the recovery room. I gave him sugar water to drink, and the nurse cautioned me that he probably would throw up because of the anesthetic.

"Do you want me to hold him?" she asked. I wondered why on earth she was asking. No way I was gonna let go. We took our son home to administer hefty doses of comfort. It was twenty-seven long hours before I could coax a smile from him, but forty-eight hours later he was back to his old tricks.

"Try not to let him climb or fall," the surgeon advised tardily, a week later when the stitches came out. I shook my head, wondering if he still believed in fairy tales.

We called relatives after the surgery, and everyone wanted to know: "Is there anything we can do?"

"Nothing," we replied. "It wasn't all that bad, and he's forgotten all about it." True, my son has forgotten. But I don't think I ever will.

The scars from his surgery had disappeared, in fact, by the second time he landed himself in the hospital. This time, in addition to the anxiety of helplessness, I also felt the burden of guilt. I allowed this accident to happen.

One evening ten months later my son, two years old, was leaping from the armchair, landing with squeals of delight on the cushion below. Delighted with his game, he repeated the maneuver again and again. My husband and I, enchanted by his excitement, were reluctant to make him stop as we had so many times in the past. Our son leaped from the chair again, lost his balance as he landed on the floor, and catapulted his head into the corner of the television. He fell screaming, and as I ran to turn him over my husband asked, "Is he all right?"

"Of course," I was ready to reply. Countless times our children have jumped and fallen, their tears always more frightening than their injuries. Instead, I looked down a triangular hole in his forehead that gave me an unobstructed view of the skullbone below.

"No," I wailed, as the elevator of my stomach plummeted. "Oh, God, what should we do?"

We called the paramedics, gratified to hear the siren sound turning into our driveway. Our son, screaming uncontrollably, did not even notice that firemen, his heroes, were actually in our house. It was not until an hour later, clutching my boy at the hospital, that my initial disbelief and panic receded. We had told our story to paramedics, emergency room personnel, and two different doctors. Persistent, but soothing, they sought to accomplish two things: to allay any suspicions that we might have busted our son's head for the sport of it, and to allay any hysteria in us.

At the hospital we were, I discovered, only a Triage Code No. 2. We were nothing exceptional in an emergency room accustomed to auto wrecks and knifings; we could afford time to fill out insurance forms. My husband came close to assaulting the youth who completed our paperwork. We waited interminable minutes because the clerk did not know how to reload the copying machine that was out of paper.

Our son, bandaged, comforted, and quieted, drowsed in his father's arms while we waited for an available hospital bed. I sat there running film in my mind, a relentless instant replay. I did the same thing a year ago when I'd had a fender bender. Faced with a split-second decision whether to slam on the brakes or go, I went—and was hit. For weeks after, I mentally replayed the scene, willing myself to hit the brakes. I did the same at the hospital. What if I had hit the brakes? What if I had stopped his jumping? We wallowed in guilt, my husband and I, thinking of how we had let our son down. As parents, our first job is to protect our kids and we had let ours get hurt. It is of no comfort to me that for most children, getting stitches is another rite of passage. Blithely I had assumed we would skip it.

The X ray was excellent, the doctor told us. Our son sliced through all of his baby fat, but he did not crack his skull. We waited for the plastic surgeon, shed a few tears of relief, and thought about the precious hold we have on life.

"I guess we have just one small chance to survive," my husband said. We shuddered at the possibilities that might have been. I cannot imagine the impact of a television set upon an eyeball. The doctors, one step ahead of us, cautioned that our son might have a scar. I cuddled twenty-four pounds of life and thought to myself, "So? Is that supposed to matter?"

We took our son home. The next day I assumed a fortress mentality. No longer a gambler, I would not take the chances I had begun to allow simply because I was tired of hearing myself say "no." I would give new meaning to the word "protective" when applied to that forehead.

"No running, no jumping," I laid down the law to all three children. It proved easy to say, impossible to enforce. Minutes after my instructions, my oldest chased my youngest, who ran into the bedroom and slammed the door. My son shoved it open so that the doorknob rammed my toddler in the head. Fortunately, it hit his ear and not his stitches. Patiently, I again explained the importance of this cut and how it must be protected. Minutes later my oldest shouted for me to come quick. My two-year-old was jumping from the coffee table to the couch. He bounced to a landing and laughed. He was having such a good time.

■   ■   ■

Obviously we cannot be there to protect our children from everything. Sometimes they must take care of themselves. While I want my children to have a happy image of the world as safe and comforting, in order to protect them I must teach them that at times it is not. Bad things can happen. We visited the ocean right after an oil spill precisely for that reason. I read them newspaper accounts of children run over in their own driveways for that reason. I show them pictures of auto wrecks as I deliver sermons about seat belts.

After years of convincing my toddlers that they are safe without Mommy at school or away from Mommy with friends, now I am teaching them that sometimes they are not. Just as we used to make our homes baby proof, now we try to make our children street smart because we cannot always be there with them. Don't talk to strangers. Don't cross the street. Call me when you get there. Don't eat that. Don't touch those. As they get older, we bombard them with slogans and merchandise morality in twenty-second spots. We want to teach them to stay out of trouble.

"Just say no," proclaims the badge on my first-grader's shirt.

"Be smart, don't start," says the sign in the preschool office. Caution has become part of the curriculum as we try to indoctrinate them young.

I do not always agree with the way it is taught. Self-esteem needs to accompany the lesson.

In first grade the children are working on their assignment to fill in the blanks. The words on the blackboard read: "I am special because _____," and the children must complete the thought. They are learning penmanship, vocabulary, and spelling. But evidently they also are learning about drugs.

As I wander around the room, helping the students with their work, it becomes obvious what they believe to be the correct answer.

"I am special because I don't do drugs," the majority of them write—requiring some help with the spelling of "drugs." Those more adventuresome write instead, "I am special because I don't do cigarettes."

The children think they are giving the right answer, but in that classroom of seven-year-olds I don't believe many of them learned the lesson. It is being taught to them backward.

"What makes you special?" I ask a boy pondering with his pencil.

"I don't do drugs," he parrots.

I should think not, I exclaim to myself. I don't know many seven-year-olds who are big users, although I suppose in this day and age I should be grateful for that.

"That's great," I reply. "But what is there that's special about only you?"

He can't think of a thing.

I go over to a girl, also stuck. "You're special because you are a terrific reader," I tell her, and her entire face brightens with pleasure.

Unable to resist, I wander over to my son's desk. He, too, is stalled after the word "because."

"Why are you special?" I ask.

He shrugs.

"Well, you're a good soccer player. You're a good big brother," I suggest. Relieved, he asks me how to spell "brother."

Recently, another parent and I were discussing whether to add basketball to our sons' already-busy schedules.

"I think it's a good idea," the father said, looking way down the road. "You know, when they get bigger they don't get into drugs if they're involved in sports."

I believe this is true—but not because basketball offers special immunity. Rather, a kid who feels valued by his team doesn't need drugs to make him feel good.

The first part of any lesson is to teach our children why they are special. The answer has little to do with slogans and more with self-esteem. At my preschool, the parents send notes to class each week describing a way in which their child was good. I overheard one mother say to another, "I forgot again. Well, he hasn't done anything this week worth writing about." Her son, standing right there, also overheard.

The second part of any lesson is to defend a child with more than a slogan. They need information. It's not enough to tell them something is bad without telling them why some people think it is good. Otherwise, how can they resist temptation? As a child I repeatedly was cautioned against strangers. But "stranger" was never adequately defined. I concluded it was some creature who popped out from manhole covers and snatched children. Consequently, I was always wary around manhole covers.

I have nothing against teaching children by slogans. They learn them easily enough, and at this age it makes sense to merchandise morality like Barbie dolls. But we need to get it right. Here's why I think the lesson was backward. A child isn't special because he doesn't do drugs. The chalkboard should say: I don't do drugs because I am special. A child refuses drugs because he realizes he's too special to need them. To protect my children, that's another lesson I'm hoping to teach them.

■　■　■

When they were little, I wanted my children to think of the world as exclusively warm and loving, like a giant family. But now that they are older, they are starting to find out for themselves that this is not always the case. My children are starting to emerge from the sheltered environment of baby-sitters, preschools, and the hand-picked friends with whom they have grown. In bits and pieces—when they see homeless people at the park or when we contribute to a food drive—they are starting to realize that the world can be unfriendly and cold. My daughter wants to know why we don't have a housekeeper. Seconds later she also wants to know why people beg for money on street corners or dig through the garbage after we place it at the curb.

For years my husband and I have emphasized how everyone is the same because people are basically good. Now my children are starting to notice that some lives are different from ours and some people are not good. Reality is starting to intrude. It needs to intrude, but now I must explain without disillusioning.

One time my daughter was playing at the park when another child asked her if she lived with her mother. After my daughter answered "yes," the other child responded, "I don't. I live with my father." My daughter was visibly shocked.

The facts of life simply happen upon us. The first thing my children have noticed is that some people look different. Clattering noisily into the doctor's office a few years ago, they were stopped short by the young woman inside. She was sitting in the waiting room reading a magazine in a wheelchair. Her hands sliced erratically through the air. My normally noisy children skidded to a halt beside her and froze in place while they subjected her to their unabashed inspection.

The woman looked at me and I made deliberate eye contact while I flashed her what I intended to be a sincere smile. That smile, I hoped, explained that with luck my children would not be too rude or hurt her feelings, but ultimately to let me know because I was responsible for them.

The kids settled onto the bench beside me, and then, loudly, they fired away.

"Why is she in that chair?"

"She cannot walk, so it helps her to move."

"How can the chair move?"

"She turns on the motor."

"How come nobody pushes her? The chair has handles."

"Somebody could push her, but with the motor she can go by herself."

Internally, I questioned myself. Should I send them over to the woman to say hello and ask their questions themselves? Would that be better or worse than letting her overhear? Just then, the woman's family came back. She flipped a switch and maneuvered her chair out of the office without a backward glance. But I looked back at the situation for a long while afterward.

"You know, that woman in the wheelchair could hear all your questions," I told my children. "When you're talking about somebody, you have to be careful not to hurt their feelings."

"What did we say," my son asked, "that could hurt her feelings?"

Good question. It stumped me for a moment because I didn't want to give him any new ideas.

"Well, you have to be careful not to say things that might make her feel bad just because she is different." I replied.

The conversation tapered off and the kids forgot about it. But I could not. Of course, that sort of thing has happened before. As children become more observant they raise more pointed questions: Why is that man using a cane? See how fat that woman is? Look at that gross guy. Why is he smoking?

The questions, usually voiced within audible earshot, are more blunt than tactful. I have tried to keep my answers honest but tactful. I confess that at times, however, I'm not always sure how. And so I don my matter-of-fact voice and simply acknowledge their observations: Yes, that man has a big bump on his nose. Yes, that girl is using crutches. Yes, that man has no arm. Sometimes when babies grow, I tell them, something goes wrong. Or, sometimes, people get hurt in bad accidents.

I try to teach my children that everybody is loved as somebody's child. I try to teach them that people are people, no matter what their differences. That's one of the lessons I want them to learn, and part of what I hope my answers say.

I want my children to have faith in the essential goodness of people. This can mean I am pleased when they fail to note differences. My children take it as a matter of course, for example, that two of their Little Tikes firemen are black. This fact is not even worthy of comment. Once my daughter played at the home of a friend whose adopted twin brothers are black.

"We played with the twins," she told me when she came home.

"Are the twins black?" I asked her—testing, I admit.

"No, I don't think so," she answered.

Other times children notice differences. When I bought her P.J. Sparkles doll I automatically bought it in white simply because my daughter is white. I tell myself it is natural to want a doll that looks like you do, but I wonder what she would have said had I bought her the black doll. Another mother tells the story of a rainy weekend at the beach when she had three girls to entertain. So she mounted an emergency Barbie doll-buying expedition. The store had only three remaining Barbie dolls: two white and one black. She bought them all, wrapped them all, and gave them to the girls. Her youngest drew the black Barbie doll. The mother says her daughter stripped the doll, put it in the corner, and didn't play with it again. This mother never mentioned her behavior to her daughter, but the story made me sad.

When my children do notice differences, I try to make sure we talk about them. Children need to understand the basis of differences before they can discount them. Often the differences are irrelevant.

"The Spanish kids wrecked my castle on the playground again," says my seven-year-old.

"The boys who wrecked it may be Hispanic," I correct him, rejecting his label, "but that is not why they wrecked it. Not all Hispanic children wreck sand castles, do they?"

Sometimes differences are not irrelevant. Children need to know when differences matter because those differences need to be respected. It is a fine line. On the one hand, I try to teach my children that people who look or act differently are still people and just as good as we are. At the same time, I want them to understand that people who are different can take pride in those differences.

Because we are Jewish, each year I find myself teaching my children to take pride in their difference as a member of the minority. Yearly we face the December Dilemma, a time when Christmas excitement permeates the air and my children know it is not for them. My children watch the Christmas specials hosted by every conceivable cartoon character; they see none about Chanukah. They feel left out.

We could all use more sensitivity. A friend, trying to be thoughtful, gave my daughter a present for Chanukah. It was a book about Donald Duck's Christmas. I try to teach my children respect for those who celebrate Christmas but pride in our celebration of Chanukah. At first it was sufficient merely to inflate Chanukah as a holiday, to make it bigger by way of competition, to give my kids equal opportunity for presents. But Chanukah is not the Jewish Christmas.

Like anyone who is different, Jewish children can find their religion embarrassing. A friend's daughter asked her mother not to put any Chanukah decorations near the window.

"I don't want anyone to see them and know we are Jewish," she said.

My daughter agreed. "I'm kind of embarrassed to let people know I am Jewish," she said last year.

I am gratified that my seven-year-old is beginning to learn pride. His friend is a Jehovah's Witness, and he does not celebrate Christmas, either.

"He doesn't want anyone to know about it. He gets angry if you ask him about it," my son explains. "But I don't care. I tell everyone about Chanukah. It doesn't bother me at all if everyone knows."

■ ■ ■

When I explain about differences, mostly I try to reinforce the feeling that regardless of them, the world is a loving place. The newspapers and television, of course, say otherwise. Never before had I considered the news X-rated, but of course now it is. Just by flipping channels my children can be exposed to graphic violence and horrible devastation (man-made or otherwise) that I would never allow them to view at the movies.

The desire to mentally evacuate our children from bad news is deeply instinctive. If we want them to be aware of what is happening, we don't want it to become the stuff of nightmares. During World War II the British evacuated their children to the countryside. The adults did it to keep the children safe as well as to give them a change of scene from war. For my children I want to nurture an optimism in the essential goodness of man, but when differences lead our country to war, my children need to be told this is not always the case.

The Persian Gulf war, obviously, brought the issue home. During the confrontation countdown before it began, we adults had been expecting war for weeks. The day it started a friend arrived to pick up her daughter who had been spending that afternoon with mine.

"They started fighting," I informed her as she walked in the door.

"Well, that's to be expected. The girls were together a long time today. Just throw them in another room until it passes," she answered flippantly.

"No, not the girls," I said. "The Gulf."

The mother was to be excused for putting the war out of her mind. Before the fighting started, most parents were torn between wanting to explain the momentous events to our children and wanting to sweep them under the rug of normalcy. But fallout from violence filters down through our days in a variety of ways, and for me there is no way to totally censor world events.

Television is the primary front upon which violence infiltrates my children's daily life. Whenever "Sesame Street" is preempted by news specials, then they realize something is in the works. They remain calm, however, since the Disney Channel stays on the air. Fine with me. The only tomahawk I want my children to know about is the kind that Indians used. So when commercial networks broadcast war, my children stick with Donald Duck. I don't want war, in short, to defeat daily life. And although my husband and I devoured a steady diet of war news during the Gulf conflict, it didn't overwhelm us. Sometimes the children's fighting in their bedroom was so loud, in fact, that I could not hear the news reports on the fighting overseas. I did not want my children to watch those reports, and yet we had to talk about them.

"How can you explain it to children? How can you defend fighting over the price of oil?" another mother asked.

"You can't," I answered. "But you can talk about the Iraqi invasion of Kuwait and how the world decided to stop it."

And so that's what my husband and I did. After dinner one night, we served a course on world affairs. Omitting the ambiguities that plagued us as adults, we told the kids that the nations of the world were fighting together to stop Saddam Hussein. (I waited for the children to catch me flat-footed by asking why the nations couldn't "use their words," instead of fight, but they did not ask.)

"When they're free in Kuwait, they're going to have to send lots of thank-you notes," my seven-year-old said, with visions of his birthday fresh in his mind.

We had to bring his conception closer to reality. War is no tea party and war is no game. Concerned about my boys' fascination with fighting, I once did some research. I have never encouraged my boys at war play (a contradiction in terms if there ever was one). I let them use sticks, but I won't supply them with an arsenal. The experts told me that boys need to feel powerful through aggressive imaginative play, but they advised giving children a more rounded conception of what fighting involves. If G.I. Joe shoots Cobra, in other words, somebody also must rush him to the hospital.

That's what my husband and I tried to do.

"A lot of soldiers are going to get killed in the fighting," we told our children. "Both sides have powerful weapons."

"Will the fighting come here?" my daughter wanted to know.

We reassured her that it would not, mentally grateful that unlike the children in Tel Aviv ours did not need to take gas masks to the playground.

My oldest was able to grasp the seriousness.

"I know what to write in my journal at school," said my uncharacteristically somber son. "I'm going to write: Today a war started and hundreds of people are going to get killed or hurt. Today is a terrible day."

Our oldest frequently complains about his father's watching the news every night.

"Why does he have to watch about bad things every night?" my son complained. "War is terrible. Why does he have to watch it?"

I wasn't sure whether he was objecting to the war or the fact that he could not watch his program.

A few days later, after he built a turbo-turning weapon out of his construction toys, I asked my son why he thinks it is fun to play with pretend weapons when he knows real fighting kills people.

He stared blankly at me for a few seconds. Then he quite rightly answered, "Yeah, but this is not real."

I see evidence of our violent world even when my seven-year-old and his buddy make paper airplanes.

"This one is a Scud missile," says his friend.

"Well, I'm aiming for Saddam Hussein," answers my son.

Sometimes television broadcasts and newspapers are filled with pictures of women and children suffering agonies. We have tried to explain that in bad times innocent people get hurt. Even when their leaders are bad, some of the people getting hurt in their countries are not bad. I don't know if the children understand that any better than my declarations that they are good kids who sometimes do bad things.

My children accept it as a matter of course that in their world the "good guys" always win and nothing unpleasant will intrude into their daily lives. They easily pack unpleasantness into the back of their minds, a concept to be opened sometime later. I am grateful that they have this ability, but I cannot do this. Some days I can feel world events hanging over our heads like a heavy black cloud. It pollutes my previous optimism that the people on this planet are getting smarter.

I can feel it in airports. Since the days of hijackings and international terrorism began, airports have never been the same. I remember the time my daughter and I flew together to visit Grandma. My daughter was unaware of it, but I felt a resigned sort of sadness with every identification checkpoint we passed.

"What's your name, little girl?" the reservation clerk casually asked my five-year-old daughter, so she could cross-check her answer against the ticket.

At the X-ray machine my daughter had to surrender her fanny pack. Then she wandered over to the wrong side of the conveyor belt to get it at the security check.

"Get back!" shouted the guard, evidently on full alert. "You can't go around there."

Before we were cleared to board our flight I had to remove the battery from my daughter's P.J. Sparkles doll. How sad, I thought to myself, a doll is the the only thing we seem capable of successfully disarming.

■ ■ ■

Sometimes, of course, we adults get all bent out of shape long before we have reason. Drugs are not yet a problem in my household, where we rarely take aspirin. Much of life's lessons simply go right over young children's heads. Just when you think your children are all set to settle down for some serious conversation, it turns out they have nothing deep on their minds at all. I'm glad. We have plenty of time to get serious.

My son comes to me with a solemn expression and asks, "Mom, what's a stepfather?"

Taking a deep breath, certain that we are treading onto serious ground, I explain about second marriages. After finishing, I ask him, "Why?"

"Just wondered," he answers. "I think Punky Brewster has one."

In the past few months, we have tiptoed through the minefields of religion, poverty and sex without exploding a single subject. Each time I am ready to dive right into something heavy, the kids manage, unintentionally perhaps, to keep it light.

My son comes home from Sunday school and asks, "Mom, what's a prophet?"

I explain that it is a person who delivers warnings about the future, a person who is able to tell others about what's going to happen. I wait for the next question.

"I get it," my son announces with satisfaction. "It's just like a news reporter."

In my son's classroom I help explain about winter holidays around the world. I light a Chanukah menorah and recite the Hebrew blessing. Then I translate it into English.

"That's really neat," a child exclaims. "What happens after you say the magic words?"

At Thanksgiving time we had a conversation about the poor and the homeless.

"Some people have no homes. They have no warm beds," I explained. "They have to sleep outside where it's cold."

"If they're cold," my daughter responded, "why don't they move to California?"

A friend had a similar conversation about the homeless with her four-year-old.

"Some people aren't lucky enough to live in houses," she said.

"Mommy, if they can't live in a house," her daughter responded, "why don't they live in a condo?"

I am always a bit relieved when children remain so delightfully innocent that nothing seems likely to get through. They remain that way, thank goodness, about sex. A friend's son requested a Ken doll for his sister. "That way," he explained without dissembling, "Barbie and Ken can sleep together."

Young children quite rightly have little sexual orientation and less modesty. My daughter took her Barbie doll to her brother's playground and announced, "Does anyone want to come here and see her boobies?"

My favorite such miss-the-point conversation took place with my daughter when we were discussing her Daddy's beard. She wanted to know why her brother had no beard.

"When you get older, then you start to grow a beard and to grow hair in other places. When you get older, your body changes," I said.

"Oh, I understand," she said. "You mean like your ears get big."

14
School Daze

Graduating from preschool

Selecting his uninspired daily attire of T-shirt and shorts, my son refused to be swayed by my suggestion that he wear something a bit more spiffy. It was his first day of kindergarten, but he didn't understand what all the fuss was about.

I do. Your first child's first day of "real" school marks the end of the preschool era and the start of serious life. From here on in, days are divided into two categories. They are either part of the school year or part of vacation. Each has characteristics totally its own.

So far as my son was concerned on that first morning, school offered nothing new. We had already visited his school the week before and met his teacher, who was busy transforming her sow's ear of a classroom into a purse. We had located the potty and test-walked his daily commute. To him, all the important stuff had been covered. And as I snapped a picture of him wearing his less-than-memorable clothes at the eminently memorable moment of his leaving the house, he grinned a bit self-consciously as if to say, "Hey, it's no big deal." The schoolyard, however, was clogged with other parents who disagreed. Their cameras and videocams were worthy of a real production.

On the Richter scale of great events, logic tells me the first day of kindergarten should not have scored a ten. It was not as if my son had never been away from home before. Like so many of today's social sophisticates, he is a graduate of several play groups and preschools. He knows how to check out a playground and cram his jacket into a microscopic cubby.

But kindergarten is different. Emotionally, it is a launching. My son was climbing aboard the escalator of education that will carry him up through high school. Gone are the intimate classes and the teachers who will ask me how he slept the night before. They will not ask, but I still want to tell. Now that he was in kindergarten, I worried that he could get lost in the crush of the crowd. At school he not only would play, but for the first time he also would have to perform. When he was in preschool, I had wanted his teachers to love him. Now that he was in public school, I knew that they would grade him.

Life has changed. Now that he has started serious school, the mornings are different. We can no longer wander late into class on a lazy morning, casually and at will. Now we are on a schedule, and like millions of families our day will be scheduled around the first bell and our summer will start when the school calendar says so.

Everything about kindergarten screams important. Adults take it seriously. At the midmorning orientation session, I was impressed to see as many fathers wearing suits as mothers wearing dresses. Earnestly I had conferred with other parents about requesting the "right" teacher for the all-important first year. As we waited in line to say good morning to his teacher, my son was full of excited anticipation. He was not nearly as nervous as I was. I suspect that meant he was ready to start school; I was the one who was not ready to say good-bye to his preschool years.

He was ready to expand his social circle, for the first time making friends beyond the boundaries of his street. He was five years old, that perfect blend of naïveté and knowledge. It is the age, he gloated, when finally he was old enough to snap his fingers. But ruefully he admitted he could not yet whistle. When I told him about his new school, he wanted to know what they would serve for snack. He did not understand he was being cast into a sea of twenty-five children where he would either sink or swim on the basis of inevitable comparison to others.

"You might get some homework in kindergarten," I solemnly informed him, adding that at last he would have something official to put into his backpack.

"Oh good," he responded with a cheerfulness never to be seen again. "I always wondered about that stuff."

For my son, the only issue of interest was picking the right lunchbox. A woman buys a party dress hoping to stand out in a crowd. A child selects his lunchbox hoping to blend in. My son (who chose Duck Tales) was confronting conformity for the first time. I wondered if he would turn out to be a follower or a leader.

As the children marched into class, more than a few parents crowded the windows and lingered for a peek. In four short hours we would have to pick up our children, but we were too excited to make tracks the way we should. A father walked by to report that he estimated the "cry rate" at about 30 percent. At first I thought he was talking about how many clinging children were crying for their mommas. But as I thought about it later, I decided I might have been wrong. He could have meant how many mommas were crying for their kids.

A few weeks later, when my son came home brandishing his first official homework assignment, I realized that school had truly begun.

A white sheet of paper with a picture of a mouse and a moon, it didn't look terribly significant. But as my son subjected the red crayon to a choke hold and began to write his version of the letter *m*, I felt a certain sense of historic importance. He was doing his first homework assignment. He and I have since sweated through many afternoons when the work was harder, the quantity greater, and his attitude more surly. But I will always remember the first time.

That was when I realized my five-year-old evidently viewed homework as a sporting competition where winning is a function of speed. He finished dashing off his row of lowercase *m*'s before I finished formulating my thoughts. His penmanship was horrible. His *m*'s resembled a row of seagulls dancing the conga. He moved on to the capital *m*'s with utter disregard for the dotted lines. Timidly, seeking to tread softly on the thin crust of his enthusiasm, I ventured a comment: "Did you notice how the uppercase *m*'s come up to this line and the lowercase letters only come up this far?"

His hand stopped and he gaped at me, astonished that I should presume to comment upon his work. Fleetingly I wondered if he stared that way at his teacher.

"I see what you mean," he finally said. But he had run out of lines on which to practice, so it was hard to tell if he really did. I reminded him to put his name on the paper, and he was even more astonished when I suggested that his *c* was backwards and he had forgotten to use a capital letter.

"I don't see anything wrong with it," he insisted.

We compared samples from his earlier work, and grudgingly he came to admit I might be right. He said nothing more as he moved on to the next sheet, but I noticed his shoulders were hunched defensively as he wrote. The air in the room was noticeably cooler, similar to my husband's reaction whenever I remind him again to load the dishwasher.

On the next homework sheet, my son scribbled blue on all the square shapes. I bit my tongue rather than point out that he had gone outside the lines so much that his squares looked more like porcupines. The last sheet came with instructions for me to read, so I felt justified in getting involved.

"You need to cut out a picture from a magazine," I told him, "of something starting with *m*.

Not until after we marched off together to take a look did I wonder whether my participation constituted cheating. I decided that the first time is an exception. We were learning how to do it for next week. After a few minutes, we settled upon a picture of Mickey Mouse.

That afternoon I decided I needed some guidance on this homework business and consulted an expert with older kids.

"Do you ever correct your kids when they're doing something wrong?" I asked.

"Never," she replied. "You criticize what they're doing now and pretty soon you won't even be able to get them to do it."

"But don't you try to teach them a little at home?" I persisted.

"No. They won't listen to me. I leave that up to the teacher," she answered with exaggerated self-deprecation. "I'm only a mother."

She was telling me, of course, that the homework is my son's and not mine. And I know she is right. In a few years I don't want to be doing his calculus with him—or any other subject about which he knows more than I do. It's just that for the first five years of his life, I had been my son's teacher. Now I had to get used to sharing the job.

My son, of course, was also new to this homework business. It turns out he needed to get used to the classroom routine. The next morning I reminded him to bring his papers back to school. He gave me a quizzical look.

"Why should I bring this work back to my teacher?" he asked. "She gave it to me to take home."

All too quickly, of course, newness gave way to familiarity and, in my son's case, a little contempt. Immediately after spring vacation he began to look forward to summer vacation as his personal deliverance. But only at the end-of-the-year open house did it dawn upon me that the year truly was ending.

Veterans now, we parents toured the kindergarten classrooms where a year ago we and our children were only beginners. The place that seemed strange and formal in the fall seemed familiar and comfortable in the spring. Open house is a chance for kids to show off their penmanship, clay dinosaurs, and art projects. In my son's classroom I recognized the names of every artist and most of the other parents.

As school ended and the children were looking ahead with excitement, I found myself looking back with nostalgia. As the first rung of the monkey bars, kindergarten had been easy—a foot bath before the cold shower of first grade. It had been a special time. Our kids would never be quite this young or this naïve again. They were still easily fooled. In kindergarten my son awaited his turn to be Child of the Day.

As a treat he would get to turn out the lights in his classroom—something I cannot make him do in his own bedroom.

In kindergarten, the teacher functions not only as an instructor, but also as a parent:

"I'm finished with my juice," says the girl. "Where should I throw the cup?"

"In the trash," answers her teacher patiently.

"Lisa said we can't climb to the top of the monkey bars," complains another child.

"No, honey. That was the jungle gym," the teacher answers with equal patience.

Next year, I wondered, will the girls still kiss their teacher good-bye? Next year, will our kids be too old to come home with notes pinned to their shirts? Next year will we take reading for granted, as commonplace as a bike without training wheels?

Kindergarten is a child's first official taste of academics.

"A salamander is a frog's nephew," my son reported after science class. He paused. "Or is it a cousin?"

A kindergartner can write, although sometimes his handwriting is easier to read if you know what he is trying to say. Reading and math have been laid out like a buffet; in kindergarten the children had only to taste. They tottered on the brink of learning.

My son hesitantly sounded out the no-diving sign at the shallow end of the swimming pool. "No dogs allowed," he guessed.

Kindergartners take their knowledge seriously.

"Do you wanna do the easy or hard work first?" a friend asked my son as they tackled worksheets.

"The easy work," my son answered. "I wanna get warmed up."

Kindergarten covered survival skills I had never imagined. In class the students learned addresses and telephone numbers, how to tell time, how to tie shoes, and how to count money. But my son, upset the first time his father traded him a quarter for twenty-five pennies, could not always accept emotionally what intellectually he had been taught.

As a parent, I have become like a dog with a bone. In kindergarten I discovered new anxieties to gnaw at night. On bad nights I tried to bury words like "hyperactive" and "learning disability." On good nights I chewed over lesser worries such as why my son could not tie his shoes or tell his right hand from his left. And in passing I fretted over birthday parties to which he was not invited. My son, living in a world of Velcro shoes and digital watches, was not nearly so concerned as I. With a healthy attitude, he always looks confidently ahead in the direction his feet are pointing.

On the last day of school, I noticed several cameras and fathers as well. I felt an unexpected sense of sadness, even as I was eager to see to which first-grade teacher my son had been assigned. I said a lingering good-bye to his kindergarten teacher, but it was the other mothers I knew I would miss the most. I wanted their children to be in my son's class so that we would be able to continue the conversations we used to start each morning. My son did not share my nostalgia or my concerns.

"Kindergarten is ending. Are you sorry?" I asked.

"No," he answered. "I've been wondering what first grade is like."

■ ■ ■

He found out soon enough. My son's second year of school turned out to be more traumatic for him, less traumatic for me. First grade was tougher than I expected it to be and quite a contrast to kindergarten. The parking lot at my son's elementary school reminded me of the drive-up window at McDonald's. Unlike kindergarten, few of the parents parked their cars to go inside. In first grade most parents began to place orders for their kids to have a nice day and dropped them off without cutting the engine. In first grade we all got serious.

I had only to compare that first day of school for my oldest and my youngest to see how far in one year I had come in my thinking.

When I was a child we used to torture each other with this riddle: Would you rather boil or freeze to death? I don't recall that we were preoccupied with death. I think we were just flaunting our discovery that not every choice is easy. The riddle came to mind during the first week of school. My son, six that fall, started first grade (real school) and my youngest, two at the time, started preschool (play school) two mornings a week. The first day I couldn't decide if I wanted my kids to cling to me for moral support or boldly go where they had never gone before.

My oldest, of course, was a grizzly veteran of his kindergarten campaign. He was savvy to wearing a backpack, raising his hand, and having homework. He appreciated the true value of summer vacation. He approached his first day of school warily—a draftee for this assignment, not a volunteer. He and his buddies had been scattered across the classrooms like wreckage from a plane crash. None of them was in his class, and he worried about piecing friendships together.

He didn't cling, this son of mine. No kisses. He marched like a soldier when his class practiced walking across the playground in a straight line. He cast me one mournful look as if to say, "See the stuff they make me do?" That night he told me first grade lasts entirely too long and recess is too short. There is no snack, he complained, adding that he was starving by lunchtime.

The first few months I worried about my oldest, the family trailblazer. I worried that he was lukewarm about reading—the same way I wonder why, when he builds with Legos, he never makes what is shown in the picture on the box. I wanted him to kiss me squarely on the lips and march off confidently with a jaunty smile, not a tortured look of submission.

My youngest, by contrast, had never been to school before. I have left him, sure, but never in a classroom where the activities do not follow his own personal agenda. I worried that after I had gone he would look up, notice my absence, and wail in a panic. I worried that he would clobber the first boy who touched a truck that he wanted. My son did not talk. I worried that he would not be understood by teachers less skilled at charades than I.

I worried, but it was wasted effort. Other frantic two-year-olds were clinging with apprehension to the safety of their mothers' knees. It is a fine art to gently pry away a child paralyzed in mortal terror. That first morning mine immediately sat down with some modeling clay. He gazed around with satisfaction. "My ship has come in," his look seemed to say. I should have known he was ready as we left home in the car when he put a seatbelt around his (Micro Machines) lunchbox. He gave me my kiss when I asked him, and then marched off confidently with a jaunty smile. Before I even left the room he had moved on to the coloring table. Sitting there, surrounded by papers, he looked just like his father, only shorter.

It is the fate of the third child, I suspect, to take everything in stride. I looked a tad wistfully at the children who were clinging to their mommas. That morning I wished my youngest had done just a little clinging. I wished my oldest had been just a little bit more cocksure. Would I rather boil to death or freeze? My answer is that it doesn't make much difference. No matter what, some people are never happy.

When my son was in first grade there were times when I wondered if he was ever happy. For months he never came home and told me the good things, or even the important things. If I hadn't helped the teacher in his classroom, in fact, I would have had little idea how he was doing, what was going on, or how it was going.

"How was school today?" I would ask brightly every afternoon.

"Fine," he would answer. "You asked me that in kindergarten. You asked me that yesterday. Are you gonna ask me that every day?"

So I tried not to, hoping instead that enough scraps of information would fall from his mouth to satisfy my hunger for information. I longed to ask: Are you excited about reading? Are you getting the idea about school? Do you realize you're going to be doing this for a long, long time?

Instead, my son would tell me the "important" things.

"If you eat a hundred times at the cafeteria, then you get to eat for free," he said.

He told me about troublemakers. His teacher gave each student green, blue, and red cards next to their names on the bulletin board. For bad behavior, she would pull the green card and substitute blue. After blue came yellow, then red and a parent-teacher conference. Fits of rage could not induce the ashen-faced reactions I saw when she would turn to a student and quietly say, "Pull a card." My son was always eager to tell me how somebody else had gotten into trouble.

"Two kids in my room had their red cards pulled," he announced gleefully but without malice. "Boy, are they are in trouble."

"John forgot to bring back his library book again," he pronounced mournfully. "He's going to have to pay for it."

Interesting information, but not exactly what I was after. And so instead I spied. I volunteered in the classroom, quizzed the teacher, and compared notes with other parents. Slowly, I found out the answers to the important questions—everything, in other words, my son never would think to tell me.

To judge by a child's perspective, sometimes I think recess is the most important—and most difficult—part of first grade. I stood in the corner of the classroom once and listened to a discussion I never could have imagined:

The teacher had not even come to a stop inside the doorway before the students were hoisting their hands in the air, waving like shipwrecked sailors, vying for her attention. Compared to these kids, the Founding Fathers were rank amateurs at the art of earnest debate.

"Those boys came and wrecked our sand castle again," my son proclaimed with a self-righteousness out of style since the Puritans. "We didn't want them to and they did it anyway."

This is serious, his teacher agreed. The classes had discussed that very problem at length just the day before. They had agreed nobody could knock over somebody else's sand castle. Everyone voted to follow the rule by standing up. Evidently some kids who stood with their legs were sitting in their hearts.

"Those boys will have to suffer the consequences," the teacher proclaimed.

"Well, Crystal wrecked my sand castle," Tony complained.

"I didn't see any sand castle. I was making a cake. I wrecked it when I was finished. You weren't even there," Crystal defended herself.

"Well, I was gonna come back," Tony lamented.

"After you come inside, Tony, it's somebody else's turn to use the sandbox," the teacher explained. "Once you leave the sandbox, you have no control over what happens to your sand castle."

While Tony digested that notion, a girl reported that two children were playing inside the kindergarten yard, where first-graders are not supposed to be. A long discussion ensued concerning whether the children were playing there or merely heading (slowly) for the bathroom.

"I was going to the bathroom and then I was trying to get the other kids to come out," Jessica defended herself.

"Nobody is to play in the kindergarten yard. It is not supervised at recess," the teacher explained. "We have talked about this over and over. I want everyone who can follow that rule to stand up."

Everyone rose. The teacher pointed to various children.

"Tell us what you are committing to," she asked. And they answered correctly—all but Michael.

"Um, I agree not to wreck sand castles," Michael answered.

With a sigh, the teacher set him straight.

"Now, does everyone understand?" she asked. Twenty-two heads bobbed up and down in the affirmative. "Now, where is the kindergarten yard?"

A stunned silence greeted her question. Turns out some of the kids weren't sure. Another discussion was required for purposes of definition.

Another girl reported that somebody was climbing over the fence—also against the rules. A boy complained somebody peeled back his fingers so he had to drop down from the monkey bars when it was still his turn. Somebody else recited the story of being hit in the face by a ball.

"I'll bet Roger did that," chimed in another child. "He's really mean."

The teacher listened and commented and then tried to focus the children's attention on the day's lesson. Hands continued to wave.

"Is it something really important?" she asked, not unkindly. It was.

"The boys were following us again. We asked them not to and they wouldn't stop," a girl piously announced, going so far as to name names.

"You must not play games like that unless everyone agrees to play. Otherwise that's teasing," the teacher lectured.

"But that's what boys do," one of the accused interjected earnestly, as if the explanation was self-evident.

That boy was confused about what's expected of him, but then I was confused about what I expected of first grade.

I expected to hear a lot about new friends, a new teacher, and new accomplishments. I expected to hear about what a change it was. I thought my son would be most concerned about his work. Instead, I heard about recess on the first-grade playground. If I asked my son what happened at school, he was likely to tell me how somebody spilled juice on him at lunchtime. He led his news bulletins with the sports.

We don't see school from the same perspective. I see recess as an interruption to the business of the day. To him, school interrupts recess. I saw first grade as a significant step in his education. To him, it was the same old stuff.

That is why I was pleasantly surprised at my first conference with his first-grade teacher. It is a time-honored and somewhat nerve-wracking experience to participate in your first, serious, parent-teacher conference. It is not easy to sit and maintain a pleasant smile while listening to a teacher tell you what your child does well—and what he does not do so well.

I'm sure it is hard on the teachers, also. Come conference time, a teacher is at once a diplomat and a judge. And come every fall, I go to hear my son's teacher diplomatically render verdict. I never have had the child who drives a teacher to distraction, who flirts with suspension, or who has his own personal chair in the principal's office. But I have had the child who clowns around, talks out of turn, and needs to "settle down." I have heard this verdict rendered in all manner of tactful phrases. I expected to hear them again.

So it was something of a shock now, in first grade, to hear nothing of the sort. The teacher had mostly nice things to say, and I found I wasn't prepared to cope. My son, I was told, is conscientious, curious, eager, and articulate.

"You mean he's talkative and bossy?" I asked, thinking of the child who is always telling his sister, his brother, and anyone else within earshot what to do. Any of my children could fill in for any of their teachers on a moment's notice.

"No," responded his teacher. "He's inquisitive, friendly, and caring about other people. In fact, I would like to see him lighten up. He seems to take life too seriously."

I sat there dumbfounded for a moment. First I wondered if we were talking about the same person. Is this the boy who won't stop clowning around at the dinner table? Is this the boy who doesn't take homework, my instructions, or bedtime seriously? Then I sat there dumbfounded again. It occurred to me that my son finally had a teacher who must like him nearly as much as I do.

As his mother, I am conditioned to appreciate beauty in the rough. I do not expect this of others. I did not know how to cope with the experience. Why else would I have sat there during the conference articulating the intellectual equivalent of "aw, shucks"? Why else did I try to argue with his teacher instead of saying "thank you" and gracefully accepting the compliment?

It is difficult to see your own children through the eyes of strangers. As parents we expect so much; we always see room for improvement. As parents, sometimes we get blinded to our child's best because all we can see is his worst. But other parents, comparing your child to their own, sometimes see yours better.

"Your son was terrific at lunch today," another mother tells me. "Somebody spilled milk on him; he got soaked. But he didn't even get upset. He handled it really well."

He did? I have seen him deck his sister for much less.

"Your son is so much fun to talk to," a different mother tells me after driving him home. "He was telling me all about his morning at school."

He was? Most days I cannot pry a word out of him.

I have tried at times to see my children as other people do. I have sneaked back to my share of windows and peeked inside hoping to catch a glimpse of my children when they are unawares. What I see is always a surprise. Is that my three-year-old sitting so straight and tall at the coloring table? I never knew he could sit still so long and apply himself so hard to anything. Is that my five-year-old smiling and greeting all of her classmates by name? I never knew she had any semblance of manners. Is that my seven-year-old working industriously on his paper without talking?

When I helped in the first-grade classroom, the other children would smile at me and the girls would compliment me on my earrings. They would show me their work and ask for my opinion or for my help. My own son did not. I am his mother and we both know it. He cannot see me as a teacher, and I cannot see him as an ordinary student. It is true that my oldest might be buckling down. He might be getting excited by learning, challenged by reading, and eager to please. He just might be. But apparently I would be the last to know.

In first grade my son had to deal with another subject besides reading and writing. As his teacher told me, my firstborn needs to lighten up. A worrier by nature, my son has always majored in stress. He's the sort of child who turns life into a vise and applies pressure to himself. I know this kid. Every question is the college boards; every game is the Olympics. In first grade I saw the first signs that he is learning to deal with stress.

My son takes it upon himself to worry about whether every detail of the world is functioning normally. Worrying about his own affairs isn't enough. He must try to manage mine. Frequently, when we get into the car, he will ask me if I am sure I know the directions to where we are going. On the way, he will check the gauge to verify that we have enough gas in the car to get where we are going. Once he confided to me that riding in cars and boats makes him nervous.

When it comes to worrying, school provides plenty of opportunity. I first noticed this tendency to take things too seriously when my son was four. One morning he was anxious to get to preschool and work on his jigsaw puzzle. More than anxious, he was downright worried.

"You'll get it finished," I reassured him. "You have most of the states finished and I know you can do the rest. What's the big deal?"

"Well, I have to finish it today," he moaned. "It's Friday and we're not allowed to keep puzzle work on the rug over the weekend. Oh, I wish I had started it sooner!"

My son, I acknowledged to myself with some amazement, was stressed. About doing a jigsaw puzzle. About the small stuff. Now I have heard modern children are subject to stress, but I blamed it on pushy parents and hyperactive lifestyles. My son is teaching me otherwise.

In grade school now, even when nothing is going wrong, he worries that it will. He still puts pressure on himself. Consider those green, blue, yellow, and red cards on the bulletin board next to his name. My son usually stayed on green, but he worried about it.

"The hard part about being on green," he confided, "is it makes you nervous worrying about when you're gonna end up on blue."

In first grade my son came home and announced he had a speaking part in the school's patriotic assembly. He had two sentences to memorize about living free in America and then to recite all by himself into a microphone before an audience of adoring parents at two performances. I greeted the news with dismay. His previous experience before a crowd was almost more than I could handle.

He was barely five when he came home from preschool and informed me that his music class was going to hold a recital. He was going to sing three songs in chorus with seven other students and then play a twenty-second keyboard solo.

"Are you ready to do this?" I asked two weeks in advance of his performance.

"Oh, sure," he blithely replied. "No problem."

It was no problem—until the day before.

"I'm not doing this recital," he announced. "I'm not gonna bow and say my name. I'm not gonna stand there in front of all the classes."

If he were a dog, his haunches would be hunkered down.

"At least sing the songs with your friends," I said.

"No!" he shouted. "I'm sitting in the audience. I won't get up there. It's all the teacher's fault. If it weren't for her, I wouldn't be in this mess."

Unbidden, the marquee in my mind flashed: "Quitter. Your son is a quitter." So we talked. I cajoled. We negotiated.

"Don't pressure him," said his teacher. "This is supposed to be fun for the students." Right.

Exasperated, I finally asked, "What terrible thing do you think is going to happen to you just standing up there?"

And in a rare moment of truth, unvarnished with anything but tears, my son answered, "I think they will laugh at me."

Once we had unmasked the enemy, conquering it became easier. Finally, we reached agreement. He would stand in front of the class, but he didn't have to open his mouth. But when the fateful day dawned, my son had hysterics. Our negotiations began anew, starting with whether he would go to school. He agreed—but only wearing his grubbiest T-shirt and shorts. He held my hand on the way into class, but amazingly he released it to go stand by his fellow performers. All the boys were dressed alike in nonchalant disarray; all the girls wore flouncy dresses.

During the entire twenty-four-minute performance, my son was a real trouper. I couldn't hear him sing, of course, because the girls sang loud and the taped music was louder. And I couldn't see if there was panic in my son's eyes because the entire time he stared at his shoes. But the caliber of his performance didn't matter. I was proud that he performed at all. One child skipped school that day and another fled the stage in tears. But, as I pointed out afterward, nobody in the audience laughed.

Since that day I had limited my son's solo performances to show and tell. So by first grade I had my misgivings about his performance in an assembly. I am proud to report that when the great day dawned he bounded up to the microphone, reeled off his lines the way he would write them (with no spaces between the words), and then escaped gratefully to his seat. I did not care a bit about his diction, however. I did not care how he said his lines. I was impressed and proud that he said anything at all. In first grade my son began to grow up.

Now, looking back at the year, I can appreciate how far my son and his classmates have come in other ways. At first, it was patently impossible for them to sit still, let alone hold their hands steady. At first, my son's class had remedial lessons to practice walking to the room in a straight line.

First grade was tough. In first grade, the teachers took off their gloves. They expected the children to work hard, no excuses accepted. The teacher had my son cowed and me as well. No longer did I feel that missing just one day of school might not matter. To my son, his first-grade teacher began to assume larger-than-life proportions. Once, when I was on the telephone, my son began talking to me in my otherwise unoccupied ear.

"Don't talk to me when I'm on the phone. I can't hear two people talk at once," I said.

"My teacher can," my son replied. "She can listen to five of us read at once."

Now my son definitely has lost that first blush of kindergarten innocence. He has stopped complaining about the longer hours of the first-grade day. He realizes that about some things he has no choice.

"Do you have homework today?" I would ask him.

"Why?" he would respond warily, although the answer was self-evident. In first grade homework became not necessarily something he had to do, but also something that I had to make him get done. Yet in other respects he remained naïve.

"Why did you have so much trouble on this spelling test?" I once asked him toward the middle of the year.

"The teacher made a mistake," he told me. "She covered up the words we were trying to spell."

By the end of the year, he became more comfortable with the program. Toward spring, his conference reports were less glowing than at the beginning of the year. My son had learned all the rules; evidently then he began trying to challenge them. He would clown around at times and talk out of turn. Although I was sorry to hear it, I reflected privately that this sounded more like the son I knew.

But most of all, in first grade he learned how to read. I thought the process would be like a flower unfolding, but now I compare it to popcorn. Once my son got warmed up, he really started popping.

I watched the children in his class stumble at reading before they could walk. Some agonized painstakingly over every word; others took flying leaps with wild guesses. It was a touchy time. I perfected an impassive face as my son faltered over the word "what," knowing he already had read it twice before in the same story. Sometimes it was a no-win situation. He grew angry if I told him a word, and angry if I did not.

"You're laughing at me!" he would shout as he would stomp away from me and the book on more than one occasion.

For months it was a frustrating struggle, much the way learning to ride a two-wheeler once remained a feat just out of his grasp. Then one day, magically, he could do it. Suddenly, something happened. He got his balance, he hit his stride, he learned to read. Now the words fall into place and he races through books. Now I can smuggle him love notes in his lunchbox. It is one of the most exciting milestones of his life. After months of faltering steps, his mind has learned to walk. The world lies before him now, shimmering with infinite possibility. Even the kids realize it.

"Reading is awesome," I overheard one of my son's classmates say. "It's even great."

My son seems older now that he can read. In a way, I am unprepared. It's like the little sister who suddenly cracks the code to Pig Latin, making private conversations impossible.

"Meet you by that black car," I tell my son.

"You mean the Isuzu?" he responds, reading the name off the bumper.

Secrets have become harder to maintain. No longer can I spell rapid-fire messages to my husband. ("Go slow," my husband jokes.) Sometimes my son is the first one to grasp my meaning. I am startled when my son reads the newspaper or a magazine over my shoulder.

"Now I guess you can read just about anything," I tease him.

"Unless it's written in cursive," he answers with a grin.

I have had to readjust my image of my son a bit, now that second grade is a very real possibility. I have to be careful of what I leave lying around and especially careful about what I write—because it just occurred to me: If my son can read books, after all, he can also read this.

First-graders make such great strides, in fact, that for a while I wondered what they could possibly learn in second grade that would be nearly so monumental as reading. Then, during the last week of school, one of the students supplied the answer. On her paper she wrote:

"I like first grade because the teacher tot us to red."

How silly of me. Now I know that next year will come spelling.

15
Seasonal Work

If there's no school,
then this must be vacation

I f school is the main course of the year, sports and summer are dessert. They are the fun times, of course, and they are ice cream. Frosty and cold, they are to be licked slowly and savored precisely because they are so different from school, which is corn chips and cheese snacks and other nonperishable goodies that can be packed inside a lunchbox. School is sitting still on a chair. Sports are running pell-mell the length of a field chasing a ball when school is out.

For my son, sports have been a spot of summer during the school year. It is during the elementary school years, of course, that a child first samples organized sports. I can picture my son in a variety of uniforms, proudly accepting a multitude of trophies awarded simply for the fact that he bothered to attend games.

Sometimes I wondered whether seven years old is too tender an age for a boy to go out for organized sports. It is possibly the only age, after all, when a boy's feet are even bigger than his mouth. It is also the age when information entering through the ear does not always get processed by the brain. I wondered whether my son was ready to go out for anything but lunch. Just as I wondered whether I could keep my three-year-old off the playing field during the endless round of practices, I wondered whether my son could grasp the object of each sport. Instead, it took me an entire year of sports to finally figure out that object for myself.

We started out gently. Beforehand I had worried that overzealous parents might put pressure on their children to perform. Except for a few agitated coaches, fuming on the sidelines, I did not see this. We delighted in the rare moments of brilliance and kept our mouths shut about the others. Nobody berated anyone. Everyone tried to put a positive face on any level of performance. My son received ribbons and trophies just for showing up. When it came time for basketball, I saw the coach count the number of kids and divide them evenly into teams. My son came home and proudly told his father, "I made the team."

The first sport my son played was Little League. I knew immediately we had a long way to go. The T-ball coach told my son to get out there and cover center field.

"Right, coach," he replied. Then he stopped, turned, and shouted to his father, "Dad, where's center field?"

Sports were a revelation for both of us.

For me, it was my first encounter with macho—as made evident when my husband insisted that he would register our son for baseball. At one practice the coach thanked the women who wanted to stay to watch and then invited any husbands to step up and help coach. (No, I would not have liked to help, but I would not have minded being asked.) Women wishing to serve in sports are welcome, of course, because every team has its "mom." I did not know there were so many fund-raisers, banners, and pancake breakfasts in the world. For the record, however, I would like to point out that it was I who purchased my son his first all-important soft cup. For the record let me also add that T-ball taught me humility. I realized that I could not recognize my own son when he was wearing his uniform without looking at his number. Across a field, seven boys with big ears wearing hats all look alike.

For my son, sports have been a revelation about teamwork and competition.

T-ball, as played by kindergartners, is hardly aerobic activity. A kid could nap in left field waiting for a ball to come his way—and some of them apparently do. My son preferred to perform a ritualistic dance that involved bouncing his left leg and gazing anywhere but in the direction from which the ball was likely to come. The scores racked up during T-ball games aren't counted, which is fine because the kids generally had no idea what they were anyway. During one game I saw a child running like crazy to home plate when suddenly his helmet slipped off. He screeched to a halt, uncertain whether he was allowed to score unless he wore it. I am told it requires several seasons before T-ball actually takes. I believe it.

Next, we tried soccer. Unlike T-ball, this was exercise. The boys would dash all over the field chasing and kicking the ball. In soccer my son finally recognized the necessity of keeping an eye on the ball, and he would try to steal it from anyone who had it—at first even from his own teammates. In soccer I watched my son digest his first taste of competition. Sometimes he found it tough to swallow. He knew the score, he knew that he wanted to win, and he knew when his team lost. We tried to teach him: "Don't get mad; get even by playing better." It was hard to convince him that if he fell down and got kicked in the head, it was nothing personal. If my son paid too little attention to T-ball, he took soccer too seriously.

Watching him, I had a sudden flashback to when my kids began playing board games in earnest. At first, losing Candy Land was so upsetting we had to stop playing. Being sent back to the Peppermint Forest when you've almost made it to King Kandy can be hard to endure. At times my son would refuse to make his move when it involved going backward. Those sessions were the only time I have ever tried to cheat—to lose. But, eventually, my son learned to play—and lose—board games with good grace. And in soccer, too, he began to learn how to win and how to lose. There was even that magic moment when he celebrated his first goal. My husband screamed so loudly a lesser man would have suffered a coronary.

Next came basketball. In first grade he had his troubles with basketball like any other sport. Just as he didn't know how to handle the stirrups in the T-ball uniform, my son got his head stuck in the armhole trying to put on his basketball jersey. All the kids suffered forms of confusion. I saw one boy come after the game was underway. He saw his team already playing, dropped his jacket, and ran out to join them as the sixth man on the court. One of the few times my son got the ball during a game, he dribbled once, tripped over his own sneaker, and fell flat on his face. ("The floor is slippery," he told me later.)

Now that we have worked our way through all the seasons, my son is older and wiser—and so am I. I have begun to see why school age is the time to start sports. School age is the time for learning lessons. My son now knows where to find center field, but he now knows even more. He has been learning that playing with his team does not mean hogging the ball. He understands that team members must depend upon each other. In basketball my son actually scored one basket. He was pleased, of course, but he was more upset that his team lost the game.

His skills still are not outstanding, but whether he excels at a particular sport is not important. The purpose of organized sports has less to do with the game and more with how it's played. He has learned how to be a better winner and loser. My son has learned that when you play on a team you all win or lose together. He still fumbles over his feet and the finer points, but he's got the main idea. Maybe not all learning takes place in the classroom, after all.

■ ■ ■

During summer there are also lessons to learn—starting with how to swim. I cannot think of summer without remembering swimming lessons. I recall my slightly shameful relief to be done with Mommy & Me classes, during which I had to brightly exclaim how much fun it was to be in the water while in reality I was freezing. I think of the bribes I employ now in order to get my kids into the water alone, and I associate it all with chattering teeth as my children emerge from the pool dripping while they wait for me to wrap them in a towel.

I cannot watch a swimming lesson at all, in fact, without remembering the first lessons my oldest ever took. He was four years old. I would watch him from the side of the pool while his two-year-old sister made me nervous by running too close to the pool and I tried to keep the sunlight from shining in the eyes of my newborn son as I nursed him on the bench. Here is how it went:

Four years old, the instructor had assured me ahead of time by telephone, is absolutely the perfect age to learn to swim. Reporting for our first lesson, I remembered those words. My son was folded accordion style with his legs in the fetal position, and his hands clutched the side of the pool in a death grip. His teacher, a sweet young thing who obviously had no children of her own or she wouldn't be doing this, coaxed him into touching the pool bottom and then announced he was doing a wonderful job. With some persuasion, he allowed her to take him away from the side. He rode her hips with his arms wrapped tightly around her neck, terror etched in every line of his body.

"Hold your breath because we are going to dunk under water," the teacher said. "Can you hold your breath?"

"Steps," he answered, surveying the vastness of the pool, which bore no relationship to his plastic version at home. "I want to go back to the steps."

"Well, first let's try this," she answered. "I won't let go of you. Just hold your breath and we're going to put your head under water."

"But wait," he said. "What's that round thing in the corner?"

"That's for catching leaves," she answered, not to be distracted. "Now you need to get ready. Remember, don't breathe."

Good advice. I watched, holding my breath with anxiety. My son did not. Coughing and sputtering he rose to the surface. He was soaking wet but I could spot which of the drops were the tears.

"Hey," she said, "that wasn't bad, was it, huh?"

"Yes."

"Why are you crying? You did it," she reminded him.

"Well," he said, "I have allergies. How come fish can breathe under water?"

"Because fish are different from people," she said. "You have to hold your breath like this. See how I do it? Now it's your turn. Are you ready?"

"No. I want to get out. It seems much safer where Mommy is sitting. I want my Mommy," he whimpered. "I want her to take me out."

"Well, Mommy wants you to learn how to swim, too," she said as I quickly ducked behind the patio furniture. "You want to learn to swim, don't you?"

"No," said the boy who pestered me for three weeks asking when his lessons would start.

"Well, let's go back by the steps," she responded. With his nose inches from the cement, he practiced putting his head in the water. Will he be the only student, I wondered, who can swim only if there are steps under him?

Numbly I watched their awkward dance as they negotiated for every inch of progress away from the steps. Panic seemed universal during this first lesson. The other students all were in the deep end, begging with their teachers even as they bobbed like corks. I no longer could hear my son's words: I just saw his head shaking furiously back and forth.

"How am I ever going to get him to come back here again tomorrow?" muttered one of the mothers watching a similar procedure. I remembered that her son had been screaming before he even got wet. This was, I perceived, one of those it's-good-for-you moments in motherhood that nobody enjoys but that have to be done. Sidling over to one of the teachers, I asked, "Is it always like this? It seems so brutal."

"The first two lessons are the hardest," she answered. "Once they aren't afraid to get their heads wet, it gets easier. The thing to do is take a walk and not watch."

The last time I heard that advice, I reflected as I turned my back on the pool, was when my son was circumcised. They were right about watching.

Aside from swimming, another lesson a child should learn during the summer is how to keep boredom at bay. I believe some boredom is necessary for contrast; it is the black that casts the white of a good time into high relief. A child needs to learn to entertain himself.

Accordingly, each year in June I anticipate how we are going to have fun—even on the summer days when the only planned activity is nothing planned at all. Summer is the reward parents as well as children deserve because school is over. It's the time when nobody cares how much noise you make or how dirty you get. I look forward to long hours soaking up the sun as I lounge, lizardlike, on my spot on the bricks and watch the kids play. At its start, here is how languid summer feels:

My daughter sees no reason to come inside the house for dinner. She has built a home for her baby doll using the lawn furniture and she has no desire to leave it. If I could locate my seven-year-old to ask him, I am sure that he, too, would not care to come inside. He is down the block playing with a nine-year-old who has deigned to notice him, and he is quite busy learning to be cool. Even my youngest, propelling his fire engine down the sidewalk using foot power, would give me an argument about coming inside. He believes fun is anything that happens out of doors.

So I do not ask any of them. We have been outside for hours, much of it spent watching the remodeling project across the street. The steam shovel and Bobcat offer irresistible attractions: movement, noise, and a giant, dusty mess more magnificent than anything ever gotten away with by my children.

It is way past time for baths and far beyond a reasonable hour for me to start dinner, and yet I do not budge off the warm bricks where I sit in a lingering patch of sunlight while the evening cools. After all, summer is starting. Shoes are giving way to sandals, easier to slip off to run barefoot through the cool grass. Slacks are giving way to shorts, and it is time to invest in a new plastic pool because the old one has a crack. Maybe this will be the year we buy one with a slide.

As the daylight lingers, so do we. The longer days already have made mockery of the early bedtimes so easy to enforce during the dark days of winter. Once again I regret not having lined my children's drapes with blackout blinds. No longer dormant during the mornings and early afternoons, the street vibrates constantly with the slamming of screen doors and shouted greetings. My children have hosted the season's first lemonade stand, at which my capital investment exceeded my children's "profit."

Each summer I expect the big kids with water pistols to begin chasing the little kids with watering cans who want to get everyone wet but themselves. Some days a water balloon war will erupt. My children will entertain themselves in a sprinkler for hours. They will "paint" the sidewalk using water, and they will water my plants by aiming for the blossoms instead of the roots. Undoubtedly, in the commotion, all the babies on the block will learn how to get their pudgy feet wet. The children will decorate the sidewalks with chalk, and once again they will try to talk me into letting them use the finger-painting set I once bought in an instantly regretted moment of weakness.

Although the atmosphere among the children has quickened with the thrill of vacation, for their parents it is slowing down. Ended are the program rehearsals, league practices, lessons, and troop meetings of the school year. Just as the children gather earlier because school has ended, so the mothers linger later to discuss summer plans for vacations, camps, and lessons. The day camp so popular last year has fallen from favor. There is talk of sports camps, nature camps, and who will feed the dog while the family is away.

I join in each summer as we mothers hold our usual street-corner forum on the relative merits of every-second scheduling versus summertime down time. Some believe in arranging absolutely nothing so that their kids can just hang out. Others want a strict schedule that keeps everyone on the move. As usual, I come down in the middle— arranging part-time activities and part-time inactivity. Swimming lessons are the only activity I deem an absolute summer necessity. The rest are open to debate.

But we all agree on the importance of reserving a certain amount of time for old-fashioned playing. Children need to learn how to cope when there is "nothing to do." As a child I hung out a lot, and we learned to turn empty hours into lemonade stands and pretend circus shows. In similar fashion my kids tend to have the most fun not when they are playing with toys, but when they are left to their own devices.

Of course this lesson is easier said than learned. Oh yes, I start each summer buoyed by the highest of hopes. But much as I anticipate its beginning, I finish each summer grateful for its end. I know full well that long before fall nips the air my children will whine about how they have nothing to do. Inevitably this will happen. I know that by the end of the summer, for want of better entertainment, even the house painters across the street will look like heroes.

Sure enough, by August, each morning before my children even brush their teeth or eat their breakfast, they want to know the daily forecast.

"What are we going to do today?" they ask after tumbling out of bed before their feet hit the floor.

Usually, I know. Keeping track of camps and lessons and dental appointments is part of my job. But sometimes—when the day ahead looms emptier than a clean-underwear drawer—I do not.

"You can find something to do," I answer, casting my children adrift in the sink-or-swim school of social interaction.

I always try to keep them busy; I am just telling them that I will not always keep them entertained. Like most mothers I have pounded the pavement via the telephone wires, hunting up a playmate for my lonely child. I see nothing wrong in that. But my role ends once the friend arrives. Two children plus one mother does not equal three playmates.

Inevitably, however, some afternoons our street is so quiet even the grass naps. And then, despite my best intentions, I find myself in the role of magician and entertainer—trying to pull out of my hat something fun to do. We go through sidewalk chalk, bubbles, and wading pools in rapid succession. I do not like those afternoons when a fun time lasts only as long as my next good idea.

About the time that I think I can stand it no longer, our family indulges in another American rite: the family summer vacation. No matter where we go, no matter for how long we go, we are eager for the change it brings.

Sometimes our enthusiasm blinds us to the realities of the situation. I believe that a rule book, inscribed where parents cannot read it, governs our lives. It is packed with truths (such as the fact that children will go to bed for the baby-sitter when they won't for their parents). We must discover these truths for ourselves. Written in this book, in the section on summer vacations, it also says every family shall make the mistake of taking a car trip at least once. This is not only the American way to vacation, but it is the cheapest way.

That is why one summer we drove round-trip from Los Angeles to Phoenix. My husband was eager to do it. He has always wanted to drive the family cross-country. He thinks this would be an adventure. I think it would be suicidal. Our children are seven, five and three: too big to sleep all the way and too little to sit still. I remember my neighbor's car trip. Her suitcase on the roof of her car blew open, and even though a truck blocked traffic on the freeway so that she could retrieve her clothes, she could not wear them with tire treads.

Needless to say, I planned for our trip as carefully as I would for an earthquake or any other disaster that might deny my children access to the television set. Let's just say that whatever we saved on airfare I nearly spent on "travel toys" (anything costing less than five dollars and weighing less than five ounces). We planned to get an early start. We were, of course, late leaving. By the time we hit the road I'm not sure I would have gone back even for the baby's blankie.

A car trip, we discovered, requires strategy when it comes to seating arrangements. I did not realize that in an automobile arm space is easily as important as foot space. We engaged in running battles over whether the armrest belongs to the elbow beside it or constitutes a footrest for the person sitting behind it. I also did not realize the supreme importance of foot space. We discovered this after the two oldest fought a virtual war over legroom across the backseat. That is how my son ended up sitting in front with his Daddy, while I was crammed behind my husband next to the car seat. As the hours dragged by, all we children grew a bit testy.

"That must be the eighth time you've leaned back and squashed my knees," I complained to my husband.

"How do you think I like feeling your knee in my back?" he snapped.

I clocked a full ninety minutes before my daughter first uttered those immortal words: "Are we there yet?" We saw this as a good time to stop for gas to fill the tank and then hit the bathrooms so the kids could empty theirs.

As the afternoon wore on, we eventually fell into a routine. I think everything would have been OK, in fact, if just about the time two of the kids finally fell asleep and I dozed off, we had not run out of gas in the middle of the desert. I write "we," but quite clearly it was the driver's fault. Still, I said nothing as my husband uttered those immortal words: "I thought we could make it."

As he left the car for help, I cautioned the children not to make him feel any worse by pointing out that we hadn't. I said nothing when he discovered that our auto emergency kit contains a snow shovel but no gas siphon. Eventually, we flagged down a truck. The kids thoroughly enjoyed riding twenty-five miles to a gas station in the cab of a flatbed truck driven by a guy known to the CB world as "Squeezer." They loved running relays in the truck stop around the junk food displays for over an hour while waiting for their Daddy to get back to the car, fill it up with gas, and drive back to us. Now we have our very own gas can. Probably, we will forget to take it on our next car trip.

On the return trip driving home from Phoenix, I foolishly believed nothing else could go wrong. And, truthfully, only one thing did. The air conditioning conked out shortly before we crossed the Mojave Desert. The good thing about the extreme heat was that even the children recognized that this was not the time to misbehave. (Would you complain about a draft if your roof blew off?) And the drive couldn't have been as bad as I remember. Nothing could. My husband piloted our portable sauna like a man possessed. My daughter sweated so much she complained that her seat had a puddle. Eventually we made it home, a bit rank, but safe nevertheless.

Soon the inevitable cycle of school, sports, and summer will start again. Next fall I will spend even more time at the grade school down the street. My daughter is heading into kindergarten, and I wonder if the world is ready for her. My son will enter second grade, and he's already signed up for soccer. I will embrace the hectic challenge of a new school year as much as I always welcome the lazy days of summer. Come next summer, contentment again will walk hand in hand with boredom. And once again we will go on vacation. And then—especially if we travel by car—we all will learn summer's final lesson. It is the same lesson my son had to learn in soccer: how to be good sports.

16
Sunrise, Sunset

What would I do without them?

y daughter has drawn a picture of her brother, which she presents to him as a gift. He begins to show her how she might have drawn it better. She gets angry and tells him she doesn't like the way he does it. He shouts at her and tears up her picture. Once again a lovely moment has degenerated into something ugly. It happens all the time. Day in and day out I have a ringside seat for the family fights. Sometimes my youngest will pick the wrong moment to try to play with his big brother. He gets a punch in the stomach for his efforts. My daughter sulked all through the Halloween parade after her brother said that her queen costume looked silly.

I see it all the time. But sometimes, if I look hard, I also see something else. Flashes of humanity, hints of camaraderie also are becoming apparent. Some days I remember why I did not want to have an only child.

My children are starting to entertain each other. My two sons walk hand in hand when I allow them to cross the street together. Attracted by their laughter, I have looked out the window to see my two boys crammed together on a tricycle careening madly down the driveway. My daughter leads her little brother on a giggly hunt for pirate treasure. A few days later they play hide-and-seek inside my closet, clutching each other tightly in the dark. My oldest and his sister open a store at which they try to sell me all the coasters from the living room table.

Sometimes, I can begin to count upon my children to help each other. At a carnival, I entrusted my two oldest with watching the youngest inside the fun house. Standing on the fairway I would catch glimpses of them helping my little guy across nets and down ladders, giving him a push from behind, or waiting patiently for him at the top. I don't know which touched me more: how solicitous they were of him, or how trusting he was of them.

My seven-year-old came home from a birthday party recently with a goodie bag crammed full of candy. My five-year-old screamed and pouted and carried on over something that wasn't hers. I was pleasantly surprised when my son, without prompting, offered her a treat.

I hesitate here to presume a trend. Certainly, the mean and petty fights continue, but I wonder if they have distracted me from seeing the good that also has taken root. Sometimes I need to take a fresh look at my all-too-familiar family. I went out with my husband recently, and while I was in another room he met an acquaintance of mine.

"Your husband is such a hunk," she said to me later.

Looking daily at the man who forgets to take out the garbage, I guess I had forgotten he is pretty cute. Sometimes it takes an outsider to see our family more clearly. When we look at old photographs, it is easy to see the way our children are growing. On a daily basis, it is not. Grandparents who visit are quick to exclaim how so-and-so has grown in just three months. They see the changes we miss because we are too close.

It is harder still to assess the changes on the inside, but I think my children are growing up emotionally as well. The other morning I prodded my oldest to eat his breakfast, get dressed, and brush his teeth.

"I've already done two things for you!" he exploded. "Why do I have to keep doing more?"

Later, when we talked, I told him I was sorry to bug him to get ready but that I had no choice. I know how he feels, but he has to do those things every morning. A sheepish look crossed his face and he muttered, "Yeah, I know." And I believe he really does.

More and more often I'm trying to take a step back from my family. With a little perspective, I'm starting to like more of what I see. If my daughter hadn't given the picture to her brother in the first place, after all, they wouldn't have had anything to fight about.

Sometimes my children themselves bring me up short and remind me to appreciate what I have. I remember one day like that. I was standing at the sink, using a wet rag and my fingernail to scrape clean the indentations on the bottom of my son's sneaker. When he would walk through water, those indentations would transform his footprint to leave a picture of a dinosaur. But a brontosaurus was not what my son's footprint had left tracked across my house. Water was not what my son had walked through. My seven-year-old, at that precise moment, was not high on my hit parade of favorite people.

But, next, neither was my three-year-old. He considers the sipper seal on his plastic cup an affront to his dignity, and foolishly I decided to honor his wishes. I should have known better. This is the same child who threw his unbreakable plastic plate on the floor with such force that it broke. All of which explains how I ended up with Lake Apple Juice in the middle of the kitchen. So a few minutes after the sneaker episode I was kneeling on the floor, wiping it for the third time, and hoping that finally it would dry without being sticky.

As I wiped I heard ominous sounds from the other part of the house. First came the clink of coins, so I knew my son was mountain climbing on the desk where my husband deposits the debris from his pockets. Then came the scraping of drawers, so I knew that he was playing with the pens and markers he is not supposed to touch. But it was the sound of the computer firing up that brought me running from the kitchen. As my son pounded furiously on the world's most expensive busy box, I chased him out of the office.

From the screaming a few minutes later, I knew he had found his sister upstairs. My five-year-old apparently is defenseless against a three-year-old.

"Momma, Momma, Momma," she wails tearfully at the top of her lungs at least fifty-five times a day. "Momma!" This ear-shattering, stress-producing behavior does not always endear my daughter to me, either. I used to come running, convinced she was in mortal danger. Now I know that she cries wolf. She cries when her brother hurts her, she cries when she thinks he might hurt her, and she cries when he hurts her feelings.

All in all, thanks to my children, I suspected the day itself was not one of my favorites. That was confirmed at dinner when my children engaged in hand-to-hand combat. It was the Battle of Iwo Jima. They were fighting for possession of the cherries in the fruit cocktail. I do not know how many cherries the average can of fruit cocktail contains, but I do know that in this particular can it was not an even number.

I was no longer a writer; I was a war correspondent. My son launched an aggressive assault upon the bowl by raiding the cherries first. My daughter responded with her own defensive action. They skirmished. My son went on reconnaissance to the bottom of the bowl and captured the last three. He ate; she howled. Desperate for silence, I snatched a cherry from his plate and put it on hers. She smirked; he screamed. As I sat there, I knew I was not enjoying my meal—and not for the first time I questioned whether I was enjoying my life. My children sap me. When I haven't any energy or patience left, they demand more. They take and take and take.

Just then my youngest came over, agitating to be held. It figured. With a sigh, I put down my fork and picked up my son. He reached up and put his arms around my neck. Then, practicing his newest skill, he pressed his soft cheek against mine and for a long minute he squeezed hard. The whitecaps in my stomach subsided. In the sudden calm, I was filled with amazement. My children take and take, but they still manage to give me so much more than I give them.

■ ■ ■

Children give a new dimension to love. All parents could stand to be reminded of that simple truth. Sometimes other parents do it for us. A reader of mine, a woman I have never met, once wrote to tell me that we used to share a lot in common. We each had a family of five. Our three children both alternated: boy, girl, boy. Each was two years apart.

"I identified with you and what was happening in your life," she wrote. "I felt a strong kinship with you. Until a year ago." That was when she and her husband took their two oldest children on a special outing. Their youngest stayed with his grandparents. As they were driving home, a car rear-ended their van and the gas tank exploded. Only after they had scrambled to safety did she and her husband discover that their five-year-old son remained trapped inside.

"The smoke was thick and flames covered the only exit from the van. We could only stand there and watch our van and our son burn," she wrote. "My husband and I couldn't even hold each other, or our daughter, because we were so badly burned.

"To make a very long story short, we are now a family of four. My daughter is four, my son is two, and my oldest boy is forever an angel."

She told me that the kinship we used to share is not the same. She said she is jealous of me and my family of five. She said that the things I write now aren't always good for a laugh. Sometimes they make her cry. She said she cries not so much for her son, who is in a better place, but for herself and all the things that would have been in his life that she is going to miss.

Then this mother asked me to give my oldest boy a hug from her. I did. For days after, whenever I hugged my oldest, my eyes would mist. Her letter was a burr, sticking in my mind. But one day, only a few weeks later, I was slamming around the house, angrily seeking a few minutes of peace. Appalled, I realized that her letter had slipped my mind. That's the way it is with good intentions. They can bloom like beautiful flowers, but if they grow in the path of a shortcut they are easily trampled.

Eight years ago I had no children, but I had the heartache of two miscarriages and of mourning for babies that might have been. Babies became almost an obsession. Jealously I used to watch other mothers, wondering if they appreciated the miracles they had produced but that I could not. If I ever became a mother, I used to promise myself, I would never take my child for granted. I would never lose my temper or my patience or my sense of awe.

On occasion, however, I now find that I have temporarily misplaced them. In the hurly-burly of daily living, I am grateful to have my children—but some mornings I would be even more grateful if they would just get dressed. Parents are contrary creatures. In the center of the storm, I yearn for quiet. Yet on the rare occasions when the house is empty, I miss my family.

When I write about my family, I do not rhapsodize about how wonderful they are. I already know it, and nobody else wants to read it. Instead, I write about the ways families learn to make peace with the madness of daily life. If I didn't complain about my children and my husband, in fact, some days I would have nothing to write about. I keep reminding myself how lucky I am to have something to say.

Writing is my way of remembering these early feelings of motherhood. But just as I use words to jog my memories, I also keep mementos. Crammed onto the top shelf of my closet, in an unwieldy pile guaranteed to tip whenever I slam the door, is my collection of special stuff. At the bottom of the pile is a baby book, placed there over seven years ago when I anticipated filling in the blanks. I intended to write about my child's dental history and what music was the rage the day he was born. Those lines remain empty.

The book itself, however, has been useful. I use it as a binder into which I stuff my memories.

At the bottom of the pile are my basal temperature charts. I am nostalgic about them now that they are nestled next to the plastic identification bracelets issued to my babies in the hospital. I have saved the signs the nurses hung on the hospital bassinets when my children occupied them. The sign for my oldest pictures a teddy bear; my daughter's displays Raggedy Ann, and my youngest's shows Snoopy. Those pictures evoke every hope and dream and fear I felt when the nurses handed me my babies for the first time.

Crammed in by the signs are the cards of congratulations sent by family and friends to welcome each baby. Some of these friends live far away and have never met my children. Some of those relatives who sent cards for my oldest did not live long enough to meet my youngest. Jammed in by the cards, I have saved locks of hair and more than a few handprints immortalized in royal blue or red paint. Other handprints make turkeys and others reindeer. I have the sticker chart that rewarded every trip my oldest successfully made to the potty.

I have a unique collection of original, unsigned, and limited edition artwork. It begins with scribbles, progresses to triangles with arms and legs, and finally entire collections of spindly legged creatures sporting smiles and holding hands. On top of the pile come my latest mementos: class pictures, a first homework assignment, and diplomas from an assortment of gymnastics, exercise, and music classes.

On rare occasions, when everything tips over or when I have an extra minute, I look through my pile. By the time I have dumped it all onto the carpet and dreamed over each scrap of paper, usually my tears spill as freely as the mess.

Something about motherhood has made me vulnerable to crying. I am a faucet with a fast flow. I cry at school concerts when I see my seven-year-old standing on the stage rigged up in a ridiculous costume singing his heart out. I cry because I know that pretty soon he'll be too old to come home from school with notes pinned to his shirt. I cry when my five-year-old suddenly looks up from her drawing and urgently says, "Mom, I want to tell you something." When I ask her what, she flashes me my sister's smile and replies, "I love you." And I cry when my three-year-old gives my knee a bear hug and then takes my hand to plant a noisy kiss on the top of it.

It's unpredictable, this side effect of motherhood. My eyes can betray me at the most unexpected moments. I cry at American Express commercials. I sniffle when the father busts through the sound barrier in order to get home in time for his child's performance. It makes perfect sense to me. I cry over newspaper accounts of children with diseases, children who drown, children who suffer—stories that as a reporter I used to cover with not nearly the depth of understanding I have now.

Most of the time, of course, I don't cry at all. I talk and I shout and I laugh and I sing—and I get so caught up in living each day that I don't notice the weeks passing. But sometimes, when the evidence spills out around me and I realize my children have gone from baby curls to flattops, then I am apt to sniffle.

My mementos I keep on a shelf. I treasure them. But I also treasure my children. I am lucky to have them.

When my children were babies, there was no doubt in my mind. Undeniably they were sweet from their heads down to their toes. But the best part of them was the back of their necks. It was softly curved, totally vulnerable, and exposed to my kisses—at least until their fuzz grew into hair.

A few months later, however, I was not so sure about my choice. There were so many other delicious parts from which to choose. For a while I was captivated by the dimples on their chubby elbows. Then it was their pudgy toes. I found endless places to admire as I would bend over the changing table, wantonly planting kisses. During the baby years I always was high on the cuddle factor. My babies were a sweet package I would wrap with love. My delight knew no bounds when they began to reach out to me with their arms. I was the elevator and they wanted to go up.

As they got older, my husband had no doubts as to what he thought was the best part. He would toss our babies high in the sky and hang them by their shirts until they surrendered to giggles of glee.

"Those belly laughs are great," he would say. "I love those belly laughs."

As toddlers, maybe their premier part was the the way my children pudged. Their cheeks were pudgy, their tummies rounded, and their short legs pumped while they walked and they surveyed the world from knee level. I loved to hold their hands, and inwardly rejoiced every time I held out mine and they automatically slipped theirs inside.

Now my children no longer pudge. They have stretched out and turned into stick figures, barely padded like the cheapest chair. Their hands are frequently sticky, and holding them most often reminds me to make them wash. Now, of course, my children's toes do not exactly cry out for my kisses.

In places, however, they still look sweet. My daughter has a special spot, at the top corner of her forehead where her hair grows back, that I smooth with kisses. And my oldest son has a cowlick at the top of his head that not even glue could tame. My youngest son has a dimple, on the left side only, that flashes when he smiles. I love those places especially. In fact, for a while I thought it was all my children's smiles that are the best. Their smiles, freely given, are the sunshine in my universe. They link us as co-conspirators in life because together we will take on the world.

But they are not the best parts of my children. As the questions came and their newborn logic began to flex its muscles, the best part, I realized, was their minds. What can be more important than to shape an intelligence as it explores and learns to reason? But another day I thought, yet again, it must be their personalities. From the moment we met, they have each carried an emotional stamp that makes them unique. Maybe it was their giggles. Who can predict what will tickle the fancy of a child and send him into peals of laughter?

Finally I decided I couldn't answer the riddle of what was best. Then, as usual, it was my five-year-old daughter who introduced me to the truth.

"You're the best mom," she said to me once for no particular reason.

"Why?" I asked her.

"Because I love you," she answered.

And now I see that she is right. The best part of my children is that they are mine to love.